Understanding Social Research

Understanding Social Research

Thinking Creatively About Method

Edited by Jennifer Mason
and Angela Dale

Los Angeles | London | New Delhi
Singapore | Washington DC

First published 2011

SAGE Publications Ltd
1 Oliver's Yard
55 City Road
London EC1Y 1SP

SAGE Publications Inc.
2455 Teller Road
Thousand Oaks, California 91320

SAGE Publications India Pvt Ltd
B 1/I 1 Mohan Cooperative Industrial Area
Mathura Road, New Delhi 110 044
India

SAGE Publications Asia-Pacific Pte Ltd
33 Pekin Street #02-01
Far East Square
Singapore 048763

Library of Congress Control Number: 2010925413

British Library Cataloguing in Publication data

A catalogue record for this book is available from
the British Library

ISBN 978-1-84860-144-4
ISBN 978-1-84860-145-1 (pbk)

Typeset by C&M Digitals (P) Ltd, Chennai, India
Printed and bound in Great Britain by TJ International Ltd, Padstow, Cornwall
Printed on paper from sustainable resources

Contents

Notes on Contributors   vii

Acknowledgements   xi

1   Creative Tensions in Social Research: Questions of Method   1
     Jennifer Mason and Angela Dale

Section I   Researching Relationships and Personal Life   **27**

2   Experimenting with Qualitative Methods:
     Researching Family Resemblance   33
     Jennifer Mason and Katherine Davies

3   Using Psychoanalytic Methodology in Psychosocial
     Research: Researching Brothers   49
     Stephen Frosh and Lisa Saville Young

4   Using Biographical and Longitudinal Methods:
     Researching Mothering   62
     Rachel Thomson

5   Using Social Network Analysis: Researching Relational Structure   75
     Nick Crossley

6   Using Survey Data: Researching Families and Households   90
     Angela Dale

Section II   Researching Place   **103**

7   Ethnographies of Place: Researching the Road   107
     Penny Harvey and Hannah Knox

8   Using Sociotechnical Methods: Researching Human-Technological
     Dynamics in the City   120
     Simon Guy and Andrew Karvonen

9   Using Participatory, Observational and 'Rapid Appraisal'
    Methods: Researching Health And Illness   134
    Sarah Salway, Kaveri Harriss and Punita Chowbey

10 Innovative Ways of Mapping Data About Places   150
    Danny Dorling and Dimitris Ballas

Section III   Researching Change   **165**

11 Using Archived Qualitative Data: Researching
    Socio-cultural Change   169
    Mike Savage

12 What's History Got to Do With it? Researching
    Sexual Histories   181
    Jeffrey Weeks

13 Using Qualitative Methods to Complement Randomized
    Controlled Trials: Researching Mental Health Interventions   195
    Anne Rogers

14 Exploring the Narrative Potential of Cohort Data and
    Event History Analysis   210
    Jane Elliott

15 Using Longitudinal Survey Data: Researching Changing
    Health in Later Life   225
    James Nazroo

Index   243

Notes on Contributors

Dimitris Ballas is a senior lecturer in Geographical Information Systems in the Department of Geography, University of Sheffield. He is an economist by training (University of Macedonia, Thessaloniki, Greece) and also has a MA (with distinction) in Geographical Information Systems (University of Leeds, UK) and a PhD in Geography (University of Leeds, UK). He is the lead author of the book *Geography Matters: Simulating the Impacts of National Social Policies* (Joseph Rowntree Foundation, 2005) and a co-author of the books *Post-Suburban Europe: Planning and Politics at the Margins of Europe's Capital Cities* (Palgrave, 2006) and *Poverty, Wealth and Place in Britain, 1968 to 2005* (Policy Press, 2007). He also has several publications in peer-reviewed international academic journals, peer-reviewed edited volumes and has refereed international conference proceedings.

Punita Chowbey is a research fellow in the Centre for Health and Social Care Research at Sheffield Hallam University. With a background in sociology, social policy and development studies, shc has been working on applied and academic projects in health and social development in India and in the UK for the last 13 years. Her research interests focus on the intersections between socio-economic disadvantage, gendered and racialized exclusion and ill-health among children and families.

Nick Crossley is a professor and currently head of Sociology at the University of Manchester (UK). He has published on a number of issues in sociology including embodiment, social movements and social networks. His latest book, *Towards a Relational Sociology*, will be published by Routledge in late 2010.

Angela Dale is Professor of Quantitative Social Research at the Cathie Marsh Centre for Census and Survey Research (CCSR) at the University of Manchester. She is an Academician of the Academy of Learned Societies for the Social Sciences (AcSS) and was awarded an OBE for services to social science in 2006. Recent work has focused on women's employment, with particular respect to ethnic differences and strategies for combining work and family life; change between generations; and the role of qualifications. In 2009 she became director of a new methods hub at the University of Manchester – methods@manchester.

Katherine Davies is a research associate in Realities (part of the National Centre for Research Methods) and the Morgan Centre for the Study of

Relationships and Personal Life at the University of Manchester. She is currently working on a project exploring the positive and negative significance of friendships and other critical associations in personal lives. She is also working on a PhD investigating sibling relationships and the construction of the self in secondary education.

Danny Dorling is Professor of Human Geography, Department of Geography, University of Sheffield. He is author, or co-author, of 25 books and 400 papers. Since 2006, Danny has been working with many others on remapping inequality worldwide (http://www.worldmapper.org). He is an Academician of the Academy of the Learned Societies in the Social Sciences and, in 2008, became Honorary President of the Society of Cartographers. In 2010, he joined the World Health Organization's Scientific Resource Group on Health Equity Analysis and Research. His most recent book, *Injustice: Why Social Inequality Persists*, was published by Policy Press in April 2010.

Jane Elliott is Director of the Centre for Longitudinal Studies. She leads the team responsible for developing the content, design and analysis of the 1958 and the 1970 British Birth Cohort Studies studies. Her main research interests include gender and employment, women's careers, longitudinal research methodology, combining qualitative and quantitative research and narrative.

Stephen Frosh is Pro-Vice-Master and Professor of Psychology at Birkbeck College, University of London. He is the author of many books and papers on psychosocial studies and on psychoanalysis, including *Hate and the Jewish Science: Anti-Semitism, Nazism and Psychoanalysis* (Palgrave, 1999); *For and Against Psychoanalysis* (Routledge, 2006); *After Words* (Palgrave, 2002) and *The Politics of Psychoanalysis* (Palgrave, 1999). He is joint author with Peter Emerson of *Critical Narrative Analysis in Psychology* (Palgrave, 2004). His latest book, *Psychoanalysis Outside the Clinic* is published by Palgrave in 2010.

Simon Guy is Head of the School of Environment and Development, Professor of Architecture and Head of the Manchester Architecture Research Centre at the University of Manchester. His research is aimed at critically understanding the co-evolution of design and development strategies and socio-technical-ecological processes shaping cities.

Kaveri Harriss is a research fellow in Anthropology at Sussex University. Her doctorate at the London School of Hygiene and Tropical Medicine examined the material contexts and consequences of chronic illness among Pakistanis in East London, engaging with issues of premature ageing and unemployment. She now works on East Punjabi transnationalism, and co-convenes the Pakistan Workshop and Pakistan Studies Group.

Penny Harvey is Professor of Social Anthropology at the University of Manchester. Her regional specialization is in South America and Europe, and she has conducted fieldwork in Peru, Spain and the UK. Her research interests focus on the modern state, and in how ethnographic work can inflect standard accounts of political economy by extending standard approaches to power, value and knowledge.

Andrew Karvonen is a research associate in the Manchester Architecture Research Centre at the University of Manchester. He combines theories and approaches from the design disciplines, urban studies and STS to study the socio-technical aspects of cities with a particular emphasis on the changing configurations of people, infrastructure and nature.

Hannah Knox is Research Associate at the ERSC Centre for Research on Socio-Cultural Change (CRESC) at the University of Manchester. Her work is broadly concerned with the anthropological study of technologies of modernization and progress. Her ethnographic research has spanned the UK and Peru, to look at the ways in which complex social, technical and expert knowledges intersect in projects of planned social change.

Jennifer Mason is Professor of Sociology at the University of Manchester. She directs the Realities Centre, which is part of the UK National Centre for Research Methods, funded by the ESRC. She is also Co-Director of the Morgan Centre for the Study of Relationships and Personal Life. She is the author of numerous articles, chapters and books on personal life and relationships, and on qualitative and mixed methods. Her books include the bestselling *Qualitative Researching* (Sage, 2002).

James Nazroo is Professor of Sociology at the University of Manchester. His research is focused on issues of inequality, social justice and underlying processes of stratification, with a particular interest in ethnic inequalities and inequalities in later life. He is pragmatic in his choice of research methods, employing methods, and combinations of methods, best suited to answer the research question. He has particular interests in longitudinal research, comparative research and mixing methods.

Anne Rogers is Professor of the Sociology of Health Care in the School of Community Based Medicine University of Manchester. Her main research interests are in the sociology of health care, mental health and more recently social networks, relationships and personal long-term condition management. Working in interdisciplinary research teams she has been interested in combining qualitative methods in trials of innovation in mental and physical health care.

Sarah Salway is Professor of Public Health at Sheffield Hallam University. Most of her work explores the interplay of gendered and ethnic identities with health-care experiences and health outcomes. She is also interested in the ethical, theoretical and methodological issues arising from the generation and application of research knowledge relating to inequalities in health.

Lisa Saville Young is a Clinical Psychologist and Senior Lecturer in the Department of Psychology at Rhodes University, Grahamstown, South Africa. She holds a PhD in Psychology from Birkbeck College, University of London, UK. Her research interests include developing psychosocial research methods and the construction of masculinities in adult fraternal relationships.

Mike Savage, after 15 years as Professor of Sociology at the University of Manchester, moved to the University of York in October 2010. His interests are in social stratification, historical sociology, and in cultural analysis. His recent book, *Identities and Social Change in Britain since 1940: The Politics of Method* (Oxford, 2010) explores in more detail the theme he raises in his chapter.

Rachel Thomson is Professor of Social Research at the Open University. Her research interests lie in childhood, youth and maternal studies, and the methods of capturing and understanding dynamic social processes. Recent publications include *Researching Social Change: Qualitative Approaches* (with McLeod, Sage, 2009) and *Unfolding Lives: Youth, Gender and Change* (Policy Press, 2009).

Jeffrey Weeks is Emeritus Professor of Sociology at London South Bank University. He is the author of over 20 books, and over 100 articles, chiefly on the history and social organization of sexuality and intimate life. Key publications include *Coming Out* (Quartet, 1977), *Sex, Politics and Society* (Longman, 1981), *Sexuality and its Discontents* (Routledge, 1985), *Invented Moralities* (Polity, 1995), *Making Sexual History* (Polity, 2000), *Same Sex Intimacies: Families of Choice and Other Life Experiments* (with Brian Heaphy and Catherine Donovan, Routledge, 2001), *Sexualities and Society* (with Janet Holland and Matthew Waites, Polity, 2003), and a third edition of *Sexuality* (2009). *The World We Have Won: The Remaking of Erotic and Intimate Life*, was published by Routledge in June 2007.

Acknowledgements

The impetus and inspiration for this book came from our experiences in organizing and participating in different kinds of research events, all of which had the aim of fostering and encouraging dialogue and debate across methodological boundaries. In particular, these include events developed under the Research Methods Programme (RMP) and the Realities 'Node' of the ESRC National Centre for Research Methods (and its predecessor the Real Life Methods Node). The Methods in Dialogue programme of workshops at the University of Manchester, organized through Realities, and theme-based workshops organized at the ESRC Methods Festivals under the Research Methods Programme have produced exciting, productive and often spirited, dialogues that have helped to confirm our view that creative tensions in method can be a very good thing indeed. We want to thank all our colleagues who have helped to organize these events, and all who have participated in them, for being so generous with their methodological ideas. Also, we are grateful to ESRC for supporting the programmes (RMP, NCRM/Real Life Methods/Realities) through which these events were able to come to life. Finally, we want to thank the contributors to this book for their enthusiasm and willingness to rise to the not inconsiderable challenge that we presented them with in writing their chapters.

Jennifer Mason and Angela Dale
University of Manchester

August 2010

ONE

Creative Tensions in Social Research

Questions of Method

Jennifer Mason and Angela Dale

Introduction

There are many different approaches to social science research, and a sometimes bewildering array of methods and techniques, each apparently with its own set of advantages, disadvantages and rules. Although there are increasing levels of resources available to help researchers learn about all of these, for the researcher wishing to research *something in particular*, it can be difficult to work out the implications of using one method over another, or of combining different methods and approaches. This is partly because some methods or combinations may be better suited to particular research questions than others. We are familiar with the idea that the methods we use influence the *quality* of the knowledge we can generate in response to specific questions, but importantly they also influence its nature and scope – that is, which parts of the phenomena under investigation it throws light upon. So, one challenge is for the researcher to know what kinds of data and knowledge in relation to *specific social phenomena* a method can potentially produce *before* being able to make a good judgement about which methods they should choose.

This is further complicated, though, by a second challenge, which is to understand how a researcher's conceptual or theoretical stance on the empirical social world leads them to choose a particular method and thus to understand the nature or essence of phenomena in a different way from researchers with different orientations. This means, for example, that two researchers may both be interested in researching the concepts of relationships, or place, or social change – the domains we cover in this book – but they might see the very fabric of *what those things are* in completely different ways. Thus not only do our substantive interests shape the methods we might choose to use, but our methods shape the thing that is the substance of our enquiry too. To borrow a phrase from two of our contributors, methods and substance 'generate implications for each other' (Frosh and Saville Young). This creates a bit of a conundrum for researchers; one that cannot entirely be resolved by reference to texts and resources that focus on method abstracted from substance.

The aim of this book is to help researchers to deal with these kinds of challenges. So instead of writing a textbook covering, in the abstract, the main methodological approaches, we have asked experts who are doing exciting and important social science research to give some insights into the methods they use, and how their methods and substantive foci generate implications for each other. We have picked three broad substantive domains – relationships, places and social change – and asked researchers with very different research orientations to describe their approaches, their logic and the kinds of knowledge their methods can yield. Yet our aim has not been to produce a book that speaks only to these substantive interests, but instead to use them as a focus to help readers to think about the interrelationship between methods and substance in a way that they can then apply more generally to their own research.

We would like the book to be useful to researchers who want to learn about, and be open to, the exciting breadth of research being practised in the social sciences. This means thinking creatively about methods (and substance), and being prepared to take on board other ways of thinking and researching, and possibly to combine methods. Sometimes this means moving outside one's comfort zone. But in order to do that, one needs not only to see the point of doing so, but also to understand the implications in terms of what kinds of knowledge might be produced, and more generally what might be involved in crossing boundaries between approaches.

The chapters that follow inform the reader about different kinds of approach, and they cover a wide range of methods including ethnography, cartography, survey methods, psychosocial methods, biographical methods, historical methods, narrative methods, visual/sensory methods and social network analysis. Each chapter will give the reader a good sense of 'the point' of using a particular method in relation to a grounded set of issues, and the kinds of knowledge that are produced. And by reading all the chapters in each section, the reader will gain a good sense of some of the different ways in which methodological approaches can define or influence phenomena under investigation.

However, to fully grasp the implications of using a particular set of methods, or crossing boundaries between approaches, it is important to discuss some core or cross-cutting issues here in the introduction. This chapter is written primarily as a guide for the reader to key points of tension, difference and, sometimes unexpected connection between approaches. These are often more implicit than explicit. In this chapter we provide a guide to 'what to look out for', or be alert to, in understanding the implications that a particular approach has for the relationship between methods and substance that we have argued is so crucial to social science research. It is a guide that can be used not only when reading the chapters in this book, but more generally in deciphering social science approaches: when making judgements about which are best suited to one's own purposes and what might be involved in using and combining them. Hence it is structured around issues that all researchers have to think through and make decisions about when choosing and using methods in real life research.

As you read through the chapters therefore, you may find it helpful to keep a critical eye on how the following kinds of questions and issues – about how the social world is envisaged – figure in the arguments of the authors, both implicitly and explicitly. We are not using conventional distinctions and 'labels' that are often applied to perspectives on social science research – such as 'relativist', 'positivist', 'realist', 'interpretivist', 'post-structuralist' and so on – for several reasons. In part we think that they are sometimes so 'broad brush' as to be quite unhelpful in practical terms, for the researcher who is trying to work out how to go about a particular project. Additionally, we are not sure that such labels are always honestly applied or attributed, and often more telling signs of a researcher's ontological or epistemological positions can be picked up in the way they write about their methods or the accounts they give of their research. Perhaps most importantly though, we think that applying labels can be a little stultifying, since it helps to construct the idea that these are discrete and clearly defined world views, or positions, with little fluidity in them. We want the reader of this book to feel a little more liberated than that, and to embrace the possibility of using approaches with which they may not be very familiar.

What kind of social world is envisaged?

Sometimes authors will spell out explicitly the kind of social world they envisage when they describe the phenomena they are investigating, but at other times this is more implicit or taken-for-granted and, in these instances, the language and vocabulary used can be a telling sign of the kind of ontology being drawn upon, as we shall show.

We set out below some different possibilities for envisaging the social world, all of which appear in some shape or form in this book. As we have suggested, however, that these are not meant to depict discrete world views or research strategies. Instead, they are more like 'ontological dimensions'. Many researchers would want to adopt a mobile view that traverses or even transcends these, arguing perhaps that the social world is made up of multiple elements or dimensions, which come more or less into view depending upon our perspectives or the methods we use. The point, however, for the reader of this book, is to be able to spot the connections between the kinds of ontology that are expressed or implied by authors (in this book and elsewhere) and the methods and approaches that have been devised to generate knowledge of them. That will enable you both to judge how good the fit is between these (ontology and methods) and also to decide on the value of particular approaches for producing knowledge about the kinds of phenomena that you personally are interested in.

A world of stories and interpretations

Stories and narratives figure in a wide range of research approaches as methods of data generation or analysis; many researchers see stories as good ways of eliciting perspectives *on* the social world, or of narrating experiences *of* it. However, here we want to draw attention to approaches where stories have a more fundamental and ontological role – where the social world is itself seen as a 'storied' entity, in the sense that stories, involving some kind of sentient composition – where people 'make' and 'tell' stories, rather than just acting a part in them – are part of its very fabric. This idea can take many different forms, and perspectives that encompass some sense of a world that is storied do not necessarily share other basic premises.

One example comes from Harvey and Knox's chapter on the ethnography of place which uses the example of road construction projects in Peru. Storytelling figures quite centrally in their chapter. Here is an extract:

> Our travels on the roads of Peru taught us a great deal about the specific materiality of roads and, as importantly, about how the layering of materials through which a road appears in the environment as a specific and relatively stable structure also carried with it histories of skills, of trade, of hopes and of struggle. These histories leave their traces in the stories people tell, in the physical make up of a place, and in the daily practices of those we encountered along the way. (Harvey and Knox, Chapter 7, this volume, pp. 116–17)

From this perspective we can see that stories (and histories) are more than just tales about the road – they are part of what the road *is*, or what a place is.

Thomson's chapter on researching motherhood provides a different kind of example. She explains that she 'wanted to capture the "zeitgeist" of contemporary motherhood'. A zeitgeist is the spirit of a particular age or period of history. It seems to us to be a concept very closely connected with stories and storytelling, and certainly Thomson's chapter is redolent with these. For example, she explains that the research 'sought to capture the ways in which women might be storying their pregnancies', and she goes on to argue that:

> women draw on publicly available narrative resources in order to 'story' their lives and make them intelligible to others (Butler, 2004; Thomson et al., 2009). New stories emerge in the confluence of developing identities and available resources that facilitate both the story telling and its reception (Plummer, 1995). The transition from private story to the generation of a public problem involves struggle and recognition of subjecthood, and the privilege to narrate oneself (rather than to be narrated by others) reflects wider dimensions of social, cultural and economic status (Adkins, 2003; Skeggs, 2004). (Thomson, Chapter 4, this volume, p. 68)

In this example, then, the aim is to investigate a zeitgeist, that involves and is implicated in processes of storying and storytelling. It is not simply that stories *yield data* about pregnancy and mothering, or about a zeitgeist, but instead that they are fundamentally bound up in what those concepts are.

A third example comes from Weeks' chapter on understanding change in sexual and intimate life. The object of Weeks' investigation is history itself, or more particularly historical narratives of sexuality. He says:

> Historians also tell each other stories, which they easily assume tell the ultimate truth about the way things were, and are. But we need to learn to understand these narratives better, and especially how they structure meanings into a more or less coherent account of what is happening to us. Narratives or stories are examples of the ways in which 'reality' is constituted through sets of beliefs, assumptions and the appropriate selection of evidence. They are powerful because they carry the unconscious assumption that what is being elaborated for the reader is a 'true history'. But I want to argue that the very act of selection can occlude a complex and more contested history. (Weeks, Chapter 12, this volume, p. 185)

Weeks wants to explore the shaping and dominating role of certain historical narratives and the hidden assumptions that can be traced within them, and to connect these with the ways in which people both live sexuality and campaign for transformation. The very essence of the social world he envisages is one where stories and histories are not simply told about the world, but are woven tightly back into the fabric of both everyday existence and societies and cultures.

We have discussed three different examples of how it is possible to have an ontological view of the social world that is storied, and there are more examples in this book as well as, of course, in the wider world of social research (see the chapters by Mason and Davies [Chapter 2], Elliott [Chapter 14], Frosh and Saville Young [Chapter 3]). We think the examples have in common the idea that the sentient composition of a story, at some level, is a core part of the reality that research seeks to investigate. But there are also many differences between them.

> Vocabulary that can sometimes be indicative of this kind of perspective includes: stories, narratives, histories, accounts, perspectives, experiences, traces, interpretations.

A world of socio-architectural structures

Another way of envisaging the social world involves perspectives that operate with some sort of 'socio-architectural' view. What we have in mind here are perspectives that see the social landscape in terms of 'structures', 'levels' or 'networks', for example. These are 'architectural' characteristics in the sense that they are seen to have a kind of social solidity, with definable and potentially identifiable properties, characteristics or effects. For some researchers who use this kind of perspective, the 'architectural' features (or the solidity) are themselves made up of dynamic elements, agency, social relations and interactions that cohere or form constellations in certain 'structural' ways, where for others the emphasis is upon more fixed and infrastructural qualities of the social world. Despite many differences between approaches, what is always present is the desire to say something about the *properties* of these architectural features, for example, a network's density, or the effect of structural or 'family level' factors, or the cohesiveness or permeability of social class structures. Here are some examples from the book.

Crossley argues that the social world:

> is a network and the pattern of connections constituting that network is an important aspect of what we mean by 'social structure' ... Different network patterns, involving different types of relations and different populations, constitute the multiple overlapping social structures that comprise a social world. (Crossley, Chapter 5, this volume, p. 75)

Here, networks have identifiable characteristics including density, and social network analysis (SNA) draws on graph theory for its concepts and terminology so that, for example, '"distances" are measured in terms of "degrees", a degree being a connection' (p. 85).

A different version can be found in Dale's chapter, where she refers to work by Jenkins et al:

> The authors use multilevel modelling (where the family is one level in the analysis and the child is a different level) to attempt to establish the relationship between shared family-level effects and differential treatment of children by parents. (Dale, Chapter 6, this volume, p. 100)

The levels in Jenkins et al.'s work, and the networks in Crossley's, are certainly not the same – indeed there are some fundamental differences between them – but we think there is a common sense of socio-architecture behind both of them. Another example can be found in Dorling and Ballas's chapter, in which they describe 'human area population cartograms' (Chapter 10). These are cartograms based on 'the spatial distribution of variables pertaining to human societies', using data drawn from surveys of individuals and households, including the British Household Panel Survey. Such cartograms can be used to map data about *populations* against different geographical 'levels' (for example, national, sub-national). Here populations are conceptualized in terms of their aggregated characteristics at a defined level of geography.

A final example comes from Salway, Harriss and Chowbey's chapter on 'putting long-term illness in context'. They express a socio-architectural view when they explain that they wanted to push beyond a focus on individual narratives of ill health in their project.

We suggest that the dominant reliance on narrative interviews [in research on chronic ill health] has meant limited attention to the social structural and cultural conditions that articulate with individual responses to chronic illness ... While we recognized the importance of listening to the personal testimonies of individuals living with long-term illness, we also aimed to understand wider contexts and processes that are commonly taken-for-granted and less open to investigation through interviews. (Salway, Harriss and Chowbey, Chapter 9, this volume, pp. 134–5)

Other chapters in this book that contain elements of a socio-architectural view include: Elliott (Chapter 14), Guy and Karvonen (Chapter 8), Nazroo (Chapter 15) and Thomson (Chapter 4).

Vocabulary to look out for: structures, underlying structures, levels, layers, networks, institutions.

A world of individuals or humans

It seems obvious that social scientists would be exploring social worlds that are made up of individuals, and groups of individuals, and certainly this basic idea permeates very many social science perspectives. Indeed, structures and levels are often conceptualized as comprising linked or aggregated individuals or patterns of behaviour. This underlying logic is particularly pronounced in social survey methodology, as the following examples help to illustrate.

Our first example comes from Dale's chapter, where she explains how surveys can build pictures of households by establishing links and connections between the individuals within them. Talking specifically of the British General Household Survey she says:

Each household has a unique serial number and, within households, each family unit and person is uniquely identified. This provides the basic building blocks for linking information between partners, or between mother and child, or aggregating information about all household members. (Dale, Chapter 6, this volume, p. 95)

Nazroo's chapter discusses the logic of 'panel surveys' (a longitudinal survey in which variables are measured on the same people [units] over time), such as the English Longitudinal Study of Ageing (ELSA), for understanding social change. ELSA collects detailed structured data from approximately 11,000 individuals in consecutive sweeps, and the rhythm of data collection, as well as the coverage of the surveys, is very intensive:

This intensity reflects the desire to collect a range of data – the causal processes we are typically interested in involve connections between different domains of people's lives (economic, social, psychological, health etc) – and the desire to observe changes as closely as possible to when they occur, so that time order can be established. (Nazroo, Chapter 15, this volume, p. 236)

Here we can see that the logic of sampling, and the topics covered (different domains of people's lives), or the 'units of investigation' and the variables used in data analysis, all work on the basic premise that the individual is the salient unit in the social world; although context – in the form of partner, family or household – are often central to any analysis. That same perspective can be traced in Dorling and Ballas's cartograms, which are often derived from standardized survey questions asking about subjective experiences or about personal and demographic characteristics of individuals. With all of these perspectives individuals, at some point, are placed into categories for analytical purposes.

A very different example comes from Frosh and Saville Young in their chapter on researching 'brothering'. They use the concept of 'human subjects', as distinct from the notion of 'individuals', to construct a view of the social world. It is clear that the human subject is not the same as the individual, and Frosh and Saville Young's in-depth psychosocial approach is very different from the survey methodology that Dale and Nazroo discuss, both in terms of their ways of generating data, and also in analysis. Frosh and Saville Young do not engage in the kind of categorical analysis that is characteristic of survey methodology. However, we nevertheless think that both share elements of an ontological perspective that sees the individual, or the human subject, as the salient unit, or receptacle perhaps, of social life (and psychic life too for Frosh and Saville Young). At the very least this means that talking to or eliciting reports or accounts from individuals/human subjects is, in both perspectives, an obvious way to proceed, even though their ways of doing this, and of 'reading' the accounts produced, are markedly different.

Other chapters in this book that contain some elements of this individual/human view include: Rogers (Chapter 13), Thomson (Chapter 4), Mason and Davies (Chapter 2) and Savage (Chapter 11).

Vocabulary to look out for: individual, respondent, cohort, household, population, variables, attitudes, or human, subject, subjectivity.

A world of behaviours, actions and events

Where Frosh and Saville Young, for example, are interested in constructions of masculinity and the ways in which subjectivities can be reflexively read from narratives and texts, an alternative world view is one that focuses on behaviours, actions and events as objective and observable or reportable things. Here the emphasis is on 'happenings' and occurrences that can be charted and mapped from the 'outside' so to speak, and that (to a greater or lesser degree depending on the perspective of the researcher) exist independently of the interpretations of the people involved in them.

Probably the classic version of this is the randomized controlled trial (RCT), discussed by Rogers in her chapter on understanding change in the self-management of health. Although Rogers' own research focuses on the use of qualitative methods to understand how patients experience a complex health intervention, she explains the conventional RCT thus:

> In an RCT patients will be invited to take part in the trial and are told that they may receive the standard treatment or a new form of treatment. It will be explained that the allocation to one or other form of treatment will be made at random – and thus the patient's characteristics will not influence which treatment they receive. In some trials neither the patient nor the person administering the trial will know which group the patient is in – in other words they are both 'blind' to the treatment that is given. The reason for this is to ensure that knowledge of the treatment does not influence the outcome. It is then assumed that, by comparing the outcomes of the two treatments, it will be possible to assess which treatment was more effective or whether there was no difference. (Rogers, Chapter 13, this volume, pp. 195–6)

In this classic version of an RCT drugs trial, the researcher is only interested in what happens in terms of the effects of drugs. To do so they control the conditions between comparison groups, and filter out any 'subjective' influences through the double blind procedure.

Probably only a minority of social scientists would adopt an extreme behaviourist position of this kind, and the experimental or 'trials' logic of introducing a stimulus and observing the result is not particularly common either. However, the chapters by Rogers, and Mason and Davies, both in different ways deploy a 'what happens if we do x' logic in different parts of their research, indicating an ontology that suggests it is possible to stimulate and observe a reaction in research – to give the social world a poke and see what happens.

A different version of an ontology that sees the world in terms of behaviours, events, and actions, can be found in the chapters by Elliott in particular, and also Nazroo. Atlhough neither uses an experimental logic, both are interested in charting events and behaviours over time, to understand social change and causality. Elliott explains that:

> Event history analysis … focuses on the timing and sequencing of events within individuals' lives … The dependent variable … is derived from the occurrence or non-occurrence of an event and the timing of that event … Examples of data amenable to event history modelling include the duration from redundancy to becoming re-employed, the duration from release from prison to re-arrest, the duration until the birth of a first child and the duration from cohabitation to marriage. (Elliott, Chapter 14, this volume, pp. 214–15)

Elliott points out that the collection of event history data needs to be standardized to allow for quantitative analysis. The ontological view she expresses is one where phenomena like the duration of redundancy to becoming re-employed, do *happen as* or *can be conceptualized as, events*. Both Elliott and Nazroo make clear that events are not somehow devoid of meaning and interpretation for those involved in them. Nazroo for example says that 'Those we study both react to and anticipate events' (Nazroo, Chapter 15, this volume, p. 237). And both chapters include interesting suggestions for working experiential or anticipated elements of events into their analyses. However, the ontological conception of a social world constituted in events remains at the heart of these approaches, and makes them distinctive.

Other chapters in this book that contain elements of this view include: Crossley (Chapter 5), Dorling and Ballas (Chapter 10) and Dale (Chapter 6).

Vocabulary to look out for: behaviour, reactions, effects, events, risk, variables.

An environmental, non-human or sensory world

By contrast, some approaches envisage a social world where various environmental, material or non-human dimensions are seen as central. These may be elements such as the visual, the auditory, the olfactory and the haptic that are perceived through the senses (sight, hearing, smell, touch), and the role of human *perception* may be more or less prominent and implicated in this kind of ontological view. Some approaches emphasize the centrality of the natural or built environment, some the physical or biogenetic embodiment of human and non-human life, and some the cultural expression of things envisaged to be somewhere between natural, material and social. Often, such approaches encompass the idea that such things can have effects, impacts, agency or life, outside of human intention or reaction, as well as being connected with them.

Perhaps unsurprisingly, this view is strongly present in three of the chapters on 'Researching Place' – those of Guy and Karvonen on 'messy urbanism' (Chapter 8), Salway, Harriss and Chowbey on putting long term illness in local context (Chapter 9) and Harvey and Knox on the ethnography of a road (Chapter 7).

Guy and Karvonen, for example, talk of the 'indelible link' between humans and technologies, pointing out that in everyday life:

> We only recognize our reliance on technologies when they break down or act in unexpected ways – when a bridge collapses under too much weight, a heat wave causes a citywide blackout, an antiquated water main finally exceeds its service life, or a hacker successfully disrupts the Internet. (Guy and Karvonen, Chapter 8, this volume, p. 120)

The social world that they want to research is a nexus between humans, technology, and their material and non-human surroundings. Harvey and

Knox's ethnography of a road similarly has place as something that involves human, non-human, material and cultural elements, and also more intangible things such as design, imagination, memory and spirits. This is what they say:

> Designed as generic networks, built to connect pre-existing places, they are material forms that produce relational dynamics that were never planned.

and then later ...

> We found it crucial to consider key non-human agents – particularly the materials (stone, earth/mud/dust, water), the inscriptions (numbers, images and written documents), the instruments and machines, the `environment' (imagined and implicated in diverse registers), and an animate spirit world. (Harvey and Knox, this volume, pp. 110–12)

Instead of seeing material surroundings as part of a nexus, Salway, Harriss and Chowbey conceptualize them more as *context* (for the long-term illness that was the focus of their study). They are interested in the physical and material dimensions of places, as well as people's sensory experience of them (what they looked like, felt like, sounded like).

These three chapters on place and space provide an interesting contrast with the fourth in that section, by Dorling and Ballas, who actually want to work against the grain of the cartographic conventions that focus too much, in their view, on aspects of physical topography and not enough on human variables. In explaining their approach they argue that:

> Human cartograms have been developed on the basis that we should focus on people, not on land and sea, when we are studying the geography of people. (Dorling and Ballas, Chapter 10, this volume, p. 151)

As a consequence, Dorling and Ballas deliberately distort conventional map projections, changing the shapes and sizes of land masses in line with human variables, to create a visually arresting human geography. This represents an almost ironic play on an environmental/non-human/sensory world view; on the one hand it strongly rejects it in favour of a focus on humans, yet on the other it requires that we are familiar with and understand the meaning of conventional cartographic projections so that we get the point when these are distorted.

Finally, Mason and Davies' chapter on researching family resemblances does not focus on place or space in particular, but does rest on a world view that sees sensory and physical dimensions as salient:

> To answer our questions about resemblances and their role in relatedness, we found we were interested in physical, visual and other sensory dimensions of existence, not all of which are accessible or exist within talk or reported behaviour and interpretation ... These dimensions cut across or move beyond conventionally understood divides in much

social research and epistemology – for example between the social, the bio-genetic, the sensory and the cultural – yet it seemed to us that 'family resemblances' are indeed played out across these domains. (Mason and Davies, Chapter 2, this volume, p. 35)

Vocabulary to look out for: places, things, nature, environment, bodies, physicality, materiality, sensory, ecology, traces, inscriptions.

A world of relationalities, connections and situations

Where environments, and non-human materialities, are part the ontology, then often the focus is more upon the situations, connections and relations where these are brought into play with human and social concerns, than it is upon the notion of the individual at the ontological centre. There are several different kinds of example of this in the book. Harvey and Knox's ontological view of the road has connections and dynamics at the centre:

> The histories of roads are the histories of the places they connect, the places they bring into being, and the places that disappear in their wake. They are also the material outcome of diverse knowledges, skills and labour practices that went into their construction, and of the markets and the conflicts that moved populations and investments around the planet in particular directions at particular times. And just as they are somewhat invisible, once attention is directed to them they are self-evidently there, constructed, open-ended, in process, and integral to modern economies. (Harvey and Knox, Chapter 7, this volume, p. 110)

Harvey and Knox's suggestion that these things are almost invisible, until we notice them and then they become obvious, is somewhat of a theme in a relational/connected/situated world view. There is sometimes a sense of an ontological struggle for recognition against an alternative and dominant way of seeing. For example, Crossley's chapter on social networks does not emphasize strongly the material or non-human dimensions of the social world, but it does give a very clear view of an ontological relationality that is often overlooked. Crossley counterposes this directly to the dominance of a more individualistic world view:

> Sociological research methods betray an individualistic bias not only in data gathering (which is understandable to a degree) but also in data analysis and reporting. The vast majority of sociological research focuses on the beliefs, experiences, dispositions, attitudes, resources etc of individuals. At the most these individual accounts are aggregated and contrasted (for example, in surveys and statistical analyses). Furthermore, where structural/relational concepts such as social class are operationalized they are generally reduced to individual attributes. Each individual has a class and the relational aspect of 'class relations' is absent ... As its name suggests, SNA focuses on patterns of connection, allowing us to explore the various ways in which they generate opportunities and constraints for both individual and collective action, advantaging some and disadvantaging others. (Crossley, Chapter 5, this volume, pp. 75–6)

So, just as we suggested that Crossley's ontology was a socio-architectural one, we can see that it also relational in that it sees the social world as made up of connections and relationalities, rather than individuals (or aggregates of individuals) possessing sets of characteristics or even experiences.

Mason and Davies also express a relational world view, although this is somewhat different from Crossley's (Chapter 2). Their focus – family resemblance – not only resides in physical, sensory, social and ethereal dimensions, but also in the experience of interactions, performances, relationality and phenomena that exist somehow *outside and between* individuals. Although in Crossley's SNA approach interactions are assumed they are not directly focused on because the aim is to bring structures to the analytical foreground. For Mason and Davies, resemblances are inherently relational; they emerge, take shape and come to life for example, in gestures and mannerisms performed over generations, in different times, as well as in interactions. They are not possessed or expressed by individuals alone.

Other chapters in this book that contain elements of a relational view include: Thomson (Chapter 4), Weeks (Chapter 12) and Frosh and Saville Young (Chapter 3).

Vocabulary to look out for: relations, connections, links, places, contexts, intersubjectivity.

The world as a singular and coherent entity, or as multiple and non-cohering?

There is a rather fundamental difference in the ontological perspectives that feature in this book, which can be expressed in two opposing poles thus:

a world that is approached as if it is a *singular coherent entity* that can in principle be categorized and measured and fully known (while acknowledging that complete measurement can in practice never be achieved).

a world that is considered to be *multiple*, such that it could not be brought into singular focus and measured completely, either because it is always dynamic, never fixed, and always contingent, or because it *exists in different planes that do not cohere* and cannot be contained within one world view.

Some examples will help to illustrate this. We think the singular/coherent view is expressed clearly in the following excerpt from Dale's chapter:

In purely descriptive terms, nationally representative surveys that record information on all members of the household can provide authoritative answers to questions such as ... The answers to these kinds of questions provide the essential information needed to understand our society and, even more importantly to understand differences between groups – whether based on age, gender, ethnicity or geography. (Dale, Chapter 6, this volume, pp. 90–1)

Nazroo also expresses something of this view in his chapter on using longitudinal data to understand change:

Which factors lead to good health at older ages, and which explain socioeconomic inequalities in health at older ages, are important causal questions. The answers to them have the potential to influence social, health and economic policy in positive ways. To answer such questions the use of longitudinal, or panel, survey data comes into its own, because it enables the identification of time order – whether the proposed cause was present before the proposed effect. (Nazroo, Chapter 15, this volume, pp. 226–7)

Nazroo's chapter contains a fascinating discussion about the value of longitudinal data for unravelling the effects of age, period and cohort in understanding poor health in old age. The logic of such a process suggests, we think, a singular/coherent ontology where causes and effects are seen to exist in (potentially) measurable form, if we can hone our methods and analyses appropriately. This same logic appears in Elliott's chapter:

A quantitative life history or 'event history' is a systematic record of *when* particular events have occurred for an individual. In this context an event corresponds to any qualitative change occurring at a specific point in time. The birth of a child, the date of starting a job and the date of getting married could all therefore be described as events within an individual's biography. (Elliott, Chapter 14, this volume, p. 214)

This contrasts with the view of the world as multiple, in flux and not cohering in a way that permits conclusive measurement, that can be seen in Harvey and Knox's discussion of 'the road', and with Frosh and Saville Young's argument that knowledge of the 'otherness' and 'alienness' of life must be contingent and open:

Throughout, we try to resist anchoring interpretation of text in certainty and narrative closure so as to hold onto the alienness of our psychic life; to allow our participants to remain 'other' might even be considered an ethical imperative. (Frosh and Saville Young, Chapter 3, this volume p. 60)

On the face of it the distinction between a singular/coherent and multiple/non-cohering view can be made broadly to equate to well known differences between relativist and positivist or realist positions, although in keeping with our approach in this chapter, we do not think that labelling them in this way does justice to the nuances and subtleties in the different perspectives, nor does it help to move the would-be researcher forward very far in practical terms. Partly that is because we suspect that many researchers never fully decide where they stand on the question of singularity/multiplicity, coherence/incoherence and that most – in a kind of pluralistic ambivalence – use research practices that might be read as suggesting allegiance with both views, at different points in their careers or indeed at the same time and in the same project. We do not want to suggest that such ambivalence is a bad thing though. We think that this is probably more productive of good research and insight, than nailing one's allegiance to a fixed and all embracing position. We think it is also possible, and sometimes positively beneficial, to approach the world *as if* it were measurable and singular for some purposes, and *as if* it were multiple and incoherent for others. The chapters by Salway, Chowbey and Harriss, and by Mason and Davies, do this explicitly, but we think if you read between the lines of the others, you may find that several of them do it to some extent.

What counts as data?

The data or evidence used by different authors vary enormously, and are influenced by the different ontological dimensions that they propose. For the reader, the methods a researcher uses to produce relevant data can be a useful signal to the kinds of social world they envisage, as we have already begun to see.

So, for example, where Harvey and Knox say that 'histories leave their traces in the stories people tell' or Thomson talks of how people 'narrate themselves', we can see how the logic of their choices of method tie in with their 'storied' ontology – both of them want to elicit narratives from the research subjects they encounter, although they do this in different ways and to different ends. Harvey and Knox's research narrative is strongly derived also from the practices and processes of material transformation that they observe. Using a different example, we saw how Salway, Harriss and Chowbey, on the one hand, and Mason and Davies, on the other, felt it was important to move beyond individual interviews, or the analysis of talk and reported behaviour, to find methods that could generate data about physical and cultural environments, contexts, interactions or performances and relationality. As Mason and Davies put it:

> We found that not all of [our] questions could be answered with conventional survey or interview methods.
> One reason for that is that these methods give primacy to – or sometimes totally rely upon – individual's reports of their experience of family life, or their accounts of the behaviour of themselves or others, or their own interpretations. ... These things, of course, are vital to understanding family relationships. ... (but) ...We were also interested in interactions, relationality and phenomena that exist somehow between individual people (Hardy's 'family face' for example), not all of which can be recounted by individuals. And we were interested in the ways in which resemblances are 'performed', culturally expressed, or how they take shape in expert knowledge and theorizing – all modes which are in some senses or at some times beyond the personal interpretation of interview or survey subjects. (Mason and Davies, Chapter 2, this volume, p. 35)

Researchers who see situations and connections as having an ontological role, such as Guy and Karvonen, or who see sensory, material and non-human elements as salient, elaborate in their chapters how they try to generate data about those elements, using methods designed to elicit them or to read their 'traces' in various ways.

Conversely, we have already seen that those authors who see individuals as having an ontological role use methods to generate data *from and about* individuals – whether that be surveys using structured questionnaires to elicit data about individuals and their households or families (Dale, Nazroo, Elliott), or interviews with people taking part in randomized health interventions (Rogers); or in-depth verbatim conversations with an individual (Frosh and Saville Young), or indeed individually narrated stories and qualitative interviews, which feature in several other chapters in this book.

The point is that researchers do need to find ways of connecting the ontological dimensions that their approach emphasizes with the kinds of data they use and produce and the methods they use to do it. If you are primarily interested in the dynamics of situations and interactions, it may not be very useful only to generate reports from or about individuals. Or if you think that elements of people's social identities, or cultural constructions of meaning, are revealed in the nuances of conversation, narratives or 'naturally occurring' talk, then it will not be so useful only to use observations of behaviour, nor indeed data from standardized surveys. Or if you think that social structures or networks or social geographies are revealed in aggregated data about many individuals and their behaviours or contacts with each other, then it will not be useful to gain unstructured (non-standardized) in depth data in only a few cases.

There can also be a significant distinction between whether researchers use data that they find – data that already exist – or whether they generate data themselves, although in practice, many researchers will use both of these strategies. Approaches that have an historical orientation, like those of Weeks and Savage, put considerable emphasis on 'found' and archived data. As Savage puts it, historians 'get their hands dirty and work with whatever material is available'. Weeks, for example, describes the breadth of materials he used to uncover the 'fateful moments' that led to dramatic changes in the regulation of sexuality in the UK in the last 50 years. He writes:

> I used a wide range of sources: personal and institutional archives, sexological texts, medical journals and newspapers, police and court records, and oral history interviews. (Weeks, Chapter 12, this volume, p. 183)

Both Savage's chapter and also that of Guy and Karvonen strongly make the point that it is not appropriate to think of the data a researcher can 'get hold of' as necessarily inferior. Guy and Karvonen explain that the 'historical record' pieced together from archival reports, books, maps, can be particularly illuminating where a retrospective or 'narrated' account might sanitize or gloss over important detail:

> When studying a particular technology, there is a tendency for the researcher to assume that the existing technology was the 'correct choice'. However, the historical record frequently reveals a palette of options that were weighed and contested by various social actors and material conditions, resulting in the success of one particular technology over others. Exploring these processes of contestation can help the researcher uncover particular influences of culture and materiality embedded in the topic of study. (Guy and Karvonen, Chapter 8, this volume, p. 125)

Crossley's chapter also gives a sense of 'piecing together' data from a range of sources, including archives, to flesh out knowledge about social networks.

> I have gathered network data by means of participant observation (health clubs project), archival analysis (suffragette and punk projects), secondary sources (suffragette and punk projects), questionnaire survey (student activism) and interviews (student activism). What I was looking for in each of these cases was guided by the requirements of SNA (in addition to the wider rationale and goals of the projects) but how I looked, the method employed, was determined by the population in question and my relationship and means of access to its members. (Crossley, Chapter 5, this volume, pp. 80–1)

These chapters demonstrate the merits of 'taking what data you can get' (although not uncritically), and show that there is scope for considerable investigative creativity in engaging with different kinds of 'found' materials in pursuit of the answers to particular types of research question.

To an extent, researchers who use survey data (for example, Elliott, Nazroo, Dorling and Ballas, Dale) are also using 'found' materials, in the sense that the surveys are often designed by others, or for more generalist purposes than any one specific research project, and the data are then made available for secondary analysis. Dale's chapter, for example, identifies some of the datasets that contain information about family relationships in the UK, and discusses the opportunities that these offer, as well as some of the constraints that working with such materials can impose. Again, some considerable creativity is involved in how the researcher seeks out and engages with the data in relation to their particular research questions.

This emphasis on found materials contrasts with, for example, Frosh and Saville Young's approach which involves generating data through an intensive narrative interview, and Thomson's 'life narratives' too:

> By inviting uninterrupted life narratives at the start of the interview we attempted to capture something of the narrative form that is the basis of the biographical narrative interpretive method (Wengraf, 2001) and the idea that in constructing a story of their lives research subjects will provide insight into both the social and psychic conditions of their lives (Hollway and Jefferson, 2000). (Thomson, Chapter 4, this volume, p. 65)

This sense that data are *constructed* or *generated* through the research process is a theme in other chapters too, including Harvey and Knox's ethnography of the road, Guy and Karvonen's socio-technical approach to researching 'messy urbanism', Mason and Davies's 'creative interview encounters' and use of experimental methods in their study of family resemblances, Salway, Harriss and Chowbey's 'rapid appraisal fieldwork' and Rogers' use of qualitative interviews in a complex health intervention.

Whether one is judging the 'ontological appropriateness' of data produced in a research study, or making decisions about the kinds of data to generate oneself, these issues in how ontologies, data and knowledge connect are of crucial importance. So too are questions about how data are read as, or turned into, knowledge – how they are taken to represent or mean something of significance, or something authoritative, for the analysis being conducted. The authors in this book each try to reflect on these questions and make them explicit for the reader, in a process that is not generally part of the usual practice of research reporting.

What makes it knowledge?

However, data do not, by themselves, produce research results or knowledge.

Again, as we might expect, the processes through which different researchers build knowledge vary, and these variations connect with the different ontological positions although they do not always directly reflect them. We cannot describe them all here, but instead are picking out two key themes and selected examples to illustrate them.

How analysis and theorizing are done

The chapters in this book do not deal in depth with data analysis, but it is clear in all of them that the way analysis is done is quite crucial for turning data or observations into knowledge.

For example, Elliott's, Nazroo's and Dale's analytical approach emphasizes systematic and rigorous procedures for handling and manipulating standardized data. Great importance is placed on the quality of the sample in terms of how representative it is of the wider population. If, for example, those who cannot be contacted or who refuse to take part in the survey are different from those who do respond, the results will be biased and thus inaccurate. If conclusions are drawn on the basis of very small numbers then there is a good chance they could have arisen simply by chance and will not be a 'true' representation. Thus the aim is always to maximize the accuracy of the data and then to analyse these data in appropriate ways. Analyses may provide descriptive accounts – for example, of household composition (Dale) or the aim may be to identify causal processes which, as Nazroo explains, call for complex methods of analysis.

The emphasis on accuracy and standardization in datasets, and rigour and quantification in analysis, combines in a practice where analysis is carried out on complete datasets, once all data have been collected and made ready. In this sense, data collection and data analysis are separate and distinct processes (or stages in a procedure). Statistical procedures are applied to intact datasets and there is no blurring of boundaries between data collection and analysis.

This formal separation is mirrored in the process of theorizing too. Theorizing comes across as very important in the chapters by Nazroo, Elliott, and Dale for example, as an activity that takes place prior to and after data collection. Theory is important, therefore, in establishing what the puzzle or set of questions are (hypotheses in some accounts), and then in building analytical models and interpreting the results. Nazroo explains this, in the context of a discussion about the 'promise of instrumental variables' for overcoming some of the difficulties of measurement error and establishing causal direction in longitudinal analysis:

> Careful design of data collection – ensuring as far as possible that relevant variables are collected, concepts are well measured and the timing of events is accurately identified – together with theoretically informed analytical models, helps to minimize these problems, often to a convincing level. But where uncertainties remain, the classic, but difficult to implement, strategy of using instrumental variables might help. ... In brief, when attempting to model a causal relationship this technique involves substituting the independent variable with an estimate of its value, separately modelled using instrumental variables that are theorized to have no causal relationship with the dependent variable. (Nazroo, Chapter 15, this volume, pp. 237–8)

This approach contrasts sharply with Harvey and Knox's discussion of ethnographic fieldwork. Although fieldwork is a stage in a bigger process, it is one that lasts a long time – usually many months or years – and significantly there is no separation of fieldwork, analysis and theorizing:

> Ethnographers try to allow the experiences of the fieldwork period to shape their research agendas, for what really matters to us are the things we know we cannot know in advance. Ethnography is a slow practice and requires patience. (Harvey and Knox, Chapter 7, this volume, p. 109)

The fieldwork experiences of the researcher, and their understandings of what is going on around them, are central in the analytic endeavour, and this takes shape for ethnographers in the writing of field notes, as Harvey and Knox explain:

Writing is a key aspect of ethnographic research. Every day we each wrote extensive field notes, describing what we had done and the people we had met, detailing the conversations we had been party to, and noting down anything and everything that seemed relevant to our project. If we recorded interviews the field notes would detail the context of the conversation, who else was there, the atmosphere, the hints and suggestions of things that might not have been said and the reactions of others. Field notes are the basis from which subsequent accounts are distilled and elaborated, they shape and supplement memory, and they direct attention in the on-going process of research. As you write you become aware of things you feel unsure about, questions you forgot to ask, details you failed to notice. They are thus not simply a record of what happened, for a reflexive anthropologist will always assume that they are only aware of some of what is going on. As narratives they shape the trajectory of the research, and they also constitute an initial analysis of the mass of small encounters and events that constitute daily life in the field. Field notes are analytical from the start, and we do not draw a strong distinction between data collection and analysis. (Harvey and Knox, Chapter 7, this volume, p. 112)

Reflexive field notes and are an important part of analysis and theorizing in other chapters, including Thomson's:

Our approach recognizes the subjective feelings of the researcher as data in their own right, and these are documented within the field notes in order to enhance meaning (Lucey, 2003). Field notes constituted an important source of data in their own right and were shared and interrogated at research team meetings and group analysis events alongside transcripts and visual data (see Thomson, 2010, for an overview). (Thomson, Chapter 4, this volume, p. 66)

The idea of long and *slow* ethnographic engagement and of knowledge building contrasts with Salway, Harriss and Chowbey's 'rapid appraisal' approach for getting to know a neighbourhood, yet some of the techniques are similar – seeking out and getting to know key people, trying to elicit local knowledge, observing the environment, observing situated social relations, asking people for their stories. Although their form of ethnography is fast, not slow, it also has in common with Harvey and Knox the idea that analysis and theorizing takes place in local and situated ways, and that they begin during, and inform, the process of data generation.

These approaches put a premium on the reflexivity of the researcher, and argue that knowledge comes from their engagement and interpretation throughout the process. In the case of Salway, Harriss and Chowbey there is an interesting layer on top of that idea, in their use of community researchers not only to gather data, but also to include their interpretations and analyses.

This idea of the reflexive engagement of an agentic researcher, blurring the boundary between data generation, analysis and theorizing, is present in a number of the chapters in the book. Guy and Karvonen put it thus:

the socio-technical researcher is often faced with the challenge of tracing networks and jumping scales to connect the micro and macro implications of technological development. The city serves as a meso-scale and the socio-technical scholar scales up and down to make connections between the global and the local. Critically, this requires the researcher to decide which connections to trace, how far to trace them spatially and temporally, and when to stop, thereby becoming another 'actor' in the network of assembly that surrounds the technical object. (Chapter 8, this volume, p. 126)

This portrayal of an energetic (acrobatic!) researcher engaged in data generation, analysis and theorizing all at the same time, is striking.

Other authors in the book emphasize the ways in which data might be 'read' to produce knowledge and understanding; *reading*, here, is seen as a highly involved, critical and analytical process of theorizing and interpretation. Whether or not this form of reading is done concurrently with data generation, the point we want to draw out is that it is seen as a particular form of reflexive theoretical engagement with the data.

Frosh and Saville Young, for example, talk about reading data (in their case, texts of interview transcripts) with a critical 'analytic attitude'. They see this as a crucial way for the psychosocial approaches that they are interested in to counter a tendency they identify for some researchers using psychoanalysis as an interpretive technique to claim 'mastery' and make 'over-blown claims to possess privileged understanding of the unconscious' on the basis of an uncritical and unreflexive theoretical dogma. They suggest that in these approaches, 'psychoanalysis proves itself because it always finds what it is looking for'. Instead they say:

> We suggest that psychoanalysis has a critical edge that it needs to retain; that this involves openness and engagement with, or 'implication' in, social research to actively block claims of expertise and 'mastery'; and that this can be operationalized (at least to a degree) by analytic procedures that are reflexive and deconstructive. (Frosh and Saville Young, Chapter 3, this volume, p. 49)

They describe their way of doing this as a 'concentric reflexivity' that:

> offers a series of analytic takes on interview text, beginning with discursive positions resisted and taken up in talk and moving 'outwards' through an examination of subjectivity as embodied and 'invested' discourse, and then to social 'context' and the knowledge-producing or research relationship (Saville Young and Frosh, forthcoming).

And later …

> Continued openness and autocritique is what is required, whether one is working as an analyst or drawing on psychoanalysis in the arena of social research. What we seek,

therefore, is an approach that asks what can be made of a social text (an interview, a set of observations, a piece of ethnography) that impacts upon both researchers and research participants. (Frosh and Saville Young, Chapter 3, this volume, p. 52)

Weeks, although using a different kind of approach, talks of his conceptualization of theory as 'a box of tools' rather than an overall framework. For him, the process of reading data involves 'reading against the grain' and, again, this is a process that involves analysis and the making of theory as you go along:

> But whatever my new theoretical assumptions, the decisive evidence came from the archive, once I began to read it in a different way: not as confirmation of the traditional assumptions, but against the grain, as the product of new processes of categorization, regulation and resistance, especially at the end of the nineteenth century, a struggle between social definition and self-definition (Weeks, 1977) (Weeks, Chapter 12, this volume, p. 184).

However, Weeks also develops an argument that analysis, and theorization, should and do involve drawing one's personal experience into the frame, in ways with which we think Harvey and Knox, albeit from a different kind of research perspective, would want to agree:

> My own experience is not local and irrelevant because personal life and macro-historical trends are inextricably combined. As I wrote in an earlier work: ... 'The changes in our own private lives are part of wider, collective transformations. The challenge lies in teasing out the hidden connections, making sense of what seems incomprehensible, or merely idiosyncratic (Weeks, 2000: 3)'. (Weeks, Chapter 12, this volume, p. 183)

To conclude this section, a question that we might ask of all of the chapters is 'do you need to be an expert' to use a particular set of methods, to analyse and theorize with them, and to produce meaningful knowledge? We have encouraged all the authors in this book to engage with the question of whether readers could 'have a go' at their approach. We think the more general answer is something like 'you need to know what you are doing', but 'beware overblown claims of mastery' and 'remember always to engage in a critical way with your own methods/methodology and look for alternative possibilities for theorizing'. So, for example, Frosh and Saville Young in some ways are telling us how to subvert a particular and dominant version of psychoanalysis, while retaining a critical edge (that psychoanalysis also helps to provide) in research. Other chapters, such as those by Rogers (Chapter 13), and by Mason and Davies (Chapter 2), give a flavour of how it can be possible to modify or work against the grain of conventional methods (RCTs in the case of Rogers, experimental methods in the case of Mason and Davies) in productive ways. The chapters by Crossley and Dorling and Ballas, using different examples, show how it can be possible to adapt or borrow ways of theorizing from other domains (Crossley shows that social network analysts borrowed from graph theory [Chapter 5] and Dorling and Ballas demonstrate that the techniques developed for human cartograms originated in the physics of heat transfer and molecular mixing [Chapter 10]). And Elliott illustrates how it might be possible to weave analytical narratives out of data that do not on the face of it take a narrative form or originate in narrations and stories. Our point really is that we think researchers should not only take a critical approach to their own methods and perspectives, but also sometimes engage imaginatively with ways of researching, analysing and theorizing, which are outside of their own sphere of expertise. We think this might be good not only for researchers, but for methods themselves, which otherwise can tend to become inward facing and self satisfied.

The approach to wider resonance and generalization

The chapter authors in this book have quite widely differing 'knowledge aims' and would take different positions on the question of whether or not the knowledge they produce in their research can be considered 'truth', or indeed to have a wider resonance or generalizability. Clearly, different knowledge aims connect to different ontologies, and you will see traces of this as you read the chapters. So for example, there are differences of emphasis in whether the knowledge sought is deemed to be total (or potentially total), accurate, factual or evidential. Alternatively there are examples in the book where the aim is to enlighten, to inspire imaginations, to raise questions, to disrupt conventional wisdom or ways of knowing, to unsettle existing assumptions, to encourage people to see things in new ways. For some, knowledge can only ever be provisional and particular, and instead of aiming for total census-style generalized knowledge, we should recognize the extraordinary richness of partiality and the particularity of accounts.

Savage makes an argument along these lines, in an interesting discussion of the differences between ideographic (particularizing) and nomethetic (generalizing) strategies for understanding social change. He argues that nomethetic strategies, where they rest on using standardized instruments to 'measure' change, can involve 'stripping away detail, possibly telling detail' and that while survey methods may appear more rigorous, for example, in their approach to sampling, in fact the rather 'messy' and unrepresentative data available from mass observation correspondents in the 1940s provide very rich detail which can generate new accounts of social change which cannot be obtained from the surveys conducted at that time.

In contrast, Dale, Elliott, Nazroo, Ballas and Dorling all use survey data that is based on a defined sample – either of the entire population or of a specific age-cohort or age-group. In these cases sampling allows generalizations to be made to a wider population and, based on sampling theory, the level of accuracy of the survey estimate can be calculated. In these cases, a sample can proxy for an entire population.

However, in stating these differences, we do not want to simplify what is actually more complex, or characterize the debate simply as one between perspectives that seek to generalize on the basis of sampling theory and rigorous statistical analyses, and those that seek to generalize perhaps more theoretically or interpretively. We think there are other elements in the ways in which researchers (including those who have written chapters in this book) seek to generalize, or to claim a wider resonance for their insights, that it is usefully to identify before we draw this chapter to a close. We are thinking of these more as *generalizing 'motifs'*, than clear cut strategies or practices. We think that sometimes some of them are used almost unconsciously, but they do have certain 'generalizing' effects that it is useful for you as the reader of this book to have in mind as you read the chapters that follow.

Visualization

Some of the chapters use visualizations – for example, Crossley's has social network diagrams, Dorling and Ballas's has 'distorted' maps in the form of human cartograms. The chapters by Mason and Davies, and Harvey and Knox contain photographs, and many more of the authors writing here use photographs and visualizations when reporting their research (rather than writing about methods as we have asked them to do here). We think it is important to appreciate the impact that visual representations like this can have. Indeed, all these sets of authors discuss the importance of this form of representation for establishing the wider significance or properties of their method and analysis.

Robust and systematic analysis

In some chapters, for example, Nazroo's, the carefully thought-out steps that take the reader through the logic of the analysis and confront all the conceivable ways in which errors may occur, provide a sense of robustness and authority. Similarly, in Elliott's chapter, the detailed reporting of sample characteristics, for example, is likely to give the reader confidence that great care and attention has been given to obtaining a high quality survey.

A world evoked through beautiful language and metaphor

We think that language is central not only to the analytical process (in the writing of field notes for example, or the naming of variables or elements in statistical model), but also in the argument that is made on the basis of the research, and the ways in which claims to a wider resonance are made.

Language does not simply have a 'rhetorical or illustrative function', as is sometimes assumed, but also a 'logical function' in both conveying the argument and convincing the reader of its authority. Sometimes this can be done with beautiful or poetic language that is compelling and that evokes a story in a vivid and gripping or authentic and authoritative way. Sometimes it can be done through the use of metaphors that appeal to familiar or resonant ideas.

'Thick description' or deep understanding

Ethnographers are familiar with Geertz's (1973) concept of 'thick description'. Harvey and Knox use the concept of 'adequate description' to convey something more contingent and relational, although actually, in our view, this somewhat underplays the powerful anthropological style through which they evoke the road and its socio-cultural and environmental relations. They want these descriptions to reach beyond the particular and, indeed, to draw on and through the particular to do this in a 'relational principle of orientation'. They explain it thus:

> By putting our descriptions out into the world we become accountable for them in ways that differ from fictional writing, as we make claims that others can judge on the basis of their experience. The descriptions are specific to the relations through which they were formed, but they are orientated to a world beyond us. (Harvey and Knox, Chapter 7, this volume, p. 117)

This idea that there is something about descriptions or interpretations that can resonate more widely, and that the relations surrounding that resonance form part of the 'adequacy' of the description, is a theme that runs through a number of the chapters, although not always explicitly.

There are, undoubtedly, more generalizing motifs than we have identified here, but our aim has been to open up the idea that generalization is done in a variety of ways for you, the reader, to engage with and think about.

Conclusion – making use of creative tensions

Overall, our aim in this introductory chapter has been to identify some of the points of connection, and perhaps more importantly of creative tension, between the different kinds of approach to social researching that feature in this book. We have touched on some core ontological and epistemological issues, and have attempted to highlight these in new and, we hope, helpful, ways.

There is, of course, a politics and ethics of research and method, with which any real life creative tensions have to engage. This is raised more explicitly in some chapters (especially Savage, Frosh and Saville Young, Rogers, and Weeks) than others, but it is a theme that is present in the background throughout.

We hope that as you read the chapters that follow, some will inspire you to have a go at using a different approach or different method in your research, or at least to think about the issues in new ways. We also hope that some chapters, and the contrasts, connections and tensions between them, will stir you to engage in a creative debate or argument with colleagues who use similar methods to you.

Reference

Geertz, C. (1973) 'Thick description: toward an interpretative theory of culture', in *The Interpretation of Cultures: Selected Essays*. New York: Basic Books.

SECTION I

Researching Relationships and Personal Life

What is a relationship?

What does each author see as a relationship? How are relationships being conceived? All the chapters in this section have relationships at their core – but, as their titles suggest, they are conceptualizing relationship in very different ways using very different methods. For some authors (Dale, Crossley) a relationship is something that 'exists' and – at least at the point of data collection – has a fixed existence that can be measured and analysed. Although for Crossley the relationship is done through interaction, the social network analysis (SNA), which he uses, focuses on the structure, rather than the 'doing'. By contrast, for Mason and Davies a relationship is a dynamic interaction that is 'done' or 'performed', as well as experienced and reflected upon, and their methods aim to capture those interactional and experiential dynamics.

Mason and Davies's research focuses on family resemblances. Relationships were investigated through observing, participating in and recording a range of different verbal and non-verbal interactions, in response to a number of different methods. These included psychological testing, 'photo shoots', vox pop encounters and creative interview encounters. Some of these methods were designed to capture a kind of 'in vivo' sense of personal relationships as they are lived or done, in ways that did not depend only individual accounts.

In Thomson's study of motherhood, relationships are contained in the stories or narratives told by the women who take part in the study. Respondents (who also included the women's own mothers and significant others) were encouraged to talk freely about their lives and their relationships, particularly in relation to motherhood. Relationships are thus presented as 'stories' within the respondents' narratives. Analysis was done in two main ways. Interrogation of the data 'horizontally' (a synchronic approach) helped to establish a 'zeitgeist' of contemporary mothering. Interrogation of the data 'vertically' (a diachronic approach) involved reading across generations in a family, to establish 'family dialogs' – through case histories – that ran over generations and time. This gave insight into how women's experience of motherhood had changed over the generations.

In Frosh and Saville Young's study of brothering respondents also produced their own narratives:

> The interviewer encouraged the participants to speak as freely as possible about their relationships with their brothers, with the aim of producing narratives or personal stories that were exploratory, focusing on continuities and transformations while also revealing detail. (Frosh and Saville Young, Chapter 3, this volume, p. 54)

Frosh and Saville Young use psychosocial methods to develop a very deep analysis of the relationship which a single 'human subject' (Grant) has with his brother. Their analysis is based on Grant's narrative account of his relationship with his brother and on extensive field notes made immediately after the interview. However, the analysis focuses not just on the content of the narrative – which they conceptualize as a discursive 'text', but also on 'structure, interruptions, linguistic formulations and reflexivity in the material'.

However, in some chapters (Crossley and Dale, in particular) relationships are defined according to pre-determined rules that form part of the methods of analysis. Thus in SNA it is the fact of relationship between one actor and another that provides the points of connection, or nodes, to construct a social network. Connections (networks) may be established for very different purposes, for example to promote political activity, or to meet for recreational purposes; and, in other studies, they may represent contacts between businesses for commercial purposes. All the examples used by Crossley relate to personal life but this is not a requirement of SNA, which may be used to study business relationships or academic collaborations. Thus SNA can be used in a very wide variety of settings and very different kinds of data can be used to construct the network matrix. Data usually need to be collected by the researcher and can come from ethnographic work, by conducting a survey, or from textual analysis, but Crossley also points out that archives can sometimes be used. This method of analysis does not imply a particular source of data. The meaning of the relationship established may be very different depending on the example selected. SNA formalizes the relationship of interest and thus provides a basis for recording information such as the frequency of contact and often the direction of the relationship (for example, through frequency of contact), so that it can come to conclusions about properties and characteristics of the network. However, it is not designed to tell you anything about the meaning or 'lived experience' of the relationships. Furthermore Crossley suggests that a linked qualitative study can often be valuable in exploring these elements.

Survey methods use a formal standard definition to describe the structure of family or household and to record information about all members of the household/family (Dale). Surveys may explicitly collect 'ego-net data' – for example, about the friends or social contacts of each respondent – which can be used in SNA but, more usually, information is collected on each member of a household, along with the relationship between each member. These relationships can then be analysed using the characteristics (conceptualized as 'variables') of two or more household members (for example mother's level of education and child's attainment) to infer relationships between them. Like SNA described by Crossley, relationships are inferred from formal characteristics, and this contrasts with the focus on interactions, psychosocial subjectivity and experiences of relationship in the other chapters.

How is relationship put into practice?

We have already seen that different authors make different ontological assumptions about the nature of relationships. Thus a relationship may be seen to be part of a formal structure – as in a social network – or to be part of a person's subjective psychosocial experience, or it may be seen to be interactive. In the first of these, the 'research data' may be collected using many different methods but the relationships are imposed by the process of data selection and the network analysis that establishes the direction and pattern of relationships. In the second two, more emphasis is placed on exploring the meaning of relationship from the perspectives of the people being studied.

Mason and Davies also use a very wide range of methods drawn from different disciplines, to answer questions about 'how family resemblances "worked" in everyday lives':

> Were they part of a politics of family or personal life – where spotting, denying or claiming them might all have implications for power relations and personal moralities? Were they and their implications easy to read or were certain expert skills required? How were they perceived, and measured? What did they look like, sound like, feel like? What was their relationship to Western conceptualizations of kinship, or genetics? We found that not all of these questions could be answered with conventional survey or interview methods. (Mason and Davies, Chapter 2, this volume, p. 34–5)

In Mason and Davies's examples people are 'performing' or recounting kinship, not in response to structured questions about pre-determined relationships but through conversations and narratives, and in response stimuli such as family photographs. While this research is informed by an idea of a 'formal structure' of kinship this takes shape and form through the interactions of their respondents, there is no pre-defined agenda for how a relationship is conceived, constructed or performed. The research methods were designed to allowed new and unexpected ideas to emerge, without the constraint of preconceived assumptions or definitions.

In both Thomson, and Frosh and Saville Young, relationships are also 'practised' by the respondent in the sense that the words or the reactions of the research subject provide the basis for an analysis of 'relationship'. Both Thomson, and Frosh and Saville Young ask people to recount their narratives and this narrative is then analysed. However, Frosh and Saville Young focus solely on 'the text' – that is, the narrative provided by one person about his brother. Their analysis examines his account as encapsulated in the text: they do not, for example, seek to make further connections, for example by talking to Grant's brother.

By contrast, Thomson recorded detailed accounts from 62 women and, for a sub-sample, followed this up with interviews with their mothers and, in some cases, grandmothers and significant others. Detailed 'case histories' were built from the narrative accounts given by mother, daughter and significant other individually. However, taken together these accounts gave a sense of the mother–daughter relationship that drew on the different generational, social and cultural context of each woman and which, through their longitudinal nature, made apparent the dynamic nature of the relationship. The focus of Thomson's analysis is on the configuration of relationships within the family, 'defined both by relationships, and by temporal processes (coincidences, history), and the individual is understood as a point from which it is possible to have a perspective' (Thomson, Chapter 4, this volume, p. 64).

In the case of survey methods, relationships are recorded at the point of conducting the survey. While it is quite common to collect information about household structure and formal relationships (for example, marital status), and separate interviews may be conducted with each member of the household, it is usual to conduct these interviews separately so that one person's response is not influenced by that of another family member. This allows for comparisons – for example, the extent to which each spouse thinks they take responsibility for child care or household tasks – but it does not allow for the interactive construction of a relationship that is achieved by methods such as photo-elicitation. The survey researcher usually construes how relationships 'work' by analysing responses from family members and making inferences from this. Thus the employment patterns and work hours of a woman may be analysed in terms of her partner's characteristics, to establish whether there appears to be a significant 'effect' of one on the other. However, the explanation of such as 'effect' cannot be easily obtained from survey data, particularly if the data are cross-sectional (that is, collected at one point in time). Often, theoretically targeted qualitative interviews can be conducted to help provide an explanation. Alternatively, greater leverage can be obtained about family interactions if longitudinal data are available. For example, by recording the timing of changes in work patterns it is possible to get more purchase on the direction of influence of one partner on another. Elliott's chapter (Chapter 14, this volume) shows how event history analysis can be used in this kind of way while Nazroo (Chapter 15, this volume) discusses the strengths – and limitations – of longitudinal data in providing causal explanations.

SNA (Crossley) may use survey data where respondents are asked, directly, to list their friends or contacts (*ego-net*) and then connections are established between the respondents and the named contacts. These connections do not have any kind of interaction but all flow in one direction, from the respondent. Often, a complete population may be defined (for example, class-mates) and all their interactions with each other may be recorded (*complete network*), and indeed much of the technical work of SNA assumes complete networks. In this case the extent to which a relationship is one-way or is reciprocated is likely to be of research interest. In other kinds of network analysis, connections may be established and relationships inferred based on textual analysis or observational studies. Social networks have formal properties based on mathematical models; the existence of a connection, the direction of flow and the density of the connection can all be measured and modelled.

The role of context

Consideration of context provides some valuable insights not only into the kinds of evidence or data used in each method but also how a relationship is conceptualised. In Mason and Davies's chapter (for example, photo-elicitation and the photo-shoots/vox pop) it can be argued that sometimes, for some purposes, the context *is* the method or the interaction it involves. The immediate situation in which respondents find themselves and the tasks they are asked to perform provide the 'stimulus' for their reactions and responses, and the whole then becomes the 'data' for analysis. However, the point of photo-elicitation is to help to 'transport' the research participant to a real world personal context by evoking a world outside of the immediate interaction, for example, their current family relationships, or memories of the past.

In Thomson's chapter the generational and social, historical and cultural context in which her interviews took place are an important part of the research, and were captured in a range of ways including detailed field notes on settings, appearances and visual documentation of preparations for the arrival of the child. Narratives by mothers and daughters can only be fully understood in the light of the broader contexts in which each are experiencing motherhood. Grandmothers were asked to reflect on the changing material culture of mothering and an analysis of cultural context was built into the study design for the new mothers:

> An analysis of popular representations of contemporary mothering was also undertaken in parallel with the interview study. Popular resources were identified in the questionnaire and integrated into the interview schedule. We also carried out a focused analysis of magazines aimed at new mothers ... (Thomson, Chapter 4, this volume, p. 67)

In survey research (Dale), context may be included in models that seek to understand particular outcomes in a family. For example, information about family income or housing quality may be included in the analysis and, more broadly, the quality of the local area (for example, schools, neighbourhoods, local labour markets) may be formally included in models using multilevel modelling. Crossley, too, uses context to understand the network (for example, punk) and, in some kinds of SNA, a multilevel modelling framework can potentially be used to include contextual effects more formally, although Crossley advocates linked qualitative analysis for this purpose. By contrast, Frosh and Saville Young's focus is within the human subject, rather than locating them in a wider context. It is not about how a relationship *works* but about the human subject, Grant, and how he narrates the relationship. However, Frosh and Saville Young also use additional contextual materials such as field notes, including the interaction between the researcher and the research subject, to inform their analysis. They also use the text itself to understand something wider – about intersubjectivities and the world in which these are situated:

> Engaging with the way in which language works in and around the researched as well as the researcher, the analysis attempts to foreground the complexity of subjectivity: the way in which, when we give an account of ourselves, our words resonate within others and also do not belong to us but rather are always already implicated in our sociality. Psychoanalysis offers a way of interrogating this sociality with its complex language for unravelling intersubjective encounters, and informs a reflexivity that takes seriously the emotionality of the interview. (Frosh and Saville Young, Chapter 3, this volume, p. 59)

Not surprisingly, personal life and relationships play a major role in a number of other chapters and contrasts can be drawn with the chapters discussed here. We hope you will explore other sections, not just for what they say about methods, but also for other ideas about researching personal relationships. For example, Harvey and Knox's (Chapter 7) ethnographic study of the building of a road is centrally concerned with the impact this has on the personal life of the multitude of people affected, as well as the agency of relationships in the whole process. Salway, Chowbey and Harriss (Chapter 9) are interested in the relationships of people with long-term limiting illness with other members of their community and with the locality itself. Elliott (Chapter 14) gives examples of how event history analysis can tease out the relationship between women's partnership formation and fertility.

TWO

Experimenting with Qualitative Methods

Researching Family Resemblance

Jennifer Mason and Katherine Davies

Introduction

Although family and relationship research is a burgeoning field, the study of family resemblance has received little attention and, where it has, it is usually treated as an aside more than a focus in its own right. Yet when we pursue the theme of family resemblance across the social and human sciences, literature and art, it is easy to find examples of its significance. For example, we can see this in Thomas Hardy's concept of the 'family face … that heeds no call to die' in his poem, 'Heredity' (Hardy, 1995: 17). In a completely different field and era, we can see it in statistical analyses of risk and the benefits or otherwise of screening for genetic diseases (Richards, 2003) – here 'heredity' has come to be a scientific term. And we can see it in research on transnational adoption which shows the work people do in 'seeing' or constructing resemblance between children and their adoptive parents (Howell and Marre, 2006). In markedly different ways, and sometimes through contrasting grammars, semantics and epistemologies, these examples nevertheless all share a common interest in questions about what it means to be related and what gets 'passed on' in families. These questions underpinned our own study of family resemblances.[1] We were interested in a wide range of ways in which resemblance could be conceived and where it might matter, for example in appearance, mannerisms, character and ways of being, outlook and philosophy, health, illness, attributes and talents.

Our study was interdisciplinary, in the sense that our team spanned a range of disciplines including sociology, psychology (psychoanalytic, social/health and experimental), socio-linguistics and visual studies. We capitalized on this mix of orientations in how we posed research questions about family resemblances, how we approached researching them and how we analysed our data. That said, we also recognize that sociology had a certain dominance overall in our project, and certainly it does in this chapter. We are both sociologists, and as director and researcher on the project, we took the co-ordinating and leading roles. Although the two of us have been fascinated by other approaches and are keen to engage with them, our own modes of thinking are nonetheless still grounded in sociology – albeit we think this is an expanded and somewhat re-orientated sociology.

Approaches to researching family resemblance

For sociologists at least, exploring family resemblances seems on the face of it a slightly odd way to understand what it means to be related. More usual are studies of care, support and contact between relatives. Here, we sociologists are in our comfort zone, assessing what kinds of care and support are exchanged, what types of contact take place, under what circumstances, how frequently, between whom and so on. There is an established methodological repertoire of tried and tested methods for these kinds of questions too. This includes social surveys (either specially designed surveys, or secondary analysis of existing datasets), and also an increasing emphasis on the undoubted merits of the qualitative or semi-structured interview for understanding the nuances, negotiations and ambivalences involved in family contact and support (Dale, Chapter 6, this volume; Finch and Mason, 1993; Gabb, 2008; Jamieson, 1998; Mason, 2002, 2007; Ribbens McCarthy et al., 2003; Smart, 2007). Other methods such as participant observation and focus groups have figured less prominently. In the case of the former, this is predominately because of the practical difficulties of spending time with people in their personal and family lives (although interviews can be quite 'ethnographic'). As Hockey argues, interviewing (with the incorporation of ethnographic techniques) is the most appropriate method for an anthropology of British family life where 'everything interesting seems to be going on behind closed doors' (2002: 209) and face to face familial relationships are rarely conducted in a readily observable way. And although focus groups can be useful in eliciting collective meanings and group dynamics, it is generally considered that they are less helpful for researchers wanting to explore the lived realities of people's everyday family lives.

We found, however, that thinking about how to research family resemblances and answer our research questions about them got us challenging some of the epistemological assumptions that underpin the reliance on these dominant or conventional methods for researching family lives. We wanted to know how family resemblances 'worked' in everyday lives. Were they part of a politics of family or personal life – where spotting, denying or claiming them might all have implications for power relations and personal moralities? Were they and their implications easy to read or were certain expert skills required? How were they perceived and measured? What did they look like, sound like, feel like? What was their relationship to Western conceptualizations of kinship or genetics? We found that not all of these questions could be answered with conventional survey or interview methods.

One reason for that is that these methods give primacy to – or sometimes totally rely upon – individual's reports of their experience of family life, or their accounts of the behaviour of themselves or others, or their own interpretations. This is common in both semi-structured interviews and survey methods, albeit in different degrees and with different emphases. These things, of course, are vital to understanding family relationships. We would not wish to argue otherwise, and we have used these methods ourselves to good effect. However, in order to answer our questions about resemblances and their role in relatedness, we were also interested in physical, visual and other sensory dimensions of existence, not all of which are accessible or exist within talk or reported behaviour and interpretation. We were also interested in interactions, relationality and phenomena that exist somehow between individual people (Hardy's 'family face', for example), not all of which can be recounted by individuals. And we were interested in the ways in which resemblances are 'performed', culturally expressed or how they take shape in expert knowledge and theorizing – all modes which are in some senses or at some times beyond the personal interpretation of interview or survey subjects.

These dimensions cut across or move beyond conventionally understood divides in much social research and epistemology – for example, between the social, the bio-genetic, the sensory and the cultural – yet it seemed to us that 'family resemblances' are indeed played out across these domains. Thus in order to derive knowledge about them, we needed to find imaginative ways of grasping family resemblances empirically, and this meant pushing and extending our methodological repertoire in certain ways.

We used a range of methods in the project which were employed to address different types of questions about family resemblance in different (and complementary) ways. For example, our 'expert study' comprised interviews with professionals whose work gave them a particular take on resemblances (including a geneticist, a genealogist and a portrait artist) in order to explore our interest in how expert knowledge is developed, applied and contested and how resemblances are theorized. This question was also addressed in part by our creative interview study where we were interested in participants as 'experts' of their own resemblance experiences and where we explored how resemblances are theorized within family contexts. Similarly, our qualitative experiment was employed primarily to look at how resemblances are measured, perceived and performed publicly, questions which were also addressed by our photo shoot vox pop encounters and a cultural analysis of resemblances in the media. We should point out that these methods and approaches emerged from our interdisciplinary collaboration on this project, rather than forming an advance blueprint that predated our joint working. We shall now describe some of the methods and approaches to generating data that we developed and used – we are going to focus on three of our methods in particular, because they help us to show the contrasting kinds of knowledge that each could produce. First, creative interview encounters, then experimental methods and then what we are calling our 'photo shoot and vox pop encounters'.

Creative interview encounters

We begin with our most conventional method – interviewing. However, we are referring to our practice as 'creative interview encounters', to hint at some of the ways in which we tried to push the boundaries of this method to help us to investigate family resemblance. The term 'creative interviewing' was coined for the social sciences by Jack Douglas (1985), to denote the kind of interview that responded to situational dynamics and was flexible, rather than following a predefined structure. It has also been used in the domain of journalism to denote an investigative rather than structured style of interviewing (Metzler, 2002). We certainly used an investigative, situational and flexible approach – and indeed have championed these ways of interviewing and doing research (Mason, 2002, 2007), but there are other ways too that creativity was part of the process, as we shall explain. Our use of the term 'encounters' denotes that we were treating our interviews as ethnographic events, in the sense that we were interested in and observed the interactions involved, the situational dynamics, the surroundings and the physical and non-verbal elements. We were not simply interested in the words spoken, or – as is sometimes assumed with interviews – the interviewees' answers to our questions. This approach continued into analysis – we tried not to just rely on written transcriptions but returned regularly to the recordings, fieldnotes, photographs and family trees and, during our regular analysis meetings, discussed what it was like to be there.

Our interviews of course involved interactive talk between the interviewer (Katherine) and the interviewees. We encouraged people to provide narratives and stories about relatedness and resemblance in their own lives. Most of our interviews were with individuals but other family members were sometimes present, and this led to real-life interactions that we could observe and be part of. These, and the one-to-one interactions between interviewer and interviewee, helped to bring to life some of the politics, negotiations and humour, as well as the strength of feeling about resemblances that we were interested in. Some of this is evident in the words and stories – and is traceable in transcripts of interview recordings, for example – but the inter-physical interactions, the touching, the gestures, the looks, the facial expressions, the intonations of voice and so on are vital parts of a resemblances 'vocabulary' that emerged interactively. This is one of the ways in which we think our interviews were creative.

Another is in the kinds of questions we asked and the lines of discourse these led to. As mentioned, we wanted to move beyond the 'relatedness' as 'care' or 'support' frame of understanding, and to ask about more than how often people had contact with their relatives, or what they did for each other. Our interest in resemblance led us to ask distinctive and unusual (for social sciences) types of experiential questions. These included questions about physical appearances and embodiment (for example, hair colour or body shape). Also we asked about ways of being, character, gestures, attributes, talents and so on, in relation to the interviewee and their relatives too. We allowed people to talk about and expand upon resemblances in their family that they could not quite put their finger on and those that they thought were magical, uncanny or ethereal. With all of these things, we went with the flow of what the interviewees were telling us about resemblances in their lives, and the way these crossed bio-genetic, social, cultural and – as it emerged – spiritual or mystical domains. As a consequence, some of our questions look like slightly odd ones for social scientists to be asking, but importantly they led to discussions and interactions that focused, among other things, on physical, sensory and sometimes mystical or magical dimensions, which were crucial to understanding family resemblance. Furthermore, they enabled people to tell resemblance stories and to proffer resemblance theories.

Here is an example:

Katherine:	Do you look anything like your mum?
Janet:	A little bit … I do look a little bit like me mum. There is that sort of you know. It's funny cos we both chose the same glasses completely different of each other when we went to the opticians. She went …
Katherine:	(Overlapping) That's interesting. Why do you think that happened?
Janet:	I don't know, it might be because of the shape of the face maybe, we thought that that would suit the shape of the face. But exactly the same frames. The style of the frames, 'oh no, how embarrassing!'

In relation to the sensory, we knew that the idea of family resemblances often evokes visualization (as people consider whether or not they look like their relatives, who is the 'spitting image' of who, and so on), and were keen to incorporate some specifically 'visual methods' into our creative interview encounters. Along with many visual researchers, we felt that encouraging visualization and using visual prompts and media with our interviewees could help us to gain access to knowledge and data that would not be forthcoming if we simply elicited largely non-visual verbal accounts from them (Pink, 2007; Prosser and Schratz, 2006). Our methods ranged from simply encouraging our interviewees to think and reflect in visual ways (for example, asking questions about visual appearances and resemblances), to drawing family trees or maps with them (as a visual aid to their sets of relationships), to photo elicitation (using their own family photographs to prompt discussions about resemblance), and visual elements of ethnography (we took photographs of their family photographs, we observed how pictures were displayed and who kept them, we observed and sometimes photographed the material objects and things in their households, we observed and sometimes took photographs of our interviewees themselves).

Looking at photographs can elicit reflections on visual and sometimes other sensory ways of resembling. We found that while looking at photographs participants were occasionally able to spot a similarity they had not seen before, articulate a resemblance more easily or were prompted by the image to move beyond the visual and reflect on other dimensions of a person, relationship or resemblance.

However, photo elicitation also imposed limits. Because our interest in resemblances went beyond resemblances in appearance, we usually saved our request to look at photographs until towards the end of the interviews so that we did not narrow our participants down to reflecting only on visual aspects too quickly. Despite this it was easy for photos to dominate the interviews and to close down discussions as well as opening them. People would often whiz through their albums and collections, merely naming the people in the photos and assuming that the image would speak for itself. Photographs were also often revealed as rather inadequate media for capturing or representing a real life resemblance. Take, for example, Faye's inability to find a photograph that can do justice to the real-life resemblance she sees between her husband and his family:

Faye: And that's Mike's (her husband's) family, they all look different there but *when people are sitting in a room* they will say 'oh you do look alike'.

Katherine: That's interesting, so the photo sort of hasn't captured the essence of …

Faye: Hasn't at all, no. And *they look different there, but in real life, you can tell.*

Of course it is still productive to explore the context of a photo and talk about what is not contained within an image as well as what is. Indeed the inadequacies of photographs for 'capturing' many of the resemblances we were told about in our study highlights the importance of intangible forms of the sensory: resemblances that exist fleetingly or in the mind's eye and cannot be reflected in a single photographic image (Mason and Davies, 2009). We tried to pay attention to these less tangible resemblances by following them up during interviews and analysis. For example, we worked with a socio-linguist, Lynne Cameron (2003), who applied a detailed metaphor-led discourse analysis to a small selection of transcriptions enabling us to explore the use of metaphor in the verbalization of elements of resemblances that participants found difficult to conceptualize.

We learned a great deal about how family resemblances are part of a cultural and personal or family politics through Katherine's experiences in these creative interview encounters. Many times she experienced first hand the social and cultural 'rules' about resemblance, or the interests that were at stake in the identification and negotiation of resemblances. This sometimes emerged where she felt a social pressure to 'see' a resemblance being offered to her, or a conflict about who to agree with in situations where there were differences of opinion between interviewees and other family members about resemblances. These situations are not neutral, and we are able to use Katherine's own experience of immersion both in the personal politics of the immediate situation, and in a wider set of norms, to derive knowledge about how resemblances 'work' and are used (Mason and Davies, 2009). Reflexive field notes were a useful source of data here, and they helped us share these experiences within our team.

Often these interactions were highly emotionally charged, for example people often wanted Katherine to see a resemblance with a deceased person whom they missed and she felt a social obligation to confirm that the resemblance was there even if she could not see it. Even in more light-hearted exchanges there was a certain pressure for Katherine to 'spot' or recognize a resemblance.

For example, during one interview Fiona (a 60-year-old interview participant) produced a photograph of her four daughters, two of whom are twins, and challenged Katherine to 'spot' the twins. This was obviously a long standing family joke or party trick playing with the unexpectedness of the lack of physical resemblance between the twins. However, despite this jovial atmosphere Katherine still felt under a certain pressure to get it right and to 'see' a resemblance between the twins in the photo. This is what Katherine wrote in her field diary:

> The photo elicitation was really interesting (if a little bit awkward) – 2 of Fiona's 4 daughters are non-identical twins and she showed me a number of photos of all 4 of them together and asked me to identify the twins – which I couldn't do and kept getting it wrong. I was feeling horribly embarrassed about it and Fiona kept pushing me to spot them but when I was eventually allowed to give up Fiona said she had done this because no-one can ever spot which ones they are.

The fact that Katherine became anxious about being unable to see any resemblance highlights some of the social norms that exist around looking through photos, commenting on resemblances in other people's families and assumptions about twinship. Katherine expected to be able to discern a special physical resemblance between the twins, marking them out from their other siblings, and because of this expectation it felt risky (slightly rude and incompetent) for her to admit to Fiona that she could not.

Overall then, we think that our creative interviews helped to yield data about ways of being and experiencing resemblances which were supplemented by data gained through observations of family interactions and the live 'doing' of resemblances. In our analyses we have used the texts of the conversations, but also the sound recordings themselves and visual materials, as well as annotated transcriptions and field notes of researcher observations and experiences of the situational dynamics.

Using the full spectrum of data in our analysis (transcripts, recordings, field notes, photographs and family tree drawings) was one of the ways that we strove to avoid flattening out the multi-dimensionality of resemblances that we had worked hard to pay attention to in our creative interview encounters (such as the sensory, ethereal, emotional and performed aspects of resemblances). We approached our analysis on a number of fronts, utilizing the interdisciplinary expertise of the wider team at various points and at other times talking together, in detail, about emerging themes. For example, we employed a thematic qualitative analysis of the interview transcriptions (an analysis method familiar to many qualitative researchers), returning regularly to the original recordings to account for such nuances as tone of voice and humorous stories that are often lost in the transcription process and linking photographs and other visual data to the transcriptions where possible. We agreed on a number of analytical and descriptive themes (or codes) and used NVivo® software to organize our data accordingly. This form of analysis helped us to explore themes running across the interviews. We also employed in-depth case study analyses of a number of interview encounters, enabling us to maintain the story of the interview interaction and generating knowledge about how resemblances are intertwined with the complexities of individual inter-personal relationships and biographies. We discussed a number of cases together to help inform the codes we used in the thematic analysis. We also used wider team meetings where the whole team analysed and discussed the same case, enabling us to incorporate different interpretations and methods of analysis at various points during the process. As mentioned earlier we also identified a small number of cases which were analysed by Lynne Cameron (a socio-linguist) using metaphor-led discourse analysis. This was particularly useful for exploring emotional aspects of resemblances that people often find difficult to verbalize without the use of metaphor.

Experimental methods

We were keen to use some 'experimental' methods in our study, in two senses of the word. First, we felt it was important to be able to experiment in our choice of methods and in how we developed and applied them.[2] We knew that our topic – family resemblances – and our research questions, were distinctive and interdisciplinary, and that we would want to move beyond the routine application of conventional methods. Second, though, we wanted to use experimental methods themselves. We were keen to observe how people would respond if presented with stimuli in experimental conditions – or at

Figure 2.1   Photo sorting in one of the qualitative quasi-experiments

least conditions were we could readily observe, so that we could derive knowledge about how resemblances are reacted to, perceived and measured. Thus we tapped into and further explored themes coming out of the creative interview encounters about perception and social norms of resemblance 'spotting' as well as the sometimes ambivalent role of the photograph in the study of resemblance that we learned about during the creative interview encounters. Initially we developed a 'qualitative, quasi-experiment' for this purpose, but later in the life of the project we also developed a new collaboration with colleagues who specialized in face recognition and psychological testing (Lee Wickham and Karen Lander[3]). This enabled us to include 'true' experimental methods as well.

Qualitative, quasi-experiments

In our qualitative experiments we asked small groups of people to engage in some resemblance spotting tasks by sorting through sets of photographs of strangers and trying to work out which ones were related. We gave them very large sheets of paper and some glue, and asked them to paste pictures of people they thought to be related together on one sheet and those unrelated on another (Figure 2.1). Once they had done this, we revealed the 'answers', and there was much discussion.

We also gave them a short self-completion questionnaire that sketched out a number of resemblance 'issues' through vignettes (see Figure 2.2). People were asked to write their responses in an open ended way onto the questionnaire.

Sofia is a 33 year old mother. She separated from her former husband and cut off contact with him 2 years ago because he had been violent towards her and unloving of their young son. Her former husband is now in prison serving a long sentence for armed robbery. Their son is now 4 years old, and Sofia has noticed that he has started to look like his father and to have some of his mannerisms.

a) How do you think Sofia is likely to feel about this resemblance?
b) Should she be worried about this resemblance? Why/why not?
c) Should she tell her son that he resembles his Dad, or just keep quiet about it?
d) How do you think her son is likely to feel about this resemblance?
e) Should her son be worried about his resemblance to his Dad? Why/why not?

Figure 2.2   A vignette from the qualitative quasi-experiment

The tasks and the questionnaires were completed individually, but in a group setting (as seen in Figure 2.1). There was a little interaction during the completion of the tasks, then also some discussion sessions with everyone in the group taking part. Unlike in a 'true' experiment, we were not trying to 'control' the conditions (or prevent conferring). Our aim was not to seek to secure 'objectivity' by ensuring that everyone had received the stimulus in the same way, nor to seek to avoid 'contamination', for example when people conferred with each other or us. Instead, we wanted to observe how people interacted with each other, for example whether they were amused, embarrassed, modest or proud about their resemblance spotting capabilities and those of others, whether the tasks were something they would be prepared to engage in at all, and so on. We videoed the qualitative experiments, and also transcribed the dialogue using Transana™ software, so that we can analyse the words and the video simultaneously. We can also link our analysis of the dynamics of the situation based on these data to the individual products of the different tasks – namely, the questionnaire responses and the resemblance spotting pasted sheets.

Overall, the qualitative experiment yielded some interesting data about the politics of perception of resemblance and how people negotiated their resemblance spotting skills (or lack of them) and identities with others in public. Participant's demeanour in showing or sometimes hiding their sheets of pasted images was fascinating, as was people's degrees of willingness to commit their resemblance judgements to paper in the first place. The qualitative experiment also gave us a sense of which factors people think are important in judging whether a visual resemblance exists or not, and what else might hinge on such judgements (they are not neutral), which helps us in understanding how perception and measurement of resemblance works. It enabled us to explore the extent to which people equate visual resemblance or similarity with 'relatedness' because, of course, there is no necessary or direct relationship between these. We are interested in questions such as whether people feel they should be able to see bio-genetic links, and whether there can be resemblance without them. This is important, given our overall emphasis in the project on what it means to be related.

Psychological testing

Our other form of experimental method was psychological testing, and here we did follow the conventional methodological 'rules' more closely, so that we could produce standardized data that could be analysed statistically. It is very unusual for this kind of method to be combined with, for example, creative interview encounters. We did, however, combine these methods, in one important way. Although the testing was done with subjects who had not been involved in any other part of the study, some of the photographs we used were drawn from our creative interviewees' family albums.

Our logic was thus. We wanted to try 'true' testing to see whether we could discern any patterns in people's abilities to spot relatedness in photographs. This is different from most facial recognition work, where the aim is to judge people's ability to spot similarity or likeness. We were interested in exploring whether relatedness itself can be perceived from the 'outside' as it were and whether, as alluded to in some of the photo elicitation interactions included in the creative interview encounters, a resemblance can be seen without knowing the living, breathing person in the photograph. We therefore conducted testing with people (individually, rather than in a group experimental session), using the same format each time. People were shown a series of photographs – first in pairs, where they had to say whether or not they thought the people were related – then in groups, where they had to say which members of the group they thought to be related. This time we did not formally observe any interactions or record any dialogue with the subjects; we were simply interested in their answers and in how 'sure' they were about them.

The link with our creative interview study enabled us to pursue the relatedness theme in ways that otherwise would not have been possible. We used photographs we had been given from people's personal collections and selected them in two different ways. First, we chose photographs of people who we had been told in the interviews were thought to strongly resemble each other (noting that the resemblance might be between the living and breathing persons and not necessarily striking in the photographs). Second, we chose photographs of people whom we knew to be related, but who had not been identified by members of the family as resembling each other particularly strongly.

The modes of 'measuring' perception of resemblance are very different in the testing and in the interviews, because the former draws on a logic of an absolute and universal (that is, not situational) judgement, that can be made in the abstract, where the latter is derived from what people say about how resemblances are lived and worked through in real lives – and these of course are full of nuances, ambiguities and conflicting interpretations. By developing a kind of *crossover* methodological approach, where elements of one method are adapted and used as part of another, we think we can find out more about the complex – and sometimes contradictory – ways in which resemblance and relatedness are perceived, assumed and connected, in different kinds of social situation. After all, the different kinds of measurement that the two approaches employ are both part of the real world of knowledge claims that we are investigating – where 'hard' scientific 'facts' are balanced against personal experience and testimony and where, we think it is fair to say, methods help to create the phenomena they are testing. Our methods were designed to help us to understand something of these complex relationships between ontology and epistemology – in method and in practical experience.

'Photo shoot' and vox pop encounters

The final method we want to discuss in this chapter formed a very small part of our study, but it is distinctive in important ways. As mentioned earlier, one of the problems in researching families and relationships is that it is difficult for a researcher to be there, literally, to conduct an ethnography of people's personal lives. Yet it is not difficult to imagine that the interactions and performance of family life might be, ontologically speaking, where the thing that we want to investigate (relationality, resemblance) *is at*, so to speak. This mode of thinking draws on ideas about performativity that have been developed in gender studies (Butler, 1997), in Goffman's still vital work on presentation of self (Goffman, 1990), and in more recent developments in family studies focusing on the significance of family practices (Morgan, 1996) and family display (Finch, 2007).

We wanted to tap into the performance of family resemblances in public – the ways that people might cultivate, celebrate or indeed deny resemblances through forms of public display. We wanted also to observe, for ourselves, whether we thought resemblances *came to life* or were *conjured up* between sets of relatives in situ as it were, while they were 'being family' and doing family life in dynamic situations. Among other things, this would allow us to use our own perceptions as another form of knowledge to inform our analysis of how resemblances are 'measured' and 'perceived'.

Of course we could explore these elements to an extent in our creative interviews, by observing interactions between relatives in the moment, by looking at whether and how they displayed photographs that might emphasize or underplay resemblance, by making our own judgements about resemblances in the interviewees' families, and by eliciting and listening to people's accounts of the performance or display of resemblance in real life. But still there were limits to this. Not everyone's interview involved interactions between relatives and, as we noted earlier (following Hockey, 2002) we recognized that we could not be there to observe most family interactions.

However, our photo shoot and vox pop encounters provided us with a unique opportunity to observe the visual and situational dynamics of display and performance first hand. We worked with a professional photographer, Ed Swinden,[4] at a university graduation party. Ed took pictures of graduates and their family groups, and Jennifer conducted short interviews on the spot with the family groups, in vox pop style using a hand held digital recorder, about resemblance in their families. The photographs began with a formally posed graduation shot, and then Ed took more pictures as the interviews were being conducted.

We chose graduation as an occasion that might be ripe for exploring family resemblances 'in public'. As university staff we had over the years regularly observed the graduation ritual and ceremony, and we had engaged in the almost irresistible practice of spotting resemblances between one's students and their mums and dads, brothers and sisters. In the creative interviews people had often recounted their version of particular events and moments where resemblances were particularly resonant, such as weddings, births, funerals. We thought graduation would be a family event that might bring together relatives who would not normally be together in a home-based interview (divorced parents and their adult children, for example). As a public event that is less 'private' than a wedding or funeral (especially for university researchers) we thought it would be more practical for us to be there, participating for a brief moment. We anticipated the presence of the photographer would help us to get people interacting about resemblances.

We did indeed find that watching families pose for a professional photograph on a formal occasion was fascinating and highlighted some of the politics around resemblances that we had picked up on during our interviews, such as disappointment or irritation about not being included in a picture or about sharing or not sharing a particular family trait or resemblance (Figure 2.3).

In analytical terms, when we run the sequence of photographs for each family together with the audio recording and the typed transcript, we have some fascinating material on the significance and performativity of resemblance, and the politics of family life and public ceremony. Surprisingly perhaps, given that each encounter lasted only around 4–5 minutes, the data are very rich and get quickly to the heart of some of the difficult as well as significant issues about resemblance and relatedness in everyday life. We think this is an important point, since social scientists might be a little disdainful of the idea of a vox pop interview, as it may seem to lack some of the scholarly qualities of a more sustained interaction. Certainly, it would be impossible to cover a large amount of ground in such a short interaction, and as such the vox pop with photographs should not be seen as a replacement for the more

Figure 2.3   Run of photographs from one of the 'photo shoot' contact sheets

conventional semi-structured interview. But we want to suggest that for this topic (or probably any topic involving performativity in 'public'), and where the aim was to produce *insight* rather than breadth of knowledge, this was an extraordinarily fruitful method.

Conclusion

To conclude, we want to suggest that the different methods we have described here have generated both distinctive and overlapping data to help us to understand how family resemblances work. Our creative interviews gave an insight into how resemblances are experienced and recounted, as well as the politics of resemblance, and how people theorize about them and make sense of them. Our photo shoot and vox pop encounters built on some of these themes, particularly around politics of resemblance and performativity, and enabled us to tap into family interactions at an event that we could witness first hand. Our psychological testing experiment enabled us to use photographs collected in our creative interview study in a different way, so that we could play with ideas around perception of resemblances and kinship. This includes the contrast between perceiving resemblances 'cold' (in a situation where one is judging resemblances between photographs of strangers), and where there is a social obligation (for example, where Katherine felt the pressure to get resemblances right in the interviews). Also it includes the contrast with people's experience as part of the family itself where they have a great deal of contextual family knowledge about who is related to who and who is said to resemble who. Here, all the politics and performance explored in the above methods come into play as part of everyday life. Finally, our qualitative quasi-experiment also helped us to explore the contrast between 'cold' or abstract situations and real life dynamics but in a different way. Here people tried to spot relatedness in photographs of strangers. They also discussed the rights and wrongs of different resemblance issues depicted in vignettes about third-party situations. The real life dynamic here was not so much their own family group or their everyday family life, but their presence in a focus group in which participants became quickly engaged in negotiating their own and others' resemblance spotting competencies and in playing out some of the humour in which talk about resemblance is often couched.

We think that these elements are all part of the complex and sometimes apparently contradictory sets of practices, understandings, interpretations, perceptions, connections and phenomena that family resemblance represents.

Notes

1. The 'Living Resemblances' study was conducted as part of the Real Life Methods 'Node' of the National Centre for Research Methods, funded by the Economic and Social Research Council, 2005–2008. The project was an interdisciplinary team effort, and we are grateful for the contributions of our colleagues: Carol Smart, Lynne Cameron, Brendan Gough, Josephine Green, Jon Prosser, Lee Wickham and Karen Lander.
2. The Living Resemblances project was part of the ESRC National Centre for Research Methods and, as such, we were charged with the responsibility to design a project that would enable us to develop innovative methods. This licence to spend energies and time developing new methods, and to be able to experiment and take risks, is not usually available in projects that are designed solely with substantive aims and outcomes in mind.
3. And thanks also to Laura Mirams who conducted the psychological testing.
4. http://www.edswinden.co.uk/. Thanks also to Carol Smart for her significant role in this.

References

Butler, J. (1997) *Excitable Speech: A Politics of the Performative*. London: Routledge.
Cameron, L. (2003) *Metaphor in Educational Discourse*. London: Continuum.
Douglas, J. (1985) *Creative Interviewing*. Beverley Hills, CA: Sage.
Finch, J. (2007) 'Displaying families', *Sociology*, 41 (1): 65–81.
Finch, J. and Mason, J. (1993) *Negotiating Family Responsibilities*. London: Routledge.
Gabb, J. (2008) *Researching Intimacy in Families*. Basingstoke: Palgrave Macmillan.
Goffman, E. (1990) *The Presentation of Self in Everyday Life*. Harmondsworth: Penguin.
Hardy, T. (1995) *Hardy: Poems*, Everyman's Pocket Library. London: Random House.
Hockey, J. (2002) 'Interviews as ethnography: disembodied social interaction in Britain', in N. Rapport (ed.), *British Subjects*. Oxford: Berg. pp. 209–22.
Howell, S. and Marre, D. (2006) 'To kin a transnationally adopted child in Norway and Spain: the achievement of resemblances and belonging', *Ethnos*, 71 (3): 293–316.
Jamieson, L. (1998) *Intimacy: Personal Relationships in Modern Societies*. Cambridge: Polity.
Mason, J. (2002) 'Qualitative interviewing: asking, listening and interpreting', in T. May (ed.), *Qualitative Research in Action*. London: Sage. pp. 225–41.
Mason, J. (2007) 'Re-using qualitative data: on the merits of an investigative epistemology', *Sociological Research Online*, 12 (3): 3. Available at: http://www.socresonline.org.uk/12/2/3.html
Mason, J. and Davies, K. (2009) 'Coming to our senses? A critical approach to sensory methodology', *Qualitative Research*, 9 (5): 587–603.

Metzler, K. (2002) *Creative Interviewing: The Writer's Guide To Gathering Information By Asking Questions*, 3rd edn. Upper Saddle River, NJ: Prentice Hall.

Morgan, D. (1996) *Family Connections*. Cambridge: Polity.

Pink, S. (2007) *Doing Visual Ethnography: Images, Media and Representation in Research.* London: Sage.

Prosser, J. and Schratz. D. (2006) Photographs within the sociological research process', in D. Hamilton (ed.), *Visual Research Methods*. London: Sage.

Ribbens McCarthy, J., Edwards, R. and Gillies, V. (2003) *Making Families: Moral Tales of Parenting and Step-Parenting*. Durham: Sociology Press.

Richards, M.P.M. (2003) 'Attitudes to genetic research and uses of genetic information: support, concerns and genetic discrimination', in B.M. Knoppers (ed.), *Population and Genetics: Legal Socio-Ethical Perspectives*. Leiden: Martinas Nijhoff Publishers pp. 567–78.

Smart, C. (2007) *Personal Life: New Directions in Sociological Thinking*. Cambridge: Polity.

THREE

Using Psychoanalytic Methodology in Psychosocial Research

Researching Brothers

Stephen Frosh and Lisa Saville Young

This chapter is concerned with the use of psychoanalytic methodology in empirical 'psychosocial' research, of a kind that is beginning to blossom in the UK and elsewhere. While supporting, and contributing to, these developments ourselves, we query the idea that psychoanalysis can be 'applied' in this domain in ways that 'add to' knowledge. Instead, we suggest that psychoanalysis has a critical edge that it needs to retain; that this involves openness and engagement with, or 'implication' in, social research to actively block claims of expertise and 'mastery'; and that this can be operationalized (at least to a degree) by analytic procedures that are reflexive and deconstructive. We are interested, therefore, in identifying an analytic attitude that provokes questioning of psychosocial method, and in thinking up ways to use this attitude in research.

On preserving psychoanalysis in social science

Psychoanalysis, as an approach to studying the human 'subject' that claims its own disciplinary status and also infiltrates other disciplines across the entire spectrum of the social sciences and humanities, has been controversial since its beginning in the late 19th century. It has waxed and waned, sometimes holding considerable hegemony across large swathes of the intellectual community and at other times being anathemized out of existence. However, even in the barren periods there have been those resisting the demise of psychoanalysis, both in the ordinary clinical grind where the committed continue their lonely work apparently oblivious to everything else, and in isolated academic territories where sudden resurgences of psychoanalytic creativity arise, sometimes infecting neighbouring areas. On top of all this, there is a reasonable claim that western culture is so saturated by psychoanalysis that one never escapes its tendrils (Parker, 1997). One possibility here is to see these times in reverse, in a kind of flip-flop: it seems like psychoanalysis is at its strongest when it is most visibly pervasive, and at its weakest when it is isolated in small corners, yet maybe the contrary is true. Perhaps it is when psychoanalysis is most *rejected* that it has most scope for challenging the norms that it finds around it.

This argument is directly relevant to the issues involved in developing 'new' methods for social research. From its inception, psychoanalysis has lived in a tension between a mode of conformity that seeks a certain kind of respectability and professional status, as against a more subversive and 'radical' position which questions the possibility of expert knowledge itself.

This tension, between knowing and disrupting knowledge, is central to current debates about how psychoanalysis might be deployed within social research: does it contribute to knowledge understood as a cumulative project in which things are waiting to be discovered, or can it be used to unsettle such claims to knowledge, and if so, in the name of what does it do that? Perhaps the dilemma here is that although the project of bringing psychoanalysis into the psychological and now the 'psychosocial' academy is an important one, both for complementing and for challenging other approaches within those disciplines, the way psychoanalysis has, historically, tended to lose its socially critical power once it is appropriated as a mode of institutional knowledge is highly troubling (Frosh, 2006). As Freud (1925) himself knew, *accepting* a disturbing thesis can be a way of denying its truth: it can become defanged, a norm, just like any other knowledge.

Another issue important for social researchers is the more methodological one of what happens to psychoanalysis when it is applied outside its area of expertise, its clinical setting. There is a long history of misappropriation of psychoanalysis that does violence to the arenas in which it is to be applied – accounts of biographical or literary (fictional) figures, for instance, or of political events or personalities, which reduces them to clinical 'cases'. In the space available here, however, we want to focus on the question of what use can be made of psychoanalysis in exploring identity-construction, in examining the ways in which people account for themselves, particularly in interview settings but in principle in all their everyday self-presentations. For example, for those seeking to deploy psychoanalysis in social research, a likely contribution derives from the sophistication of its ideas about emotional investment and fantasy, which can offer a 'thickening' or enrichment of interpretive understanding brought to bear on personal narratives (Frosh et al., 2003). This may offer a more complete (because more individualized as well as emotion-inflected) interpretive re-description of interview material with helpful links to clinical perceptions and practices. However, in some recent work, we (Frosh and Saville Young, 2008; also Frosh and Baraitser, 2008) have expressed concern about the manner in which psychoanalysis undergoes distortion when it is brought to bear in this way on this kind of talk – on how people make sense of themselves outside the very specific context of the psychoanalytic clinical encounter. The example we have worked with comes from a recent British tendency to draw on psychoanalytic ideas in order to offer biographically rooted interpretations of the defensive strategies observable when people talk about themselves, particularly when they talk about their anxieties (Hollway and Jefferson, 2005). Our criticism is not only that the way in which this work proceeds tends to be too 'top down', too much in line with its own theoretical premises, so that psychoanalysis proves itself because it always finds what it looks for. It is also that even when the work is sensitive to this and offers a genuine challenge to more normative approaches, its use of psychoanalysis to produce academic knowledge results in the banalization of psychoanalysis as an interpretive technique rather than as a critical force. There are also methodological difficulties that emerge once psychoanalysis is removed from the setting in which it can be tested by the patient's responses. Interpretations, for example, are difficult enough to validate when the patient is there to respond to them; when what is being interpreted is a text or a social event, the invitation to wildness is almost impossible to resist.

Perhaps a way forward here is offered by the parallel case of psychoanalysis and literature, where historically a similar problem has occurred. Psychoanalysis *applied to* literature has both made egregious claims for expertise and has undermined them by demonstrating an incapacity to recognize literature's disciplinary specificity (how it has its own traditions and forms out of which it is crafted, rather than being some direct expression of the 'unconscious'). This has been commented on almost since the beginning of applied psychoanalysis, but is expressed especially clearly by Shoshana Felman (1982) in a famous examination of the 'and' in 'psychoanalysis *and* literature'. Felman points out that psychoanalysis' approach to literature has been one of attempted mastery, with literature being called on to take a subservient or 'slave' position, in which interpretation is the key to unlock what literature has to say, in which, that is, psychoanalysis knows literature better than literature knows itself, so that psychoanalysis 'occupies the place of a *subject*, literature that of an *object*' (1982: 5). The alternative to this, Felman argues, is to seek a way in which psychoanalysis and literature can genuinely invest in each other as equals –not one mastering the other, either as psychoanalysis speaking the truth of literature or literature exposing the narrative assumptions of psychoanalysis, even though both disciplines do have something to say to the other from these 'expert' positions. For Felman, the 'notion of *application* would be replaced by the radically different notion of *implication*', of psychoanalysis and literature – studying what each discipline does to the other, how the strategies of reading involved in textual and clinical work draw on one another and produce new ideas (1982: 8–9). It is this question of *reading* that is perhaps central: not just the masterful analyst reading the patient's discourse for its unconscious significance or the sophisticated literary critic reading the text for its nuances and resonances, but the awareness present in both disciplines that reading is a process of involvement that draws the reader in – it is a productive process that changes the reader/analyst as much as it explores any text.

Translated into the field of social research, this leaves us with a commitment to psychoanalysis as a process of reading the social in order to explore the patterns of desire that flow across it, while also maintaining an openness that allows psychoanalysis itself to be challenged and changed and that constantly disrupts any claims to be 'the one who knows', the master with expertise over what is happening. In comparison with the 'British school' psychoanalytic approach mentioned above, there is a stronger influence of Lacanian psychoanalysis here. Lacanian approaches to text (Frosh, 2007; Parker, 2005), rather than trying fully to understand and bring order to narrative accounts, are concerned with how meaning is always 'deferred', how the 'significance' of an account can never be fixed or restricted to one causal 'truth'. Narratives are 'estranging' because 'the feeling remains that whenever we try to say something completely, the saying of it misses the point' (Frosh, 2007: 641). Indeed, language itself produces gaps and differences – there is always some other way in which something could be said, and hence there is always a set of meanings that are 'repressed' or excluded when one speaks. Language is therefore not something that we use to express what we 'really mean'; if anything, language with its rules and syntax, limiting how and what can be said, functions to obscure so that we become 'playthings of language, and are duped by language' (Fink, 1995: 14). From this perspective, using psychoanalysis to uncover defence mechanisms or psychic processes in discursive work is an illusory goal, for we are always subjected to language and therefore can never occupy a position that offers a final pronouncement on it. An analysis of text does not convey hidden meaning because *there is no final hidden meaning*, but 'the fundamental openness of utterances' (Georgaca, 2001: 226) so that the subject can never be fully known or fixed, but remains resistive. Continued openness and autocritique is what is required, whether one is working as an analyst or drawing on psychoanalysis in the arena of social research. What we seek, therefore, is an approach that asks what can be made of a social text (an interview, a set of observations, a piece of ethnography) that impacts upon both researchers and research participants. Another literary analogy might be clarifying here, this time from Thomas Ogden (1999). For Ogden, examining the parallels between how one might listen to a poem and how one might listen to a patient, the task of the analyst is no longer to unearth the truth of what lies behind the patient's or the poem's words; it is simply to find a way to listen and respond that brings 'feelings and ideas to life in words that will advance the analytic process' (1999: 66). In line with much contemporary psychoanalysis, this moves the discipline towards more openness and more of a focus on 'intersubjectivity', the engagement between interacting 'subjects', with responsiveness rather than knowingness being a core attribute of the analyst. This general goal, to bring feelings and ideas to life in words, is perhaps the most that we might hope for in our deployment of psychoanalysis in empirical work.

A final introductory point here concerns the 'expertise' of the researcher. One recurrent issue in the psychoanalytic movement is that of training and in particular of who should be recognized not only as a legitimate analyst, but also as having the 'authority' to train others. Controversy over this point has led to some acrimonious disputes, including several involving Lacan (see Frosh, 2009, for an example). This is because it is the Lacanian movement that has been most vociferous in its critique of issues of 'mastery' in psychoanalysis, identifying the attribution of special knowledge as a mode of 'imaginary' functioning that hides the reality that no-one can know the 'truth' (Lacan, 1991). More prosaically, there is a question about what is demanded of the analyst or – as here – the researcher for her or him to be able to 'inhabit' psychoanalysis sufficiently to use its procedures. In clinical work, the requirement is for a full personal analysis and extensive training; in much academic work deploying psychoanalysis, it is familiarity with psychoanalytic *ideas* seems to be all that is necessary. Our suggestion is that there is no particular 'authorization' of psychoanalytic research practice that can operate outside the structures of the institutions of psychoanalysis, particularly as we are advocating a self-reflexive approach that not only feeds back onto the researcher her or himself, but also to the discipline of psychoanalysis, in that it queries that discipline's own methodology and claims to knowledge. It is not a free-for-all, of course, in that one can use psychoanalysis 'wrongly' in the sense of making misleading claims about one's adherence to its principles; and one can also use it aggressively and destructively, rather than with openness and reflexivity. However, there is no magical transformation of the researcher required before one can experiment with psychoanalytic ideas and methods, just the need for caution in relation to over-blown claims to possess privileged understanding of the unconscious.

Bothering 'brothering'

Elsewhere, we have described the procedures that we employ in trying to use psychoanalytic ideas alongside critical narrative analysis (Emerson and Frosh, 2004; Frosh and Saville Young, 2008) in research on spoken material. We have also described a mode of 'concentric reflexivity' that offers a series of analytic takes on interview text, beginning with discursive positions resisted and taken up in talk and moving 'outwards' through an examination of subjectivity as embodied and 'invested' discourse, and then to social 'context' and the knowledge-producing or research relationship (Saville Young and Frosh, 2010). Concentric reflexivity is always unfinished because we can never reach a point where we are able to stand outside of assumptions and knowledge; therefore, the end point is not so much an outcome as a process of engaging in these reflexive interpretations and movements, recognizing narratives as ambiguous and equivocal and moving to new ways of reading text.[1]

The extract below is taken from a narrative style interview (conducted by the second author) with 'Grant',[2] a white, middle-aged, British man, around the nature of his brother–brother relationships and the meaning of being a brother. Partly due to findings that emphasize the emotional closeness of sisters over brothers (Spitze and Trent, 2006; Von Volkom, 2006), fraternal bonds have been relatively neglected in the literature, despite a few studies pointing to the centrality of brothers in some men's lives (Bedford and Avioli, 2006; Floyd, 1996, 1997). The interview material presented here was collected as part of a broader study, which focused on how men construct their brother–brother relationships through their talk and specifically on how constructions of masculinities might inhibit, promote or maintain the brotherly bond (Saville Young, 2006). The interviewer encouraged the participants to speak as freely as possible about their relationships with their brothers, with the aim of producing narratives or personal stories that were exploratory, focusing on continuities and transformations while also revealing detail. Directly after the interviews, extensive field notes were made detailing observations of the participant's 'performance' in the interview context (drawing on Riessman's (2003) performative narrative analytic approach) focusing on gesture, association and action in the interaction between the participant and interviewer that might influence the interpretation of the text. These field notes also prompted a mindfulness of the researcher's personal and theoretical frameworks that were being brought to bear on the research material. Grant has one older brother and the following narrative was his response to a question asking for a description of him.

Extract[3]

1. **Grant**: Well he's, I suppose, he's completely professional in life.
2. Um he's three years older than me.
3. When um, when we were very young, I think that my experience was that he probably resented my arrival, probably felt that I stole the lime, limelight and (pause)
4. I think he spent a lot of time ignoring me, trying to not acknowledge my presence.
5. Um (pause), and I never really had much contact with him at all.
6. I remember he always used to push me away and tell me to go away, so I did.
7. Um [**LSY**: this was as a child] as a child.
8. Then when he left school, three years before me, he had exceptional grades in his O levels,

9. went on to A levels, then on to university, studied

10. and got a professional job as a um (long pause) kind of bridge design. Not an architect as such but building, creation of bridges.

11. And now he has a company that um designs and builds all types of bridges.

12. He has many people working for him

13. and he's done quite well for himself.

14. But there, there is a strange anomaly in our family because

15. I, I, I was very rebellious at that age.

16. When I was fourteen I had encephalitis

17. and when I returned to school I found that I was kind of more alienated than before

18. and I couldn't really adjust to being back with people.

19. So I used to spend more and more time completely on my own (pause), until,

20. such a time that I left school that I really didn't want to socialize anymore

21. and I used to spend a lot of time just staying away from home, sleeping out in the parks, um not returning.

22. And my brother was completely the opposite.

23. He was studying.

24. He stayed at home.

25. Um, had a proper relationship with a woman, got married.

26. And I got a girl pregnant, at nineteen

27. and by twenty, I'd left her.

28. Um my family, in their um benevolent attitude,

29. looked after the mother of my child and the child so that she wouldn't really need very much [**LSY**: yes] and

30. **LSY**: You mean looked after financially or actually had her in the home?

31. **Grant**: Well, just in terms of, no because she, she wouldn't actually live with my family but they kind of arranged things like finding a property to live in,

32. making sure the child had um daycare and such like.

33. And basically because my wife was Greek

34. her family were in Greece

35. she was quite um distraught about the situation that we'd created

36. and she couldn't return to her family

37. because she felt very ashamed.

38. So she was quite isolated in Bristol.

39. So I think my fa-, my family kind of put a, you know, a protective belt around her so that she could live and work and raise a child as a single parent.

40. And she would come to..

41. You know I, I, I felt so awful that I um

42. I, I actually didn't see my family, for many years after that and (pause)

43. I went down the route of taking drugs and being a rock and roll musician etcetera and (long pause)

44. I found out years later that she was...

45. She, she would return to Christmas, weddings, you know birth, death and this kind of thing

46. and she ended up marrying my brother. [**LSY**: Okay]

47. So he petitioned me ten, fifteen years ago if he could adopt my son

48. and I said that would be fine.
49. So that's the relationship I had with my brother.
50. A very alienated relationship when I was young and (pause)
51. because of the nature of how he now is the father of my child, it, we don't really speak at all. We don't have any communication.

How should we respond to the above extract drawing on the analytic stance described earlier? Our approach is to attend sequentially (and gradually more 'psychoanalytically') to *content, structure, interruptions, linguistic formulations* and *reflexivity* in the material. To begin with we want to focus on *content* by interrogating the discursive positions Grant constructs in his talk, drawing on two opposing discourses: a discourse of hegemonic masculinity constructing his brother's success through multiple, 'traditional' subject positions including academic achiever, professional, builder, *'proper'* (l. 25) husband and boss; and a discourse of non-hegemonic masculinity constructing Grant as rebellious, ill, a loner, homeless, an abandoning husband and father, and a drug-user. Juxtaposing the two discourses in the narrative highlights the differences between these two brothers: where Grant fails, his brother succeeds, including successfully usurping Grant's wife and child. Nevertheless, while the non-hegemonic discourse constructs Grant as the 'failed man' it also partially works to position him as unconventional and alternative, thus inhabiting another recognisably 'masculine' position: he is after all a *'rock and roll musician'* (l. 43). In this way, later on in the extract it is possible for the listener to relocate Grant's 'failure' as developing in opposition to normative and oppressive gendered practices thereby giving structure, credibility and meaning to parts of Grant's life when he used drugs and lived a fairly nomadic lifestyle.

Paying attention to the narrative *structure* in the extract highlights Grant's skill as an orator and his capacity to tell a well-crafted story that increases the likelihood of a listener's identification with, or at least sympathy for, him. He introduces the 'title' of the story, the *'strange anomaly'* (l. 14) early on in the narrative and then keeps the listener guessing with each new event that is introduced. Is the 'strange anomaly' that he was a loner or that his brother was different to him; that he got a girl pregnant and left her or that he lost touch with his family? At each stage the listener is left to think that *this* is the anomaly that Grant is talking about, so that the revelation of his brother's marriage to his girlfriend or 'wife' (the shift from one to the other is unexplained), when it comes, is climactic and has the effect of shocking the listener, possibly echoing his own feelings at the discovery.

Our next step is to bracket off the seeming-coherence of Grant's tale in order to draw attention to the *interruptions* in the narrative which point to a more motivated telling. Interruptions, or 'breaches' (Emerson and Frosh, 2004: 131), are often given weight both in narrative and discursive approaches, where they are seen to reveal moments of active sense-making work by speakers, and in psychoanalysis, which takes them to be key indicators of a breakdown of routine 'egoic' speech in the face of pressing unconscious material. In our example, the first interruption disrupts chronology: it occurs at the beginning of the extract when Grant moves from the present, describing his brother as a '*professional*' (l. 1), to the past, describing his brother's reaction to him when he was very young (l. 3). This early, troubled relationship carries an important meaning for Grant's story: his brother resented Grant *first*, possibly hinting at a motivation for the later appropriation of his wife and child. The interruption can therefore be read discursively, as a rhetorical move to prepare the ground for a shift of responsibility from Grant to his brother, or psychoanalytically, as revealing a long-standing background of envy that is seen retrospectively always to have inhabited the brothers' relationship.

The second interruption arises when Grant describes his abandoned wife accepting his family's support; Grant suddenly breaks off to recount what he was doing at the time (l. 41). Suggesting guilt and self-imposed exile ('I felt so awful' [l. 41]), he describes moving into a life of 'taking drugs' and 'being a rock and roll musician' (l. 43). The pauses before and after this sentence suggest both a piece of active narrative work (how will he account for what happened?) and a covering-over of his response: rather than expand on the acknowledgement that he 'felt so awful that I um/I, I actually didn't see my family, for many years after that' (ll. 41–2), he switches to a 'normative' statement about his choice of 'route' (l. 43) before returning to the narrative about his wife. There is some clear rhetorical work going on here: by switching subject-positions from his wife to himself (l. 41) and particularly by focusing on his own 'awfulness', the story works to increase the listener's sympathy for Grant's position as the husband and father who was wronged; but there is also more than a hint that something in his own actions remains hard for him to think about.

There is a further revelatory shift of subject positions that leads into the next layer of analysis, which focuses on *linguistic* work. Towards the end of the extract, Grant points to why the brothers do not have any communication – 'because of the nature of how he now is the father of my child' (l. 51). Whereas Grant has previously referred to his son as '*the child*' (l. 29 and l. 32) or 'a child' (l. 39), he now, in the context of a proposed adoption, refers to him as '*my son*' (l.47) and 'my child' (l. 51) claiming ownership and emphasizing that his brother has taken something which originally belonged to him. This reinforces a reading of Grant's account as a motivated tale of difference, fraternal hate and dispossession. But language also corrupts; in other words, there are moments in the text in which language 'uses' Grant, producing its own effects. For example, the extract contains frequent references to departure or return: 'go away' (l. 6), 'not returning' (l. 21), 'staying away' (l. 21), 'left her' (l. 27), 'couldn't return' (l. 36), 'come to' (l. 40) and '*return*' (l. 45). Grant's narrative from this perspective seems to be providing a commentary on crossing boundaries, those between the self and other as well as kinship boundaries between man and wife, father and son, brother and brother.

Certainly, in Grant's story the kinship boundaries are transgressed but, from this reading, there is also some acknowledgement of the way in which the other impinges on our subjectivity. Grant and his brother are implicated by and in one another. The otherness of his brother is felt deeply by Grant to the extent that he describes himself developing in reaction to or defence against him – in some sense he is therefore paradoxically rooted *in* his brother. We are reminded here of theoretical approaches that recognize the other as primary in the formation of the self (Butler, 2005; Frosh, 2002; Laplanche, 1997) so that subjectivity cannot be thought of outside of sociality; we are imbued with the other before we are even aware of ourselves as a 'self'.

Without 'tying up' the fragments of analysis we have traced thus far, we want to move concentrically outward to the *reflexive* level in which we consider Grant's performance in the interview context and, related to this, to think through how the story affected the interviewer and subsequent listeners. The interviewer's talk in the extract above is minimal; however, the field notes suggest that while identifying with Grant and feeling deeply for him at the time of the interview she also brought a particular 'sense making' stance that undercut this responsiveness. An extract from the field notes reads:

> At one point in the interview I wondered if Grant had a psychiatric history of schizophrenia, especially as he was describing a period in his late adolescence where he spent a lot of time away from home, sleeping in parks etc. I almost seem to be adopting the role of clinician/therapist in my thinking around Grant.

We might reflect on this through recourse to the difficulty of making contact with others, and the way in which symbolization 'gets between us under the guize of allowing us to communicate' (Frosh, 2008: 315). Here the interviewer's defensive desire is to *diagnose* Grant, placing him in a particular mental health category or symbolization that has the effect of creating distance, establishing a professional relationship between therapist/clinician and client. This defensive manoeuvring is also apparent in the extract where the revelation that Grant 'got a girl pregnant' (1. 26) and then 'left her' (1. 27) a year later is followed up with a question that aims to clarify information ('You mean looked after financially or actually had her in the home?' [1. 30]) as a step away from the emotional valency of the talk. We note here that on presenting this particular case study in public a common response is for audience members to question the credibility of Grant's story. We are not interested in arguing here whether or not Grant's account is true, rather we are intrigued by the evident desire to reject Grant's narrative. What is so threatening about this narrative that it is defended against to the point of disbelief?

Perhaps a partial answer to this question lies in what is absent in the story. In Grant's telling there is little overt emotionality: he had a particularly deliberate way of talking which comes across in the numerous pauses suggesting words are carefully chosen rather than bubbling forth. This absence of emotion is captured in Grant's response to his brother's request to adopt his son: 'I said that would be fine' (1. 48). Elsewhere in the interview, Grant goes so far as to inform the interviewer of an absence in his narrative: 'I will tell you that I'm holding something back.' This 'threatening presence' (Frosh, 2008: 316) of absent speech and absent emotion leaves one feeling 'full' of emptiness. It is a painful story to read, because of the sense of dispossession it invokes but also because of the invasiveness of the fraternal relationship on Grant's identity and his powerlessness to protest against it. There is something deeply uncomfortable and almost menacing about the way in which his brother who is absent in Grant's life in that they 'don't have any communication' (1. 51) is also threateningly present. The other (as the unconscious or the external other) is full of excess, even intrusive, so that it is frequently difficult to bear; consequently, we might try to 'understand', cohere or colonize it, through diagnosis or through interpretations which question the very credibility of the narrative itself.

This might also reflect the research process: what, one can ask, is being sought here? The troubled nature of an account such as that presented by Grant leads us to seek explanatory concepts and methodological strategies that place his text safely as a mode of rhetoric, a retrospective sense-making or a diagnostic sequence. This individualizes the account (the speaker as exception) or normalizes it (the apparent-exception as adopting the routine strategies of all other speakers), as a means of backing away from the disturbance of its effect. We, too, have stopped short here, relinquishing the opportunity to make interpretive leaps to the level of the social (what does this material say about conventions of kinship, parenting and marriage, for example, as well as about brothering and masculinity, the topics of the research project itself?), as well as expressing caution about invoking the 'unconscious'. This is because as we read, so we encounter the breaking-forth of moments of dissatisfaction and recalcitrance, in which what stands out is not a 'truth' of speech that can be revealed by psychoanalytic or any other technology, but a deferral of meaning in which it is clear that something happens, but never certain exactly what that is.

Rather than yielding a particular kind of replicable knowledge, the approach put forward in this chapter hopes to disrupt knowledge; instead of adding meaning to text as interpretive approaches claim to do, our aim is to interrupt subjectivity in narrative accounts through recourse to affect and the way in which it 'agitates' communication. Engaging with the way in which language works in and around the researched as well as the researcher, the analysis attempts to foreground the complexity of subjectivity: the way in which, when we give an account of ourselves, our words resonate within others and also do not belong to us but rather are always already implicated in our sociality. Psychoanalysis offers a way of interrogating this sociality with its complex language for unravelling intersubjective encounters, and informs a reflexivity that takes seriously the emotionality of the interview. Lacanian psychoanalysis, specifically, offers us a way of engaging with the unconscious as located in texts and therefore informs an interest in what the text signifies 'beyond, despite and regardless of the speaker's intentions' (Georgaca, 2005: 84). Throughout, we try to resist anchoring interpretation of text in certainty and narrative closure so as to hold onto the alienness of our psychic life; to allow our participants to remain 'other' might even be considered an ethical imperative.

Notes

1. This text is a transcript of the narrative produced in the interview; we stress that the analytic unit is the text rather than the narrative or interview 'talk' as a way of recognizing that the analysis is a reading process that is influenced by the analysts' own subjectification of language which begins at the transcription stage. In other words, the narrative co-produced in the interview context is transformed through the transcription and reading process.
2. A pseudonym is used to protect the anonymity of the participant and particular identifying details have been changed.
3. Drawing on the traditions of 'critical narrative analysis' (Emerson and Frosh, 2004) the extract is divided into small spurts of speech or numbered lines, with each line containing a chunk of information or an 'idea unit' as well as a pitch glide (a movement in the pitch of the voice) or 'tone unit'.

References

Bedford, V.H. and Avioli, P.S. (2006) '"Shooting the bull": cohort comparisons of fraternal intimacy in midlife and old age', in V.H. Bedford and B.F. Turner (eds), *Men in Relationships: A New Look from a Life Course Perspective.* New York: Springer. pp. 81–101.

Butler, J. (2005) *Giving an Account of Oneself.* New York: Fordham University Press.

Emerson, P. and Frosh, S. (2004) *Critical Narrative Analysis in Psychology.* London: Palgrave.

Felman, S. (ed.) (1982) *Literature and Psychoanalysis: The Question of Reading: Otherwise* Baltimore, MD: Johns Hopkins University Press.

Fink, B. (1995) *The Lacanian Subject: Between Language and Jouissance.* Princeton, NJ: Princeton University Press.

Floyd, K. (1996) 'Brotherly love I: the experience of closeness in the fraternal dyad', *Personal Relationships,* 3: 369–85.

Floyd, K. (1997) 'Brotherly love II: a developmental perspective on liking, love, and closeness in the fraternal dyad', *Journal of Family Psychology,* 11: 196–209.

Freud, S. (1925) 'The resistances to psycho-analysis', in *The Standard Edition of the Complete Psychological Works of Sigmund Freud, Volume XIX.* London: Hogarth Press. pp. 211–24.

Frosh, S. (2002) 'The Other'. *American Imago,* 59: 389–407.

Frosh, S. (2006) *For and Against Psychoanalysis.* London: Routledge.

Frosh, S. (2007) 'Disintegrating qualitative research', *Theory and Psychology*, 17: 635–53.

Frosh, S. (2008) 'Elementals and affects, or on making contact with others', *Subjectivity*, 24: 314–24.

Frosh, S. (2009) 'Everyone longs for a master: Lacan and 1968', in G. Bhambra and I. Demir (eds), *1968 in Retrospect: History, Politics, Alterity*. London: Palgrave. pp. 100–12.

Frosh, S. and Baraitser, L. (2008) 'Psychoanalysis and psychosocial studies', *Psychoanalysis, Culture and Society*, 13: 346–65.

Frosh, S. and Saville Young, L. (2008) 'Psychoanalytic approaches to qualitative psychology', in C. Willig and W. Stainton-Rogers (eds), *The Sage Handbook of Qualitative Research in Psychology*. London: Sage. pp. 109–26.

Frosh, S., Phoenix, A. and Pattman, R. (2003) 'Taking a stand: using psychoanalysis to explore the positioning of subjects in discourse', *British Journal of Social Psychology*, 42: 39–53.

Georgaca, E. (2005) 'Lacanian psychoanalysis and the subject of social constructionist psychology: analysing subjectivity in talk', *International Journal of Critical Psychology*, 14: 74–94.

Georgaca, E. (2001) 'Voices of the self in psychotherapy: a qualitative analysis', *British Journal of Medical Psychology*, 74: 223–36.

Hollway, W. and Jefferson, T. (2005) 'Panic and perjury: a psychosocial exploration of agency', *British Journal of Social Psychology*, 44: 147–63.

Lacan, J. (1991) *The Other Side of Psychoanalysis: The Seminar of Jacques Lacan Book XVII*. New York: Norton.

Laplanche, J. (1997) 'the theory of seduction and the problem of the other', *International Journal of Psycho-Analysis*, 78: 653–66.

Ogden, T. (1999) '"The music of what happens" in poetry and psychoanalysis', *International Journal of Psychoanalysis*, 80: 979–94.

Parker, I. (1997) *Psychoanalytic Culture*. London: Sage.

Parker, I. (2005) 'Lacanian discourse analysis in psychology: seven theoretical elements', *Theory and Psychology*, 15: 163–182.

Riessman, C.K. (2003) 'Performing identities in illness narrative: masculinity and multiple sclerosis', *Qualitative Research*, 31: 5–33.

Saville Young, L. (2006) '"Doing brother" and the construction of masculinities: a psychosocial study', PhD thesis, Birkbeck College, University of London.

Saville Young, L. and Frosh, S. (2010) '"And where were your brothers in all this?": a psychosocial approach to texts on "brothering"'. *Qualitative Research*, 10: 1–21.

Spitze, G. and Trent, K. (2006) 'Gender differences in adult sibling relations in two-child families', *Journal of Marriage and Family*, 68: 977–92.

Von Volkom, M. (2006) 'Sibling relationships in middle and older adulthood: a review of the literature', *Marriage and Family Review*, 40: 151–70.

FOUR

Using Biographical and Longitudinal Methods

Researching Mothering

Rachel Thomson

The increasing participation of women in further and higher education, and in the labour force since the Second World War has transformed the shape and meaning of women's biographies (Lewis, 1992), reflected in a trend towards later motherhood. Yet this change has been uneven, with stagnation in social mobility and widening inequality heightening differences *between* women, reflected in differential patterns of family formation depending on educational and employment status (Crompton, 2006). The social polarization of motherhood is one of the most distinctive demographic trends of the post-war period, reflected in a movement towards later motherhood for the majority, and early motherhood for a minority. The transition to motherhood in the contemporary era is an arena where socio-economic differences between women are defined and compounded through the creation of distinct cultures of child-rearing (Byrne, 2006; Clarke, 2004; Tyler, 2008). The Making of Modern Motherhood[1] study set out to capture and relate two dimensions of social division – divisions that exists *between* generations (as captured in relationships between grand-mothers, mothers and daughters) and divisions *within* generations (as captured by women simultaneously becoming mothers for the first time). Recognizing the complexity of this task we maintained a relatively narrow substantive focus for the study on the experience of first-time motherhood. In this chapter I outline the research design that we employed, explaining how this developed in practice and the kind of data that it generated.

Inspiration and resources

Karl Mannheim's (1952) essay on generations is generally seen as 'the classic' sociological account', the potential of which has not yet been exhausted (Kohli, 1996). Developing a musical metaphor, he suggested that the 'zeitgeist' of a period is not a single sound, but instead can be understood as a combination of sounds, 'an accidental chord' (Mannheim, 1952: 284). This chord is comprised of the notes that express the distinct *units* that exist within a generation. As with melody, the combination of these notes subtly changes over time. Drawing on the positivist tradition, Mannheim begins with the idea of a generation as constituted 'by a similarity of location of a number of individuals within a social whole' (1952: 290). Through a shared social location, members of a generational unit are also likely to share values and attitudes, primarily formed in childhood and adolescence. For Mannheim, generations are in a state of constant *interaction* focused on the negotiation of the present.

One of our inspirations for this research project was a study undertaken by Harriet Bjerrum Nielsen (2003) and (with) Monica Rudberg (1994, 2000), who traced 22 intergenerational chains of Norwegian women in order to capture something of the historical changes in women's position within Norway in the post-war period and how change and continuity are mediated within families. Drawing on interview material Bjerrum Nielsen and Rudberg suggest that at any one time there will be a lack of fit between gender identities (the kind of woman that one wants to be), subjectivity (one's sense of 'me') and the social and cultural possibilities available to realize these. The focus of their analysis was cross sectional – identifying common themes in the accounts of the different generations (grandmothers born 1910–1927, mothers born 1940–1948 and daughters born 1971/2). This enabled them to characterize what was distinctive about the account of each generation, and to suggest how successive generations could be understood as reacting to each other. Norway is a less diverse country than the UK and we were aware that we could not assume such coherence within our generations, nor could we map family generation neatly onto historical generation. Following Mannheim's musical metaphor, we wanted to capture the 'zeitgeist' of contemporary motherhood, made up of the many different notes that are struck by distinct yet contemporaneous generational units. For our study, it was a priority to map this diversity, at least for the contemporary generation of first time mothers.

Where Bjerrum Nielsen and Rudberg read across their generations to understand something about the historical periods during which these women were growing up, we were interested in our intergenerational chains as case studies. Our approach was influenced by work in the life history field where a family is taken as the unit of analysis and as a route into the wider social and historical landscape. An important example is Daniel Bertaux and Isabelle Bertaux-Wiame's (1997) analysis of single French farming family over five generations, which explores interdependency of destinies and the complex interaction of psychological and social factors over time. We are also indebted to Paul Thompson's adaptation of the family systems approaches of John Byng-Hall (1995) – that conceptualizes the family in terms of a continuous contractual relationship, where unresolved emotional dynamics can be transmitted through the 'symbolic coinage' of family stories, within which motifs, patterns and difficulties are repeated and the 'very phrases echo down the generations' (1993: 30). Our hope was that by collecting and juxtaposing the accounts of different generations of women about the experience of their first pregnancy and birth, that we might both capture the echoes of a family dialog while gaining insight into how solidarity is maintained between women in the context of changing opportunities and expectations.

A third influence on our research design was an interest in capturing change as it happens. The arrival of a new generation in a family is a dynamic moment, where expectations hit realities, old roles are shed and new relationships formed. Here we have drawn on Norbert Elias' (1978) conception that the configuration rather than the individual is the basic unit of analysis. The configuration is defined both by relationships, and by temporal processes (coincidences, history), and the individual is understood as a point from which it is possible to have a perspective. We envisaged a longitudinal component to the case studies, designing the research around a critical moment of personal and family change (Holland and Thomson, 2009; Thomson et al., 2002). The prospective dimension of the research brings with it a new range of methodological and epistemological questions arising from how respondent accounts change over time, the significance of the researchers' subjective responses and reflections as a source of data in it's own right and the impossibility of analytic closure (McLeod and Thomson, 2009; Thomson and Holland, 2003, Thomson 2009a).

Research design and methods

The research questions for The Making of Modern Motherhood study were as follows:

- What does motherhood mean to first time mothers? Are there differences between women relating to age, social class, ethnicity and sexuality?
- What are the intergenerational narratives concerning motherhood? How do they resonate with theories of individualization or shifting patterns of interdependence?
- How does being a mother change women's identities? What forms of entitlement (or loss) does it bring and what social practices/actions and forms of solidarity does it incite?
- How have women of different generations imagined and practised motherhood? What resources and advice do they draw upon (texts, people, products, community) and how does this fit with other identities, life plans?
- What part do men play in influencing women's expectations and experiences of motherhood?

In order to answer these questions we combined longitudinal and cross-generational research designs, enabling us to capture an interplay of historical, generational and biographical processes.

Questionnaire

A pre-selection questionnaire was developed, piloted, refined and distributed through settings in a new town and inner-city research sites including: Mothercare shops; public and private antenatal classes; Sure Start; young mothers projects and specialist networks aimed at disabled and lesbian mothers. The primary aim of the questionnaire was to assist us in identifying a diverse interview sample of expectant first time mothers. In addition to demographic data and a basic reproductive history, we also collected information concerning the respondents' mother, preferred sources of advice, media consumption, antenatal activity, birth plans and feelings about pregnancy. In total 144 questionnaires were completed and data was coded and entered into SPSS and basic descriptive statistics were run on an initial sample of 131. The resulting report guided our analysis of media texts and informed our selection of interviewees.

Interviews

From the volunteers we identified a sample of 62 expectant mothers for interview. Volunteers were followed up fulfilling the requirements of a quota sample constructed primarily in relation to age, but providing diversity in terms of social class, ethnicity, work status, living situation and proximity to family support. An interview schedule seeking to capture biographical narratives was generated, piloted and refined. We sought different forms of data from the different stages of the interview. An initial invitation to respondents to tell the stories of their life and pregnancy was followed by a discussion of the resources that they drew on in preparing themselves for motherhood. By inviting uninterrupted life narratives at the start of the interview we attempted to capture something of the narrative form that is the basis of the biographical narrative interpretive method (Wengraf, 2001) and the idea that in constructing a story of their lives research subjects will provide insight into both the social and psychic conditions of their lives (Hollway and Jefferson, 2000). We deliberately sought to capture the ways in which women might be storying their pregnancies, inviting them to retell family stories of their own births and accounts of 'conception' that must be produced for family, friends and professionals (Thomson et al., 2009). Visual prompts were then used to facilitate an exploration of sensitive issues including sexual relations, body image, breast feeding and dis-identifications with other mothers on the basis of social class, age, ethnicity and disability (Kehily and Thomson, 2011). The final section of the interview involved discussion of the respondents' expectations of motherhood and their birth plans. Interviewees were also asked about preparations for the arrival of the baby and, with their consent, photographs were taken to record these.

Consents for recording and archiving were negotiated before and after the interview, which was generally conducted in women's homes and recorded digitally. A coding frame was generated through an analysis of a subsample of interviews, and an agreed approach was established before the full sample was coded using a computer based qualitative analysis software. After the interview, detailed reflective field notes were made documenting access, setting, appearances, emotional dynamics and emergent themes. Our style of recording field notes was guided by ethnographic note taking and the use of case profiles in qualitative longitudinal research (Thomson, 2007; Thomson and Holland, 2003). Our approach recognizes the subjective feelings of the researcher as data in their own right, and these are documented within the field notes in order to enhance meaning (Lucey et al., 2003). Field notes constituted an important source of data in their own right and were shared and interrogated at research team meetings and group analysis events alongside transcripts and visual data (see Thomson, 2010, for an overview).

Case studies

Twelve women were invited to take part in case studies. In making our selection we sought a diverse sample as well as considering the resilience and enthusiasm of potential participants. Case studies included interviews with grandmothers, great-grandmothers and 'significant others', and were completed with a second interview with the expectant mother at least one year after birth. Interview schedules were generated through a combination of standard questions and themes identified from the expectant mother interviews. Grandmothers and great-grandmothers were asked to recall what they knew of their own mother's experiences of pregnancy and birth before providing a detailed account of their own first pregnancy and commenting on their daughter's experiences. They were also asked to share images and objects from their own mothering and photographic records were made with their consent. In most cases all stages of data generation in case studies were undertaken by a single researcher. Multidisciplinary analysis workshops were enormously productive in helping us create a common framework for the analysis and representation of case study data.

The task of creating case histories from case archives in a qualitative longitudinal study is labour intensive yet a necessary means of condensing data. Case histories operate as a data management tool for a complex and mixed media dataset and as a vehicle for narrating and interpreting the whole case. In creating the case histories we were guided by the following principles:

- That the overall purpose of the case history was to enable understanding of different lives in relation, and over time.
- That the case history should bring together the different parts of the case.
- That each research encounter should be featured in its own right.
- The case history should maintain the temporal sequence of the research process (for example, the sequence in which interviews were conducted).

- That the case history is written in the voice of the researcher, integrating an account of the interview dynamic and including the explicit reflections on meaning.
- That the case history also operates as a thick description, as far as possible using the interview subject's own language, seeking to capturing family scripts/dialogs.

Cultural analysis

An analysis of popular representations of contemporary mothering was also undertaken in parallel with the interview study. Popular resources were identified in the questionnaire and integrated into the interview schedule. We also carried out a focused analysis of magazines aimed at new mothers during the period September 2004–April 2006 (Kehily and Thomson, 2011).

Analysis and interpretation – reading data in two directions

The study generated a large, complex and rich dataset, with endless possibilities for analysis and interpretation. In this section we provide two examples of the ways in which we have interrogated this data and the kinds of findings that it gives rise to.

Reading horizontally across the sample: talking about generation

In order to answer the first of our research questions: 'What does motherhood mean to first time mothers?' we interrogated the initial dataset of interviews with 62 expectant first time mothers, as well as the visual data that we had generated when at the women's homes and our analysis of pregnancy magazines. We were also able to draw on our field notes where researchers had systematically reflected on the significance of each interview encounter for our key research questions. We searched for an 'affinity of responses' (Mannheim, 1952: 306) within the accounts and data sources, using constant comparison to find whether these cohered around the axes of difference that we had identified. One finding that emerged strongly in this analysis was the significance of age in shaping women's accounts of motherhood. We summarized this cross sectional analysis of the interviews with expectant mothers in the following way:

> Researchers interviewed women aged between 15 and 48 as they prepared for the birth of their first child. These interviews capture the very different 'situations' of expectant mothers – defined in terms of their bodily, socio-economic and relationship circumstances. Our analysis suggests that age has become *the* master category through which popular notions of mothering are constituted: with women of different ages narrating their transitions in terms of 'the end of childhood', the centre of a 'project of self' and the 'last gasp' of fertility. Getting motherhood 'right' in contemporary times involves synchronizing the

biographies of the individual, couple, family and peers; with the timetables of work, education and care. In focusing on 'choice', this construction of motherhood marginalizes the experiences of younger and older mothers (who are seen as suffering from insufficient or excessive agency respectively), and obscures underlying patterns of social class, and the salience of sexuality, ethnicity and disability. (Thomson and Kehily, 2008: 7)

This analysis draws primarily on the interview data and on the kinds of narratives employed by women to describe their situations. By comparing accounts we were able to discern patterns within the data, suggesting that the way women tended to talk about their impending transition to parenthood emphasized life stage and downplayed other potentially important differences which might also be important in shaping women's experiences. We have conceptualized the status of these kinds of narratives in terms of 'intelligibility', suggesting that women draw on publicly available narrative resources in order to 'story' their lives and make them intelligible to others (Butler, 2004; Thomson et al., 2009). New stories emerge in the confluence of developing identities and available resources that facilitate both the story telling and its reception (Plummer, 1995). The transition from private story to the generation of a public problem involves struggle and recognition of subjecthood, and the privilege to narrate oneself (rather than to be narrated by others) reflects wider dimensions of social, cultural and economic status (Adkins, 2003; Skeggs, 2004).

The relatively large size and diversity of our initial interview sample meant that we were able to explore patterns in the ways in which people talked about becoming a mother and to map these against various axes of difference. Asking our respondents to identify and discuss the books, magazines, websites and television programmes that they drew on in their pregnancies, and then conducting an analysis of pregnancy magazines helped us to locate interview narratives within a common popular culture and to begin to understand how this privileged particular experiences (Kehily and Thomson, 2010). Reading data horizontally in this way privileges socially oriented analyses that help us locate individuals in relation to wider cohorts and their historically located circumstances. Other cross generational studies have attempted to repeat this analysis with different family generations, although this gives rise to many challenges in terms of controlling the sample with demographic features complicated by social mobility (Bjerrum Nielsen and Rudberg, 1994, 2000; Brannen et al., 2004). Our design did not provide us with sufficient numbers of the older generation to make this a valid undertaking. Instead we focused on understanding our data vertically, exploring the complex interaction of psychological and social factors over time.

Reading vertically within the case: capturing family dialogs

Although we had questioned our 62 expectant mothers about how parenthood might affect their family dynamics, it was only through the family case study data that we could engage empirically with research questions that sought to identify intergenerational narratives concerning motherhood. By relating the successive accounts of women, their mothers and significant others collected during a period of intense upheaval, we hoped to capture the 'symbolic coinage of family stories' in the making (Thompson, 1993) and what Gabriele Rosenthal (1998) conceptualizes as the 'family dialog' that can only be discerned by exploring the family as a collective and dynamic whole. As I have already suggested, the idea that families produce and negotiate their own distinctive scripts does not mean that these exist in isolation from wider popular narratives. One of the ways in which we sought to capture these dialogs was by asking about whether women knew the story of their own birth. The following extracts taken from pilot interviews, illustrate how family motifs (such as gardening) can resonate across and between generations. Thirty-three-year-old Sarah Carter[2] was nine-months pregnant at the time of the interview:

> Sarah: I was early and mum's waters broke when she was doing the gardening and granny was there at the time, she didn't tell me that until we had this conversation. Her own mother was there when her waters broke and she didn't tell her, she let her go home, she didn't want to worry her, I thought that was really funny, cause that's probably what I would have done. Oh mum, see you later, everything's fine.

I also asked her about how her relationship is with her mother at this very late point of her pregnancy:

> Sarah: We've had literally two conversations, what she's been doing, she says, 'Ooh I'll come round and do some weeding' and that's basically her way of coming over to make sure I'm alright. But she does the weeding as well and next door is just like, 'look at your mum out there, doing the weeding' and it's weird because she doesn't want to talk, in a way she's not even there to talk to me, in the garden weeding, as long as she knows I'm alright. It's a bit bizarre and I have to sit her down and force her to have a cup of tea and have a conversation with her, and then she's like, it's like she doesn't want to intrude basically, she doesn't want to, but she wants to come over …

Some weeks later (after the baby is born) I interview Sarah's mother, Connie, inviting her to tell me what she knows about her own birth.

> Connie: It's Boxing Day, so the whole Christmas my granny kept chickens had a big vegetable garden, so it was reasonably you know they had reasonable money, and (they were) sitting by the fire through Christmas Evening eating raisins and the contractions came and they chatted a bit more. Time went by and mum must have gone, it must have almost gone into second stage very, very quickly. And dad was sent off for the midwife, which obviously didn't come in time obviously, I was born just after midnight that was in the wrong place at the right time.

I then asked Connie about the birth of her first child (Sarah) and she tells me this story:

> Connie: Well it started on a Sunday, my mum was over and we were gardening. I was planting bulbs and I squatted down to plant the bulbs and my waters went. But then being, this is the difference between Sarah's generation and mine, I didn't actually tell my mum (laughs). I just sort of carried on, thinking, I went in and got the meal and she had the meal with us and then she went home and then I told husband (laughs). And I was leaking all that time so I knew something was going to happen.
>
> Rachel: That's interesting. Why do you think that you didn't tell your mum?
>
> Connie: Well in a way I kind of wanted her out of the way. I didn't actually want to bother her with the thought of it and, I thought well it is going to take a while so I will just wait till she had gone.

These extracts convey a sense of the complex relationship between continuity and change within families. Gardening provides a point of continuity between generations of women, yet it is also a medium through which generational difference can be expressed. The decision to exclude her mother from her birth is an important gesture for Connie, who was part of a vanguard of women who remade birth as an intimate couple experience rather than part of a separate sphere of women's business. Yet her reticence places her outside the culture of disclosing intimacy that characterizes the contemporary moment. Sarah and Connie are both similar and different, and well worn family stories about birth are one of the ways through which these connections and distinctions are negotiated.

The inclusion of family case studies certainly enriched the findings of the original Making of Modern Motherhoods study (Thomson, 2009b). In the final report on the first stage of the study, we summarized the contribution of the case studies as follows:

> Case studies also provided insight into how women's experience of motherhood had changed over generations. Women becoming mothers in the 1950s, 60s and 70s generally recall a time when mothering was more taken for granted ('we just got on with it'), with less reliance on antenatal classes, or independent research. The dominant discourse of 'choice' that shapes contemporary constructions is less evident in their accounts, with ideas of 'life planning' applied in retrospect. Grandmothers told a story of progress concerning the changing situation of mothering, emphasizing the increased involvement of men in birth, and an increasingly sociable, public and material enactment of mothering – captured in practices of baby massage, support groups and the availability of labour-saving products. Yet these gains were also associated with losses – including the creation of pampered and demanding babies and an intensification of the rhythms of daily life. Deliberation over childcare and whether women 'would' or 'could' stay at home with babies was the most sensitive of all intergenerational conversations. Whatever the strategy adopted by mothers and father, it was constituted in conversation with their own experience of being parented. (Thomson and Kehily, 2008: 8)

Interviews with grandmothers and significant others generally took place after the birth of the child, and we began to build a picture of the ways in which the wider family were responding to and narrating the arrival of a new generation. Re-interviewing the mother a year after our first meeting provided an opportunity for her to reflect on and describe this process. At these second interviews women reported profound changes that were less easily narrated that the changes that they had anticipated on our first meeting. In our final report we described this in terms of 'transformations to the temporal, spatial and emotional fabric of their lives, described in terms of "being more connected to the world" and like being "the same person in a different country"' (Thomson and Kehily, 2008: 8). In a second phases of the research, in which we have followed six of our 12 case studies over another two-year period, we have undertaken second interviews with both grandmothers and significant others, spent a day observing the mother and child and conducted a fourth interview with the mother, constructing our interview schedule from fragments of data taken from our series of conversations. As our longitudinal dataset grows, the case history methodology becomes an increasingly important tool for enabling us to manage the dataset and to gain a sense of the family case as a dynamic and related whole that can be viewed and narrated from different positions within the constellation (Elias, 1978; Thomson, 2009) including that of the child (Thomson et al., 2009).

Conclusion

In this chapter I have presented the design and methods of the Making of Modern Motherhoods study in order to show the potential of biographically based research in understanding how social changes are negotiated and experienced within the personal lives of individuals and families. My focus has been on how to capture the interplay of two dimensions of generation: horizontal (captured in interviews with a diverse group of 62 expectant first time mothers) and vertical (through 12 intergenerational family case studies, followed longitudinally). Our research questions demand that we interrogate the dataset in different directions, synchronically in order to capture the 'zeitgeist' of contemporary mothering, and diachronically in order to pursue the family as a unit of analysis. Mapping the zeitgeist of contemporary mothering involved an analysis of patterns in narratives across the dataset, making links between personal and popular discourses. Forging family case histories demanded a different approach in which capturing echoes in the family dialog over time was the objective. The chapter aims to show how it is possible to operationalize research questions that engage with questions of continuity and change, and the kind of insights that this research design can produce. Influential social theories of individualization and de-traditionalization tend to forge coherent and linear narratives about social change. Yet these narratives are increasingly disrupted by empirical projects such as this which point to complexity (in the past as well as present) and the significance of wider cultural narratives (Goodwin and O'Connor, 2005; McLeod and Thomson, 2009; Savage, 2005, 2007). Exploring motherhood in two directions – cross-sectionally as experienced by a generation, and longitudinally as experienced by a family – produced an understanding of continuity and change as mutually constituted, with discourses of change and continuity arising respectively from identifications within and between generations.

Notes

1. The research project The Making of Modern Motherhood: Memories, Identities and Representations (Res 148–25–0057) was funded by the Economic and Social Research Council as part of the Identities and Social Action research programme (http://www.identities.ac.uk). The project was directed by Rachel Thomson and Mary Jane Kehily and involved Lucy Hadfield and Sue Sharpe. A subsequent stage of the study 'The Dynamics of Motherhood' has been funded by the ESRC as part of the Timescapes initiative (http://www.timescapes.leeds.ac.uk).
2. All names have been changed to protect the anonymity of participants.

References

Adkins, L. (2003) 'Reflexivity: freedom or habit of gender', *Theory, Culture and Society*, 20 (6): 21–42.

Bertaux, D. and Bertaux-Wiame, I. (1997) 'Heritage and its lineage: A case history of transmission and social mobility over five generations', in D. Bertaux and P. Thompson (eds), *Pathways to Social Class: A Qualitative Approach to Social Mobility*. Oxford: Clarendon Press. pp 62–97.

Bjerrum Nielsen, H. (2003) 'Historical, cultural, and emotional meanings: interviews with young girls in three generations', *NORA: Nordic Journal of Women's Studies*, 11 (1): 14–26.

Bjerrum Nielsen, H. and Rudberg, M. (1994) *Psychological Gender and Modernity*. Oslo: Scandinavian University Press.

Bjerrum Nielsen, H. and Rudberg, M. (2000) 'Gender, love and education in three generations', *The European Journal of Women's Studies*, 7 (4): 423–53.

Brannen, J., Moss, P. and Mooney, A. (2004) *Working and Caring over the Twentieth Century: Change and Continuity in Four Generation Families*. Basingstoke: Palgrave Macmillan.

Byng-Hall, J. (1995) *Rewriting Family Scripts: Improvisations and Systems Change*. New York: Guildford Press.

Byrne, B. (2006) 'In search of a "good mix". Race, class gender and practices of mothering', *Sociology*, 40 (6): 1001–17.

Butler, J. (2004) *Undoing Gender*. London: Routledge.

Clarke, A. (2004) 'Maternity and materiality: becoming a mother in consumer culture', in J. Taylor, L. Layne and D. Wozniak (eds), *Consuming Motherhood*. Rutgers University Press. pp. 57–71.

Crompton, R. (2006) *Employment and the Family: The Reconfiguration of Work and Family Life in Contemporary Societies*. Cambridge: Cambridge University Press.

Elias, N. (1978) *What Is Sociology?* New York: University of Columbia Press.

Goodwin, J. and O'Connor, H. (2005) 'Exploring complex transition: looking back at the "Golden Age" of school to work', *Sociology*, 39 (2): 197–200.

Holland, J. and Thomson, R. (2009) 'Gaining a perspective on choice and fate: revisiting critical moments', *European Societies*, 11 (3): 451–69.

Hollway, W. and Jefferson, T. (2000) *Doing Qualitative Research Differently: Free Association, Narrative and Interview Methods*. London: Sage.

Kehily, M.J. and Thomson, R. (2011) 'Displaying motherhood: representations, visual methods and the materiality of maternal practice', in E. Dermott and J. Seymour (eds.) *Displaying Families*, Basingstoke: Palgrave.

Kohli, M. (1996) 'The problem of generations: family, economy, politics', Public Lectures No. 14 Collegium Budapest: Institute for Advanced Studies. Available at: http://www.colbud.hu/main_old/PubArchive/PL/PL14-Kohli.pdf (accessed 4 February 2008).

Lewis, J. (1992) *Women in Britain since 1945*. Oxford: Blackwell.

Lucey, H., Melody, J. and Walkerdine, V. (2003) 'Project 4:21 transitions to womanhood: developing a psychosocial perspective in one longitudinal study', *International Journal of Social Research Methodology*, 6 (3): 279–84.

McLeod, J. and Thomson, R. (2009) *Researching Social Change: Qualitative Approaches*. London: Sage.

Mannheim, K. (1952) 'The problem of generations', in P. Kecskemeti (ed.), *Essays on the Sociology of Knowledge*. London: Routledge & Kegan Paul. pp. 276–323.

Plummer, K. (1995) *Telling Sexual Stories: Power, Change and Social Worlds*. London: Routledge.

Rosenthal, G. (1998). *The Holocaust in Three Generations: Families of Victims and Perpetrators of the Nazi Regime*. London: Cassells.

Savage, M. (2005a) 'Revisiting classic qualitative studies', *Historical Social Research*, 3 (1): 118–39.

Savage, M. (2005b) 'Revisiting class qualitative studies', *Forum: Qualitative Sozialforschung/Forum: Qualitative Social Research*, 6 (1). Available at: http://www.qualitative-research.net/index.php/fqs/article/view/502/1081

Skeggs, B. (2004) *Class, Self, Culture*, London: Routledge.

Thompson, P. (1993) 'Family myth, models and denials in the shaping of individual life plans', in D. Bertaux and P. Thompson (ed.), *Between Generations: Family Models, Myths and Memories*. Oxford: Oxford University Press. pp. 13–38.

Thomson, R. (2010) 'Creating family case histories: subjects, selves and family dynamics', in R. Thomson (ed.), *Intensity and Insight: Longitudinal Methods as a Route into the Psychosocial*. Timescapes working paper. Available at: http://www.timescapes.leeds.ac.uk/assets/files/WP3_final_Jan%202010.pdf (accessed 16 June 2010).

Thomson, R. (2009a) *Unfolding Lives: Case Histories in Personal and Social Change*. Bristol: Policy Press.

Thomson, R. (2009b) 'Thinking intergenerationally about motherhood', *Studies in the Maternal*, 1 (1). Available at: http://www.mamsie.bbk.ac.uk (accessed 16 June 2010).

Thomson, R. (2007). The qualitative longitudinal case history: practical, methodological and ethical reflections. *Social Policy and Society*, 6(4), 571–82.

Thomson, R. and Holland, J. (2003) 'Hindsight, foresight and insight: the challenges of longitudinal qualitative research', *International Journal of Social Research Methodology*, 6 (3): 233–44.

Thomson, R. and Kehily, M.J. (2008) 'The making of modern motherhoods: memories, representations, practices', RES-148-25-0057, final report to the ESRC.

Thomson, R., Bell, R., Holland, J., Henderson, S., McGrellis, S. and Sharpe, S. (2002) 'Critical moments: choice, chance and opportunity in young people's narratives of transition to adulthood', *Sociology*, 36 (2): 335–54.

Thomson, R., Hadfield, L., Kehily, M.J. and Sharpe, S. (forthcoming) 'Acting up and acting out: encountering children in a longitudinal study of mothering', *Qualitative Research*.

Thomson, R., Kehily, M.J., Hadfield, L. and Sharpe, S. (2009) 'The making of modern motherhoods: storying an emergent identity', in M. Wetherell (ed.), *Identity in the 21st Century*. Basingstoke: Palgrave Macmillan.

Tyler, I. (2008) '"Chav mum, chav scum": class disgust in contemporary Britain', *Feminist Media Studies*, 8 (1): 16–34.

Wengraf, T. (2001) *Qualitative Research Interviewing: Biographic, Narrative and Semi-structured Method*. London: Sage.

FIVE

Using Social Network Analysis

Researching Relational Structure

Nick Crossley

Indroduction

The social world comprises interaction and relationships between multiple human actors. It is a network and the pattern of connections constituting that network is an important aspect of what we mean by 'social structure'. Or rather, different network patterns, involving different types of relations and different populations, constitute the multiple overlapping social structures that comprise a social world. Agents, furthermore, are never isolated atoms but always embedded in relations which variously influence, support and de/stabilize them. Indeed, since socialization, thought and self-hood (identity) are all fundamentally dialogical in nature (Mead, 1967), agency is itself produced in and sustained by networks.

It is somewhat odd, given this, and given that such arguments can be traced right back into the history of sociological thought, to Durkheim, Marx and Simmel, that sociological research methods betray an individualistic bias not only in data gathering (which is understandable to a degree) but also in data analysis and reporting. The vast majority of sociological research focuses upon the beliefs, experiences, dispositions, attitudes, resources and so forth of individuals. At the most these individual accounts are aggregated and contrasted (for example, in surveys and statistical analysis). Furthermore, where structural/relational concepts such as social class are operationalized they are generally reduced to individual attributes. Each individual has a class and the relational aspect of 'class relations' is absent. This may be necessary and I do not deny that it is sometimes productive but it also destroys the integrity of the object of sociological theory and research; the complex web of connection that is the social world.

In this chapter, I discuss a set of methods and techniques which offer an alternative: social network analysis (SNA) (Scott, 2000; Wasserman and Faust, 1994). As its name suggests, SNA focuses upon patterns of connection, allowing us to explore the various ways in which they generate opportunities and constraints for both individual and collective action, advantaging some and disadvantaging others.

Like the other contributors to this book I intend to blend a straightforward account of SNA with illustrations from my own work and some statement of my own personal take. To this end I begin with a brief description of four projects in which I have used SNA. All but one of these projects (the health clubs project) are on-going. However, all but one (student activists) are at a sufficiently advanced stage to have yielded publications. The published papers are my key reference points. All measures discussed in the chapter have been derived and all network graphs drawn using the Ucinet software package (Borgatti et al., 2002).

Projects

Punks and post-punks in Manchester and London

This project analyses local music scenes as networks, focusing specifically upon the UK punk and post-punk scenes of the late 1970s and early 1980s. Publications to date have focused upon: (1) the (pre-existing) social network which, I argue, facilitated the emergence of the punk scene in London (Crossley, 2008a); and (2) the formation of a social network in Manchester, which was coterminous with and constitutive/facilitative of the emergence of the post-punk scene for which the city is celebrated (Crossley, 2009).

(Net)working out

In the context of a wider ethnographic analysis of the practice(s) of working out in a private health club (Crossley, 2004, 2006), I explored the social relationships formed in this context, particularly within a number of circuit training classes, and mapped networks within and across classes (Crossley, 2008b). My contention was that sociability and the doing of social relations is central to the social world of the health club, shaping the way in which exercise is done and constituting an important motivation for it. My work explored the positive social capital generated in this process but also the 'dark side' of social capital. Specifically, I explored insider/outsider figurations and conflicts, and also low level conflicts between competing insider groups.

Suffragettes ties

This project, which builds upon an extensive body of literature exploring the significance of networks in collective action (Crossley, 2007), a theme also analysed in the punk project, seeks to map and explore the network of informal connections linking participants in the UK suffragette movement during its period of heightened militancy (1904–1914).[1] In addition to engaging with substantive issues regarding the role of networks in relation to movements, the project involves a methodological reflection upon ways of combining qualitative and quantitative strategies. To this end it focuses, among other things, upon letters written to and from suffragettes. A paper from this work (Edwards and Crossley, 2009) pilots the ideas of the broader project, utilizing the ego-net (see below) of a little known Nottingham suffragette: Helen Watts.

Student activist networks

This work seeks to test and further explore some of my own published hypotheses regarding the role of networks and network structure in the politicization of university students (Crossley, 2008c). It will explore the network structure of both the activist community and the wider student community, and will investigate the role of network ties in processes of mobilization and recruitment.[2]

These projects overlap in various ways. Even where they diverge, however, each is inspired by a combination of theoretical enthusiasm for SNA and uncertainty as to whether it can achieve, in empirical practice, the promise it appears to hold. They are my attempts to 'give it a go'; strands of a personal experiment focused upon 'networks' as a concept and SNA as a methodology. That experiment has some way to go yet but the preliminary 'findings' are promising and I hope that this chapter will encourage others to 'give it a go' too. To that end I will attempt now to explicate the key features of the method. Specifically I discuss: (1) different types of network; (2) data gathering; (3) recording and visualizing network data; and (4) network measures and the need to integrate them into a broader, mixed method approach, which includes a qualitative aspects.

What is social network analysis?

SNA is a set of techniques for handling, analysing and visualizing 'relational data'; that is, data concerning relations between a set of social actors or entities. It is a structural method that examines the pattern of connections between the entities. As such it can be applied to any type of relationship between any type of relevant entity. We might study relations within sets of individual human actors, roles, corporate actors (for example, firms, national governments or pressure groups), cities, websites, animals; anything that is capable of engaging in the type of relationships which are of interest to us. And the relations in question might be relations of friendship, sexual contact, economic exchange, bullying, aggression, migration, URL connection, acquaintance; again, any type of relationship which is possible between our specified actors and relevant in terms of our research questions and interests.

Historically SNA emerged in an overlap between a number of social science disciplines (chiefly sociology, anthropology and social psychology) and a branch of mathematics known as graph theory (Freeman, 2003; Scott, 2000). Over time it has extended into other social science disciplines and has incorporated other mathematical aspects, most notably statistics (by which I mean both statistical modelling and a variety of clustering, scaling and data reduction techniques). In addition, the growing popularity of the concept of networks and of graph theoretical methods of analysing them across the academic field has led to various interdisciplinary debates (and turf wars), most notably with physicists (see Freeman, 2003; Crossley, 2005, 2008d). For reasons of space I limit my focus in this chapter to the appropriation of *graph theoretical ideas* for *sociological purposes*.

As the above synopsis suggests, the techniques of SNA are mathematically based. Lest this causes qualitatively disposed readers to consider skipping on to the next chapter immediately, a brief elaboration is necessary. There is no reason why SNA techniques cannot be combined with qualitative methods. I have argued elsewhere that they can and very often should be (Crossley, 2010). It is interesting in this respect that SNA has a strong root in anthropological ethnography. A casual glance at any of this early work nicely demonstrates how SNA fits within a qualitative–quantitative, mixed methods approach (Mitchell, 1971). However, the fact that the anthropologists began to look beyond qualitative ethnography, towards mathematics, is indicative of two unique strengths of SNA.

First, SNA affords a systematic means of handling relational data; that is, recording and presenting it. Relational data is very difficult to describe and store systematically in a discursive manner. In a small group of 10 people there are a possible 90 directed or 45 undirected (on 'direction' see below) relationships to account for and even simple situations in which, for example, 'John knows Jane's brother's friend's uncle's cat', are difficult to capture, communicate and intellectually process in discursive form. If sociological research is to transcend the individual focus and become truly relational than it needs methods for handling relational data and SNA offers this.

Second, SNA entails a set of concepts and algorithms for thinking about, identifying, describing and measuring structure. It enables us to reflect upon the pattern that the multiple actors and relations involved in a situation form and the significance of those patterns. This is important for sociological purposes, not least because it affords us a way of operationalizing the concept of social structure. It is not clear how it could be done without SNA.

It remains only to say, as a final plea to those who equate quantitative approaches with a slow and painful death, that though SNA increasingly draws upon statistics for various purposes its mathematical roots are not statistical and neither are its procedures. It is, as noted, rooted in graph theory. At the very least this makes it a different type of quantitative approach and one which the qualitative researcher might find more appealing than statistics.

Data

There are several types of data commonly analysed in SNA. In this chapter I limit my focus to 'complete network' data. To set this in context, however, it is necessary to briefly describe the four main types.

- *Ego-net data*. An ego-net is a network that forms around a particular actor. Typically an analysis will focus upon and perhaps compare the network of a number of different egos. This requires that for each ego we derive a list of relevant alters and a list of all relevant relations between those alters (relevance, in each case, being a matter for the researcher to decide in accordance with their theories, questions and objectives). As noted above, the published work on our suffragettes project, to date, has involved ego-net research. We have focused our attention upon one militant suffragette (Helen Watts), exploring 'her archive' in an effort to determine both her contacts within and outside of the movement and their relationships to one another. In addition, a questionnaire in the student activists project asked each respondent to specify certain characteristics of their five closest friends, including the relations of these friends to one another. This allowed us to ascertain whether students tend to bunch into tightly knit friendship groups or 'spread themselves thinly' across various circles. It also allowed us, because we asked, to determine where they met their best friends and whether friends were typically studying the same subjects.
- *Complete network data*. In this form of network analysis we define a population, specify the type of relationship we are interested in and investigate which members of the population have that type of relationship. In my punk project, for example, I surveyed a range of secondary sources in an effort to identify the key actors in the early London and Manchester punk scenes and I sought to ascertain which of them enjoyed a professional and/or close personal relationship. Similarly, in the student activist project we sought to identify (by means of ethnography) a population of key political activists whose relations we attempted to determine by means of interview. Furthermore, in an effort to map wider student networks, we surveyed individual tutorial groups from a range of subject areas, presenting students with a full class list and asking them to tick where they had any of a number of types of relationship with any of the others.
- *Blockmodels*. In this form of network analysis we usually begin with a complete network. We then 'block' the nodes using a clustering algorithm and we study the relationships between the clusters ('blocks') as constituted by the relationships between their members. Blocks are usually formed in accordance with the similarity in patterns of connection between their members ('structural equivalence'), such that John and Jane will be included in the same block if they have ties to (mostly) the same people. Whether any two clusters are deemed to be related is sometimes left to the discretion of the analyst and is usually decided by reference to a threshold value. For example, if two clusters have four and five members respectively then there can be a maximum of 20 'undirected'(see below) relationships across them: each of the four members of one cluster having relations with each of the five in the other. An analyst might decide to count the two clusters as related if 50 per cent of these relations (that is, 10) are realized but they might equally decide upon a threshold of one relationship or 20. In other cases, including the punk example discussed below, algorithms automatically assign ties where doing so minimizes an error term.[3] We used this technique in the suffragettes project. This is slightly unusual as 'ego-nets' are generally too small to merit clustering and the data reduction it facilitates. Our net involved 96 actors, however, and we felt that the structure of the network would be better revealed in a reduced (blocked) format. In this case, though some blocks were difficult to interpret, blockmodelling revealed the different

social circles that Helen Watts moved in and also showed those circles to be closely inter-woven. Blockmodelling is often presented as a means of identifying and analysing 'roles'. I have some reservations regarding this claim but the technique does often reveal important network 'positions', as we found in the suffragettes projects. The clustering identified actors who traversed different social circles, for example, thus occupying a position which would allow them to 'broker' between those circles.

- *Two-mode analysis.* Typically the 'modes' in question are actors and events, actors and organizations or actors and places. The underlying idea is that actors are connected through, for example, their common participation in the same events, and events are con-nected through the participation of the same actor(s) in them. I am a link between the uni-versity I work at, the gym I belong to and the local shops I use, for example, and the university, gym and shops each link me to others who also use them. Technically two-mode networks can be decomposed into two complete networks: for example, research on the links between people and places might produce a network of people (linked through common places) and a network of places (linked by common people). Reference to 'two-mode net-works', however, generally suggests an attempt to deal with both types (people and places) in the same network. None of my projects, to date, have used two-mode networks. In the health club project, however, I did borrow some of the logic of this approach. The project involved a complete network, whose population comprised every individual who had par-ticipated (at least once) in a twice weekly circuit training class over a specified period. Ethnographic evidence had pointed to a sub-group of actors within this population who not only mixed in the class but also met afterwards in the saunas, sometimes then going on to the pub or a curry house. One of the ways in which I assigned ties to pair of actors (or not) was by observing their common participation (or not) in these extra-curricular activities. I used common participation in events (sauna, pub and curry sessions) to link the actors involved. Likewise, in our suffragette project we have linked activists who were arrested at the same protests and imprisoned together.

These different types of network inevitably complicate any discussion of net-work analysis. Procedures differ in accordance with the type of network involved. In what follows I take complete networks as my paradigm example, unless I indicate otherwise.

Data gathering and network representation

SNA is a method or set of methods of data analysis. In most of its forms it requires data which confirms (at least) the absence/presence of a specified type of relationship between every possible pairing of actors within a given population. As such, it presupposes a systematic survey of that population. But that survey can be conducted by way of any of a wide range of traditional social scientific methods of data gathering. In my own work, for example, I have gathered network data by means of participant observation (health clubs project), archival analysis (suffragette and punk projects), secondary sources (suffragette and punk projects), questionnaire survey (student activism) and interviews (student activism). What I was looking for in each of these cases was guided by the requirements of SNA (in addition to the wider rationale and goals of the projects) but how I looked, the method employed, was determined by the population in question and my relationship and means of access to its members.

Given the very specific information required for SNA it is not usually possible to use it to analyse the major archived surveys drawn upon in much quantitative analysis. Nor could such surveys be easily adapted, in the future, to facilitate SNA. However, there is a trend at the moment for including questions on respondent's key contacts and social capital. These are sometimes sufficient to allow rudimentary ego-net analysis and certainly provide additional relevant information on relations that SNA itself might not be capable of gleaning.

The actors who are linked in a network are commonly referred to as 'nodes' or, following graph theory, 'vertices'. SNA is a method for analysing the pattern of connection between a set of vertices. This requires a means of recording and representing such patterns. SNA has two basic means: adjacency matrices and graphs. Table 5.1 is a hypothetical adjacency matrix.

Table 5.1   A hypothetical adjacency matrix

	(1) Tom	(2) Dick	(3) Sally	(4) Harry	(5) Mary
(1) Tom	0	0	1	1	0
(2) Dick		0	1	1	0
(3) Sally			0	0	1
(4) Harry				0	1
(5) Mary					0

In a simple adjacency matrix we list our vertices both across the top row and down the furthest left hand column. We indicate the presence/absence of relations between them by way of 1s (present) and 0s (absent) where their rows and columns intersect. A relationship between Dick and Sally is indicated, for example, by a 1 at the intersection of his row (row 2) and her column (column 3). Technically, if we call our matrix A (the capital and bold face both being conventional), we call this intersection 'a_{23}', using lower case to indicate that we are referring to an element of the matrix, rather than the matrix itself, and indicating in subscript the row number followed by the column number (always in that order).

In many cases it will be meaningless to ask if vertices have a relationship to their self. In such cases, by convention, we record such relations as absent – note the string of 0s in Table 5.1 running in a diagonal from the top left of the matrix (a_{11}) to the bottom right (a_{55}). It might be meaningful to ask about reflexive relations, however. We might, for example, want to know if Sally likes the others in her group but also if she likes herself. In this case the diagonal becomes operative and records genuine information.

Note that a square matrix allows two intersections between any two vertices. Dick and Sally intersect both where his row meets her column (a_{23}) and where her row meets his column (a_{32}). This allows for the possibility of recording non-reciprocated relations. If Dick sends a Christmas card to Sally but she does not send one back, and this is the interaction we are interested in then we would record a relationship on Dick's row (that is, put a '1' in a_{23}) but not Sally's (that is, put a '0' in a_{32}). In some cases relations are necessarily reciprocated and the information below the diagonal replicates that above it.

Our matrix **A** (Table 5.1) is very basic. It records the presence/absence of relationships only. This can be elaborated in a number of ways. I have already noted reciprocation or 'direction'. Some relationships are, by definition, reciprocal and thus 'undirected': if John *lives with* Jane then Jane *lives with* John; if Sally *plays golf with* Lucy then Lucy *plays golf with* Sally. Other relations, however, such as *liking, emailing* or *passing on a virus* are not necessarily reciprocated and, in some cases (for example, *bullying, dominating, serving*), might be necessarily unreciprocated. Where both the nature of a relationship and our method of gathering and recording data allow for non-reciprocation we have a 'directed' relationship; direction meaning that the relationship goes from one vertex to another. Directed relationships may be reciprocated but if we elect to treat relations as directed we leave this option open and record it in our matrix in the manner noted above.

A further complication is weighting, which might be either ordinal or interval. In a questionnaire, for example, we might ask respondents to rate their level of trust in others on a scale of 0 to 5, giving us an ordinal score to include in our matrix in place of the simple binary recording of absence/presence. Alternatively, in an ethnography or archival trawl we may count the number of recorded meetings (or letters or emails) between two parties, giving us an interval measure of (in this case) their frequency of interaction. Again this figure is put into the matrix at the relevant intersection.

Finally, and usually for the special purpose of addressing 'structural balance theory', we can distinguish positive and negative relations (signed relations). Typically this is done by using the mathematical symbols, '+' and '−' in matrix entries. A record of '+1' at a_{12} would indicate that vertex 1 likes vertex 2 (or whatever the relation is), for example; '−1' would indicate dislike; and a '0' would indicate absence of a (relevant) relation.

In the case of two-mode networks we use an *incidence* rather than an *adjacency* matrix. Here we list actors down the first column and events (or whatever) across the top row, indicating participation (or not) with 1s and 0s. Most network software packages can either analyse this data directly or convert it into two adjacency matrices. In addition, an incidence matrix can be analysed (for example, with cluster analysis) and visualized (for example, with multidimensional scaling), for network analytic purposes, using standard statistical packages (Crossley, 2008c).

A graph (also called a 'sociogram' or 'network diagram') records the same information as a matrix and sometimes further information too. In the simple case vertices are represented as circles and the absence/presence of relationships between them is represented by the absence/presence of connecting lines between them. Figure 5.1 is a illustration of relations between the 46 most central protagonists in the London punk scene in late 1976. Vertices are tied if they had enjoyed either a strong friendship or a professional relationship (for example, band mates) before December 1976, when punk exploded into the national music scene.

When relationships are undirected they are referred to, following graph theoretic convention, as 'edges'. When they are directed they have arrow heads indicating direction and they are termed 'arcs'. In some cases a reciprocated directed relationship is represented by two arcs, one moving in each direction between vertices. In other cases there is a single arc with arrowheads pointing in both directions. Weightings are represented either by the thickness of an arc/edge or a numerical label. Signs are also indicated by arc labels.

In addition to this information, vertices can be differently coloured or shaped to indicate attributes, and sized in accordance with an interval or continuous measure. We might indicate gender, for example, by colouring female vertices pink and male vertices blue or representing them as squares and circles respectively. And we might set the size of nodes in accordance with annual earnings. Likewise edges/arcs can be colour coded to indicate the type (if more than one is under consideration) or ordinal strength of a relationship.

In Figure 5.1 attributes are indicated by shapes: square for musicians, triangle for friends of band members and circle for actors who possessed and used resources such as money, managerial skills and contacts outside of punk circles to nurture and promote punk. Vertices are sized in accordance with their number of contacts in the network ('degree'). To anticipate a later point, note the two very large circles towards the centre of the graph. If circles are large then actors with resources are popular!

The position of the vertices on a graph is usually irrelevant from an analytic point of view and may be arbitrary or conventional in any case. The graph theory that SNA draws upon operates with a different conception of space to our usual Cartesian conception. 'Distances' are measured in terms of 'degrees', a degree being a connection. Likewise, 'positions' in a graph refer not to standard spatial coordinates but rather to patterns of connection. Having said this, various scaling and data reduction techniques can be used in graph construction, which, for example, position those vertices close to one another which have a similar pattern of connection, and researchers will often manipulate graphs (legitimately) in an effort to make patterns of connection and the underlying structure of the network, as revealed by network measures, apparent.

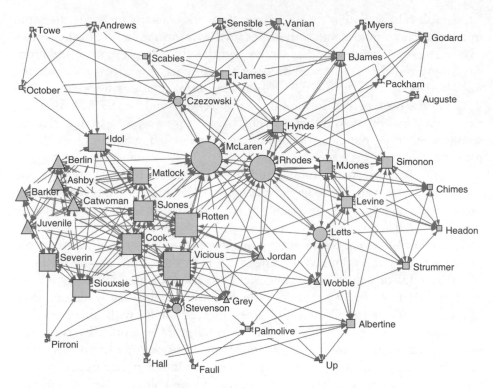

Figure 5.1 Network of punk pioneers in London

Numbers and narratives

In what follows I explain and illustrate some basic SNA measures by summarizing aspects of my analysis of the punk network visualized in Figure 5.1 (see Crossley [2008a] for the full analysis). In addition, I hope to show that, though measures are very important, they are most effective when brought into dialogue with qualitative data and analysis. In this case that involves conversing with archival and secondary sources on the emergence of the London punk scene during 1976.

Note that Figure 5.1 forms a single 'component'. Every vertex has a path of connections linking it to every other. The shortest path between the two most distant vertices, the 'diameter' of the network, is 3 degrees.[4] As this suggests, however, not every node is directly linked to every other. In fact, of the 1035 ties possible in the network only 246 are present (23.7 per cent), giving the network a density of 0.237. We have no norms by which to ascertain if this density is high or not but I argued that it is, given the nature of the ties involved and the size of the network (Crossley 2008a). Moreover, following convention, I took a high density, combined with a low diameter in a single component, as evidence of cohesion in the network. And following network studies of collective action, I suggested that this cohesion is one important reason why the network was able to nurture a 'punk revolution'. Short path distances meant that cultural innovations did not have far to travel and made it relatively easy for would-be bands to search for members. In addition, I found archival evidence to support the widely accepted claim that high density generated the level of trust and cooperation needed for successful collective action, while both closing networks off from the wider world, such that a deviant sub-culture could take form, and protecting them from threats posed to their deviance by 'outsiders'.

Further evidence for my argument is provided by the comparative timing of the emergence of Manchester's celebrated punk scene. Manchester's punk protagonists were equally primed for action in the mid-1970s. There is evidence of many of the same sentiments and aesthetic preferences that fuelled punk in London, for example. Manchester's key players were not linked in a cohesive network in 1976, however, and it was only after they had become connected in a network that their scene began to take off; or rather, the emergence of their scene was coterminous with a process of network formation (Crossley, 2008a, 2009).

Of course punk was not just about networks. It was about what people did in interaction within networks. To research that I had to conduct qualitative analysis of archives. Moreover, I was only able to find evidence of, for example, cooperation, to support my cohesion hypothesis, by way of a qualitative trawl of the historical record. Network structure was important, however, and SNA afforded a powerful purchase upon it.

Cooperation was not the whole story of the London punk scene. Power and conflict played their part too. SNA was extremely useful for analysing these aspects. One way of beginning to explore power and influence in a network is by reference to the 'centrality' of particular vertices. SNA offers many definitions and measures of centrality but three are especially important. We can measure how many connections each vertex has, deeming those with more connections more central (*degree centrality*). We can examine the chains of connections linking every vertex to every other, deeming those with the shortest distances to travel more central (*closeness centrality*). Or, again focusing on the chains, we can examine who most often lies in the path connecting other pairs of vertices (*betweenness centrality*). In addition, in an attempt to measure the capacity of vertices to 'broker' between their alters we can measure their '*aggregate constraint*'; that is, the extent to which every possible pair of others to whom they are linked are themselves linked (in contrast to the centrality measures, a low score on this is generally held to indicate advantage).

There is no necessary correlation between these various measures in general but in our network the same three vertices (Malcom McClaren, Bernie Rhodes and Sid Vicious) score 'best' for each measure, often by a considerable margin. We see in Table 5.2, for example, that their scores are often several standard deviations away from the mean.

Table 5.2 Centrality and constraint

	Degree	Closeness	Betweeness	Aggregate constraint
McClaren	29	0.738	0.203	0.112
Rhodes	24	0.681	0.164	0.116
Vicious	25	0.692	0.116	0.131
Mean (for the whole network)	10.78	0.5927	0.02095	0.2665
SD	6.092	0.0741	0.041	0.104

Each of these positional properties can confer both opportunities and constraints upon the vertex in question. I do not have the space to discuss this here but note that these opportunities/constraints are only potential and depend in some part upon the actions of both the actor and others in the network. Moreover, note that both the fact of their realization (or not) and its mechanisms are sometimes best revealed by qualitative analysis. My reading of the archive and secondary literature, for example, suggested that while McClaren and Rhodes were, indeed, key movers and shakers in the network and exploited their centrality and lack of constraint, Vicious, though popular, was not and did not. Either he did not recognize his centrality, chose not to use it or perhaps subtle differences in the nature of his ties, not picked up in the analysis, gave his centrality a different meaning and potential to that of McClaren and Rhodes.

There is some archival evidence to support the latter hypothesis. Vicious' centrality in the network was largely due to his drift across several bands and failure to find a lasting role. McClaren and Rhodes were central, by contrast, because they held resources (chiefly money, know-how and important contacts outside of the immediate punk circle), which others wanted and needed in order to succeed. This ensured an advantage in their relations with others, tipping the balance of power, and it made them targets for connection that, in turn, afforded them a central position in the network which each enjoyed the wherewithal to exploit. This is only one dimension of the power configuration in the network and only one factor affecting interactions, relations and network structure but it is important. Moreover, the contrast between Vicious and McClaren should remind us that reducing relations to zeros and ones in a matrix entails a loss of important information. Social relations are multiplex and sometimes very particular. SNA has to be attuned to that fact if it is to prove useful.

Power imbalances were one source of conflict in the network but not the only one. Other actors enjoyed varying degrees of positional advantage, sometimes generating resentment, and a qualitative reading of the 'gripes' aired by protagonists at the time point to the existence of sub-groupings in the network and relative exclusion. Many complained of 'cliquishness', for example, and *The Damned* (a group) complained that they were outsiders.

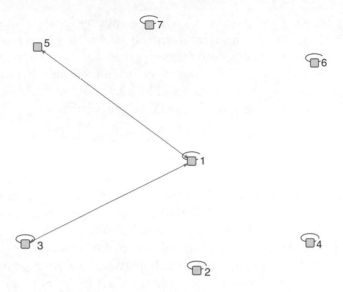

Figure 5.2   Blockmodel of the network from Figure 5.1

SNA supports such claims and allows us to explore them. A 'k-core'[5] analysis, for example, reveals a clique[6] with 14 members within the network; that is, it identifies 14 vertices who each have a tie to the 13 others. A clique is a highly cohesive cluster within a network, whose cohesion may afford them a greater capacity for action while also making non-members feel excluded (Crossley, 2008a, 2008b). Qualitatively we can confirm that this was a sub-group (involving McClaren, Rhodes and Vicious) who hung around together, particularly at an in-crowd bar (Louise's), where they schemed and 'planned the revolution'. Weaving SNA and a qualitative narrative together, therefore, we begin to identify forms of segregation which may have caused tension.

Other measures allow us to extend this analysis. Blockmodelling, for example, reveals seven blocks (see Figure 5.2). The only connections in the model[7] are between block 1, which includes McClaren, Rhodes and Vicious, and blocks 3 and 5, respectively. This allows us to see that cohesion in the network is uneven. There are in-crowds within the in-crowd and thus some, including *The Damned* (whose members are in block 4), are indeed *relative* outsiders. They may have been cut off from decision making process, been slow to receive new information and innovations and so on

Note also, however, that the internal density of block 5 was sufficiently low that the algorithm deems it internally unconnected. This is indicated on the graph by the absence of a reflexive (circular) tie around this block. The vertices in Block 5 are clustered together in virtue of the similarities in their patterns of connection but, in contrast to the members of all other blocks, they do not have sufficient connection to one another for the model to deem them a connected cluster. This is interesting because it suggests that members of block 5 lack the internal cohesiveness to act as a group. One might conjecture that they are a cluster of marginal actors united only by way of their peripheral involvement with members of block 1. But we could only explore that hypothesis by returning, qualitatively, to the archive.

Conclusion

I have done no more than scratch at the surface of SNA in this chapter but I hope that I have done enough to demonstrate its value as an analytic toolbox for a genuinely relational form of sociological analysis: that is, an analysis focused not only on individuals but also upon the relations between them. The tools of SNA are, in large part, mathematically based. However, I hope that I have also demonstrated both their significance in terms of key sociological concerns (for example, cohesion, power and influence) and the ways in which they might be incorporated within a mixed-methods approach to analysis which includes a qualitative dimension. Indeed, had I the space I would have argued that for many (not all) purposes a qualitative dimension is necessary in SNA in order to add essential and consequential concrete detail to what would otherwise be too formal and abstract to properly serve a sociological purpose (Crossley, 2010). That said, however, my efforts in this paper are best described in converse terms: I have argued that the abstraction, formalization and mathematization involved in SNA can make a highly significant contribution to relational sociology.

Notes

1. I began this project with Gemma Edwards. The project team also now includes Rachel Stevenson and Ellen Harries.
2. The work on activist networks is being conducted with Yousaf Ibrahim. The tutorial-based network survey aspect of the project, discussed below, was conducted with Rachel Stevenson.
3. If less than 50 per cent of the ties across members of two blocks are present then we make fewer errors by claiming that the blocks themselves are not tied than by saying that they are. If more than 50 per cent of the ties are present then we make fewer errors by saying that the blocks are tied.
4. As noted above, a degree is a connection. In this context, distances are measured in degrees, such that, for example, if i is connected to j (but neither k nor l), j to k (but not l) and k to l, then i is linked to l at a distance of three degrees.
5. In SNA a k-core is a sub-network ($n > 2$), all of whose members are connected to a specified number (k) of others. A five-core of size $n = 10$, for example, is a sub-network of 10 vertices within a network, each of whom are connected to five others of the 10.

6. In SNA a 'clique' is a sub-network ($n > 2$) within a network, all of whose members are connected to one another.
7. As noted with respect to blockmodels above, this doesn't mean that there are no connections between members of the groups, just not enough to cross the threshold of the model.

References

Borgatti, S.P, Everett, M.G. and Freeman, L.C. (2002) *Ucinet for Windows: Software for Social Network Analysis*. Harvard, MA: Analytic Technologies.

Crossley, N. (2004) 'The circuit trainer's habitus: reflexive body techniques and the sociality of the workout', *Body and Society*, 10 (1): 37–69.

Crossley, N. (2005) 'The new social physics and the science of small world networks', *The Sociological Review*, 53 (2), 351–8.

Crossley, N. (2006) 'In the gym: motives, meanings and moral careers, '*Body and Society*, 12 (3): 23–50.

Crossley, N. (2007) 'Social networks and extra-parliamentary politics', *Sociology Compass*, 1 (1), 222–36.

Crossley, N. (2008a) 'Pretty connected: the social network of the early UK punk movement', *Theory, Culture and Society*, 25 (6): 89–116.

Crossley, N. (2008b) '(Net)working out: social capital in a private health club', *British Journal of Sociology*, 59 (3): 475–500.

Crossley, N. (2008c) 'Social networks and student activism: on the politicizing effect of campus connections', *Sociological Review*, 56(1): 18–38.

Crossley, N. (2008d) 'Small world networks, complex systems and sociology', *Sociology*, 42 (2), 261–77.

Crossley, N. (2009) 'The man whose web expanded: network dynamics in Manchester's post-punk music scene 1976–1980', *Poetics*, 37 (1): 24–49.

Crossley, N. (2010) 'The social world of the network: qualitative aspects of network analysis', *Sociologica*. Available at: http://www.sociologica.mulino.it/main (forthcoming).

Edwards, G. and Crossley, N. (2009) 'Measures and meanings: exploring the ego-net of Helen Kirkpatrick Watts, militant suffragette', *Methodological Innovations On-Line* 3 (2): 37–61. Available at: http://www.methodologicalinnovations.org/viewissue.html

Freeman, L. (2003) *The Development of Social Network Analysis*. Vancouver: Empirical Press.

Mead, G.H. (1967) *Mind, Self and Society*. Chicago, IL: Chicago University Press.

Mitchell, C. (1971) *Social Networks in Urban Situations*. Manchester: Manchester University Press.

Scott, J. (2000) *Social Network Analysis: A Handbook*. London: Sage Publications.

Wasserman, S. and Faust, K. (1994) *Social Network Analysis*. Cambridge: Cambridge University Press.

SIX

Using Survey Data

Researching Families and Households

Angela Dale

Introduction

At first the use of survey data for researching family relationships may seem unlikely – what can a survey tell you about a mother–daughter relationship? Or about how siblings relate to each other? However, in this chapter I shall argue that it can be a very important method of enquiry and yield understandings that cannot be established by other methods. Survey methods can often be used in tandem with other methods – for example, depth interviews based on theoretically selected samples, where the two kinds of information can often amplify and complement each other.

In purely descriptive terms, nationally representative surveys that record information on all members of the household can provide authoritative answers to questions such as:

- How many people in Britain live in three-generational households? And does this vary by ethnic group?[1]
- Are lone parents with dependent children more likely to be single, divorced, widowed or separated?[2]

Surveys can also provide more tentative answers to fundamental questions such as:

- How do parental resources influence the educational attainment of children?[3]
- Does parental break-down have long-term consequences for children?[4] (Answers in the endnotes.)

The answers to these kinds of questions provide the essential information needed to understand our society and, even more importantly, to understand differences between groups – whether based on age, gender, ethnicity or geography. Effective policy needs to be based on a clear picture of the composition and characteristics of families and households in Britain today. Equally important, and a lot harder to achieve, is an understanding of the processes by which family members impact on each other over time. This kind of research, usually requiring longitudinal data, provides fundamentally important information for formulating policy initiatives. However, one has to be very cautious in claiming causality, even using longitudinal data (Cox and Wermuth, 2001; and Nazroo, Chapter 15, in this volume).

This chapter begins by setting out some of the opportunities – and also the constraints – of using surveys to study family relationships and provides examples of the kinds of relationship information typically collected in major surveys. This is followed by some examples, drawn from published research, in which survey methods have been able to demonstrate relationships between family members, sometimes between partners and sometimes between the parents and their children, which are of considerable relevance to policy. These examples, although only skimming the surface of some very complex analyses, aim to provide an indication of the diversity and complexity of survey-based research. The final section gives some information on how to have a go yourself.

Opportunities and constraints of using survey data to analyse family relationships

Opportunities

There are a large number of readily available, high-quality datasets that hold a great deal of information about family relationships: for example, all the large government household surveys, the British Household Panel Survey and the British cohort studies. Similar data sources can be found in the USA and in Europe (Dale et al., 2008). There is also an excellent ESRC-funded support service, the Economic and Social Data Service (http://www.esds.ac.uk) that not only provides access to many UK surveys but also advice, training and other backup to researchers using these surveys.

Most of the large publicly funded UK surveys provide information on all members of the household. This allows one to look at the relationships between couples or between parents and children. For example, do couples hold similar political views or similar life values? With a longitudinal study such as the British Household Panel Survey you can examine whether couples with shared values stay together longer than those with very different values.

Surveys often ask for a surprisingly large amount of detail on relationships. Perhaps the most detail is found in the 1958 British cohort study (discussed in Chapter 14 by Jane Elliott) in which respondents were all born in one week in 1958 and are still being followed, although now in their 50s. Details of the study are available online (http://www.cls.ioe.ac.uk/studies.asp?section= 000100020003).

It is possible to choose your unit of analysis, for example, children, adults, the elderly, women, couples. So, for example, one can focus on elderly people and the extent to which they live with other kin members; or couples and their joint retirement behaviour. Many surveys have a sufficiently large sample size that they can support valid analyses of relatively small groups such as one-parent families or have sufficient consistency over years that respondents can be pooled over three or four years to increase sample size.

You can construct your own definitions and classifications. For example, you can build a measure of household deprivation based on theoretically informed measures; or a new classification of the life-course that reflects the distinctions relevant to your research. You are not confined to classifications used in published reports although you are, of course, limited by the questions asked in the survey.

Constraints

There are also, of course, constraints on all survey-based research. Survey data relies on the respondents' answers to pre-defined questions, often with pre-coded answer categories. Although open questions are sometimes asked, they are very expensive to code and it is usual to develop a coding frame based on a fairly small number of pilot studies.

Surveys are therefore limited in the kind of information they can ask for. Questions need to be understood across the sampled population; they need to be relatively straightforward and avoid being overly intrusive (although questions about income and contraceptive practices are routinely asked!). However, they are not usually the best method for gaining a detailed understanding of how family relationships are perceived and practised. Respondents do not have their own 'voice' and cannot usually raise issues not covered in the questionnaire.

Surveys usually collect information on all family members who live in the same household. Some surveys ask for information on, for example, whether you give help or receive help from family or friends outside your household. But detailed information is usually collected only for those living in the same accommodation. Also, while one can obtain a nationally representative picture of patterns of part-nership and living arrangements, one cannot infer from this the importance attached to particular relationships and one is rarely able to establish information about important others (related or not) who live outside the household. However, the concept of couples who are 'Living Apart Together' (LAT) is now widely recognized and sometimes captured by surveys.

Basically, surveys are only as good as the data collection exercise. Questionnaires must be well-designed and thoroughly tested; response rates must be adequate and biases from non-response established; inferences can only be made to the population sampled.

Examples of family and household relationships

Many of the surveys best suited to analysing family relationships record information on all household members (defined as the people who usually live in the accommodation) and ask questions that allow individual relationships to be distinguished. Box 6.1 shows all the relationships captured in the 2006 General Household Survey – and these are also captured by many other UK household surveys. The numbers against each relationship records the response of the second person in the household to the first person – where there is more than one person in the household. Typically each household member is asked their relationship to each other member of the household. Thus most people are either the spouse, son or daughter of the household reference person. However, step-children and foster children are also separately identified (but not adopted children) and many other more unusual family relationships are recorded. It is thus possible to establish the formal relationship of each person in the household to every other person in the household.

Box 6.1   Relationships of other household members to person 1 (households with more than 1 person)

How are the people in your household related to each other? Response 1

1	Spouse	4905
2	Cohabitee	892
3	Son or daughter	6319
4	Step-son/daughter	272
5	Foster child	11
6	Son/daughter-in-law	42
7	Parent/guardian	99
8	Step-parent	3
9	Foster-parent	0
10	Parent-in-law	23
11	Brother/sister	86
12	Step-brother/sister	2
13	Foster brother/sister	0

(Continued)

This 'relationship matrix' can then be used to define many different derived variables that record, for example, how many families are in the household (92 per cent of households in the UK have only one family but 8 per cent have two or more); how many children are in the family; the age of the youngest child in the family. A large number of these variables are usually available on the datasets, prepared by the data collectors. For example, the GHS contains many different household classifications (some with up to 57 different categories) that have been derived for different purposes, often for different government departments. Box 6.2 illustrates a household classification with only 12 categories.

Box 6.2   Household type F (grouped)

1	1 person only	2722
2	2+ unrelated adults	549
3	Married couple, dependent children	7267
4	Married couple, independent children	1661
5	Married couple, no children	5208
6	Lone parent, dependent children	1937
7	Lone parent, independent children	579
8	2+ families	460
9	Same sex cohabitees	71
10	Cohabiting couple, dependent children	1265
11	Cohabiting couple, independent children	53
12	Cohabiting couple, no children	1054
	Valid cases	22924

Notes: This is also available as a 57 category variable that gives breakdowns based on the number of children and age of husband/wife.

Source: GHS, 2006: http://www.esds.ac.uk

While the derived variables already available are very helpful to the analyst, the surveys also allow you to make your own linkages between family (or household) members. Each household has a unique serial number and, within households, each family unit and person is uniquely identified. This provides the basic building blocks for linking information between partners, or between mother and child, or aggregating information about all household members.

Using surveys to understand family relationships

Survey data can raise issues that are of major significance – for example, how family relationships (such as, a partner; children) affect women's levels of economic activity and how this differs between ethnic groups or between age-cohorts. Large sample surveys can provide robust estimates for the main ethnic groups and thus give an authoritative, nationally representative, picture of differences in family relationships. In this section I provide some detailed examples of ways in which surveys may be profitably used to understand family relationships.

Combining survey data with interview data

Survey data can be used in tandem with qualitative data. Each may provide very different kinds of understanding of the same topic but, used together, can complement each other and provide a more powerful research base than either method alone.

For example, survey information about all members of the household shows that Black Caribbean women (aged 19–60) are much more likely to be single parents than either Indian or White women. About 27 per cent of Black Caribbean women aged 16–60 are single parents with children under 16 by comparison with 3 per cent of Indian women and 11 per cent White women (Dale et al., 2006). However, unlike White women, the majority of Black Caribbean women are not single parents because of partnership break-down but have never married. Single, Black Caribbean mothers are also much more likely to be economically active than their White or Indian counterparts.

This raises questions over the meaning of single parenthood for these women. Are Black Caribbean women more likely to choose to be a single mother? Do they have a long-term relationship with the baby's father that is not captured by the survey? (If so, this may suggest that surveys need to include additional questions to capture this information.) Do their higher levels of employment imply a more 'individualized' or at least a more self-reliant attitude to life? All these questions can be best answered using in-depth interviewing of theoretically sampled women. Although the survey analysis can provide detailed and accurate information about the circumstances of single mothers of different ethnic groups, a much greater depth of understanding can be gained by exploring with women who fall into these particular categories their feelings about single motherhood and their views about employment.

Combining qualitative and survey methods can also help to answer some puzzles. It is well established from many different surveys that, in the UK, marriage or cohabitation no longer has a negative effect on women's employment and that a woman with a partner in paid work is more likely to be working, herself, than a woman whose partner is unemployed. It is also well established that married Pakistani women, especially if they have children, are much less likely to be in paid work than any other ethnic group (except Bangladeshis) (Dale et al., 2006). Many UK-born Pakistani women marry men from their countries of origin, who move to the UK on marriage. It is widely suggested that these husbands are likely to be more traditional than UK-born men, and will want their wives to stay at home and take care of the family rather than taking paid work. We conducted interviews with 15 Pakistani women who were UK-born. Six of these women were married and all had gone back to Pakistan to marry (and then returned to the UK with their husband). Among other topics we asked about barriers to taking paid work. Some of the reports from these interviews are produced, below, and are described more fully in Dale and Ahmed (2008). Our respondents unanimously portrayed men from Pakistan to be traditional and unsupportive of women's employment.

> I think a lot of the girls that get married from back home, their husbands would like them to sit at home and have the family – the children. (Interview 7)
>
> Well, my younger sister, she … she actually doesn't work – her husband's like a bit strict – he doesn't really want her to work or … I think maybe it depends on the husband as well – because they're from back home, they think differently … (Interview 2)

However, the women we interviewed, themselves married to a man from Pakistan, all reported how supportive their husband was:

> I've always had loads encouragement from my family. My husband, too, he's been brilliant, he has never stopped me doing anything. (Interview 7)
>
> My husband, he's alright – he's quite good. I mean, he's my best friend as well – I can talk to him about anything and I can tell him I want to work and he won't mind if I study … (Interview 2)

Of course, as we had a very small sample of women who had been recruited through organizations that were facilitating employment opportunities, it was perfectly plausible that these women were married to men who were supportive of their work but, in general, men who migrated from Pakistan for marriage were not.

By using survey data from the Labour Force Survey we were able to show that marriage to an overseas born man who came to the UK at age 18 or over has no negative influence on a Pakistani women's employment. Whether a UK-born woman had a husband who was UK born or brought up, or a husband who came to the UK as an adult, made no significant difference to her chances of being economically active. This result is important because it can refute some of the more alarmist media stories that suggest that the migration of men from Pakistan to the UK for marriage has a negative impact on their wives ability to take paid work.

This analysis used the Quarterly Labour Force Survey, conducted by the Office for National Statistics, with an annual sample of 60,000 households. All adults in the household are interviewed and questions include details of education, employment, country of birth and date of migration to the UK. Although the sample size is so large, we combined data from 1998–2005 to get a sufficiently large sample of minority ethnic groups. We selected women aged 19–60 as the unit of analysis and attached, to each woman, information about her partner (if she had one) that was theoretically relevant to the analysis. In this case we used the age of arrival of the partner in the UK. In related analyses we also attached information about the employment status and the qualifications of the partner. The survey did not ask the reasons for migrating to the UK and so we could not be certain that migration was for marriage. However, because the year of migration was recorded we could calculate the respondent's age at migration and distinguish those who arrived at 18 or over from those who arrived at a younger age. (The age of 18 was used as, during the period 1998–2005, both the UK sponsor and the spouse had to be 18 or over at the time of entry to the UK.)

A logistic regression model was then used, where the outcome or dependent variable was binary – whether or not the woman was economically active. Explanatory or independent variables included the woman's age, her qualifications; whether she had a child aged under 5; aged 5–15; and a composite variable that distinguished the following categories:

- Single UK born (reference category).
- Single born overseas.
- Partnered, both woman and partner UK-born or came to UK before 18.
- Partnered, woman UK born or came before 18; partner came to UK 18+.
- Partnered, came to UK at 18+; partner UK born or came before 18.
- Partnered, both woman and partner came to UK 18+.

The coefficients from the model showed whether a woman's probability of being economically active was significantly different to that of single and UK-born women (the base or reference category), taking in account (or holding constant) the other variables in the model.

The results showed that only where the women was, herself, born overseas was there a negative and statistically significant difference from being single and UK-born. Marriage to a man who came from Pakistan at age 18 or over did not have a significant negative effect on the woman's likelihood of being economically active. This evidence was sufficiently strong that we could refute any claims that, for Pakistani women, marriage to a man from 'back home' had a negative effect on their employment. A full paper is available online (http://www.ccsr.ac.uk/publications/working/2008–02.pdf).

Change over time: intergenerational relationships

Longitudinal data, that records information on the same individual and their family circumstances over a long time period, can be very valuable in helping to explain some of the factors that influence outcomes such as educational or occupational attainment in adulthood.

A question with both theoretical and practical policy relevance, concerns mechanisms of inter-generational relationships. The 2009 Millburn Report (Cabinet Office, 2009) has raised major concerns that those entering the higher professions are over-whelmingly likely to come from higher income families with parents who are themselves professionals – and that this relationship has grown stronger in recent decades rather than declining. Using data from two British birth cohorts, the report found that 'Across the professions as a whole, the typical professional grew up in a family with an income well above the average family's: today's younger professionals (born in 1970) typically grew up in a family with an income 27 per cent above that of the average family, compared with 17 per cent for today's older professionals (born in 1958). In the cases of 9 of the 12 professions recorded, the data shows an increase in people coming from better-off families between the 1958 and 1970 birth cohorts' (Cabinet Office, 2009: 18).

Unravelling the processes of inter-generational transmission is of enormous importance if we wish to create a society with greater equality of opportunity. The British cohort studies record detailed information about parents' education, income, occupations, style of parenting, the cohort member's schooling and educational attainment at different ages, and the characteristics of the area of residence. Longitudinal data from the British Household Panel Survey also provide detailed information that can be used to establish the relative importance of parents' education and parents' occupational classes as determinants of children's attainment of service class occupations (Lampard, 2007). Over time, some fairly clear evidence has been established to show the different roles played by mothers and fathers, the role of parental income and the extent to which low family income can be offset by parental interest in the child's educational attainment (Chevalier et al., 2005; Ermisch, 2008; Ermisch and Francesconi, 2001); and the effect of family size on a child's educational attainment (Iacovou, 2001, 2008).

Effect of family size on a child's educational attainment

Iacovou (2001, 2008) used longitudinal data from the National Child Development Study (NCDS) – a survey of children born in 1958 who have been surveyed at regular intervals since birth to ask: 'does family size make a difference to the educational attainment of the children?' (This question was part of a larger piece of work that also included the effect of sibling order.) The question tested two different theoretical positions, one which argued that the greater the number of children the less time parents had to spend on any one child (the dilution theory) and a 'confluence' model that argued that a large family size lowered the average intellectual ability of the family (assuming children had a lower mental age than parents).

The main analysis used ordinary least squares regression with children's test scores in mathematics and reading at ages 7, 11 and 16 as the outcome measures. By using outcomes at different ages and for different kinds of tests it was possible to check whether results were robust over time and with different measures. (An additional part of the research also examined attainment in O levels and also educational attainment at age 23.) Because the data were collected from birth, explanatory variables were available that were all earlier in time than the outcome variables. As expected, by comparison with the scores for an only child, children from larger families scored less well as the number of siblings increased – but with the notable exception that children with only one other siblings did better on all tests at all ages than only children. Of course, these effects of family size may be explained by other family characteristics – for example, the parents' age, their level of education, social class and whether the child's father left the family at any point in the child's life. However, when these controls were added the relationship with family size was reduced – but generally still present. A much fuller set of explanatory variables were also available, including the extent of parental interest in the child's education, measured at different ages; whether the parents' read to the child; the kind of secondary school the child attended. The very wide range of information collected by NCDS over the childhood years allows the role of both 'structural' factors such as the type of school attended and 'personal' variable such as parents' reported involvement with the child to be included in the analysis. The size of the coefficients on the variables used in the model indicates the strength of each in explaining the child's attainment.

One extension to the analysis was aimed at getting a better understanding of why an only child did less well than a child with one sibling. One explanation was that these children lacked interaction with other children and, in particular, lacked the opportunity to teach a younger sibling. To try to address this, Iacovou used information in NCDS about the extent to which only children interacted with other children. When children were aged seven parents were asked: 'Does the child meet other children outside the household? (Exclude going to and from, and in school).' Iacovou's analysis showed some evidence to indicate that only children who experienced interaction with others had higher attainment scores, at least on some measures, than children who did not. The richness of the dataset also allowed the author to test whether the findings on family size were the same for children from different class backgrounds and with different levels of family income. The full paper can be downloaded online (http://ideas.repec.org/p/ese/izerwp/2001–12.html).

Longitudinal surveys that record family relationships are also used by developmental psychologists to understand the dynamics of family interaction and, in particular, how parents and children interact. Work by Jenkins et al. (2003) has sought to distinguish the effect of family-level characteristics (for example, socio-economic status; marital conflict) from 'child-effects', which are characteristics of the child such as age, gender or temperament, all of which might influence how the parent relates to the child. Important questions include:

- Do family-wide or child-specific aspects of the environment predict change in child behaviour?
- How similar are children's experiences in the same family? Does this vary with family level characteristics?
- What is the child's own contribution to the family-level environment?

The authors suggest that family context may increase or decrease the likelihood that children will be treated differently by their parents. For example, children who live in families with high levels of stress may be more likely to experience different treatment from their parents than children living in families with low levels of stress. The authors use multilevel modelling (where the family is one level in the analysis and the child is a different level) to attempt to establish the relationship between shared family-level effects and differential treatment of children by parents. The data are rather similar to the 1958 cohort – a longitudinal sample of 8476 Canadian children, between 4- and 11-years-old, in 3762 families.

The results are extensive but include the finding that the child's age was the strongest child-specific predictor of receiving positive attention from the parents. Children's temperament was one of the most important predictors of parental negativity and the strength of this association varied significantly across families, partially explained by family socio-economic status. The greater the socio-economic disadvantage the more reactive parents were to the children's difficult temperament. Differential parenting was higher in families with lower socio-economic status, marital dissatisfaction and larger family size.

Data sources and methods – how to have a go

In the UK we have a large number of excellent surveys which support research on family relationships. Many are funded by government and designed to cast light on families, their income and their resources – for example the Family Resources Survey which is repeated annually but with different samples. Others, such as the General Household Survey (General Lifestyle Survey) are conducted annually but have a longitudinal element that allows individuals to be followed over four years. Other surveys such as the Labour Force Survey are designed to provide information on education and employment.

Longitudinal studies, which include the British cohort studies and the British Household Panel Survey (now being replaced by the UK Household Longitudinal Survey) follow the same individuals over very long time periods, with considerable information on others in the household. Software packages such as STATA are now widely used in universities and provide a great deal of flexibility in making linkages between family or household members.

Researchers can begin to explore family relationships in survey data by going to the web-site of the ESRC's Economic and Social Data Service (http://www.esds.ac.uk) and locating a dataset such as the General Household Survey. These pages contain a great deal of information about the survey and contain a simple and clear 'Starting Analysis' guide that gives a walk-through of the steps involved:

• Which dataset do I want?
• Consulting the documentation.
• Explore the data online.
• Registering for the data.
• Downloading the data.
• Analysing the data using an appropriate analysis package.

ESDS run regular awareness raising workshops, hands-on introductory workshops as well as higher level methodological workshops. Online resources also provide detailed information on using hierarchical data, matching files and pooling data, weighting, analysing change over time, as well as guides to using STATA and SPSS.

Surveys can play a useful role in understanding family relationships and can be analysed very simply and easily to obtain some descriptive information, or, with increasing degrees of complexity depending on the questions being answered.

In the USA, researchers have access to a range of excellent surveys, for example through the ICPSR at the University of Michigan or more specific datasets such as the National Longitudinal Study of Youth, based at the University of Ohio. Many data sources can be downloaded very quickly and easily from the web.

Notes

1. In Great Britain, about 2 per cent of women aged 16–59 lived in three-generation households in 2001, compared with about 10 per cent of Pakistani and Bangladeshi women aged 16–59 (http://www.ccsr.ac.uk/sars/resources/ethnicityrpm/rpm.doc).
2. In 2001, 39 per cent of lone parents with dependent children in Britain were single (never married); 35 per cent were divorced; 18 per cent were separated and only 5 per cent were widowed. However, 71 per cent of Black Caribbean lone parents were single and 29 per cent of Bangladeshi lone parents were widowed (Dobbs et al., 2006).
3. Chevalier et al. (2005) found that, after controlling for the endogeneity between parental education and income, income was more important that parental education in determining children's school attainment at age 16 and in whether or not children left school at 16.

4. Chase-Lansdale et al. (1995) using the National Child Development Survey, concluded that parental divorce during childhood led to a small increased risk of emotional disorder at age 23. This operated indirectly through higher emotional problems at age 16, and lower school attainment and lower family status at age 16.

References

Cabinet Office (2009) 'Unleashing aspiration: the final report of the panel on fair access to the professions'. Available at: http://www.cabinetoffice.gov.uk/media/227102/fair-access.pdf (accessed 18 June 2010).

Chase-Lansdale, P., Cherlin, A. and Kiernan, K. (1995) 'The long-term effects of parental divorce on the mental health of young adults: a developmental perspective', *Child Development*, 66 (6), 1614–34.

Chevalier, A., Harmon, C., O'Sullivan, V. and Walker, I. (2005) 'The impact of parental income and education on the schooling of their children (February 2005)', IZA Discussion Paper No. 1496. Available at: http://ssrn.com/abstract=673407 (accessed 18 June 2010).

Cox, D.R. and Wermuth, N. (2001) 'Some statistical aspects of causality', *European Sociological Review*, 17 (1): 65–74.

Dale, A., Lindley, J. and Dex, S. (2006) 'A life-course perspective on ethnic differences in women's economic activity in Britain', *European Sociological Review,* 22 (4): 459–76.

Dale, A. and Ahmed, S. (2008) 'Migration, marriage and employment among Indian, Pakistani and Bangladeshi residents in the UK', CCSR Working Paper 2008–02.

Dale, A., Wathan, J. and Higgins, V. (2008) 'Secondary analysis of archival and survey data', in P. Alasuutari, L. Bickman and J. Brannen (eds), *The SAGE Handbook of Social Research Methods*. London: Sage.

Dobbs, J., Green, H. and Zealey, L. (2006) *ONS Focus on Ethnicity and Religion*. Basingstoke: Palgrave Macmillan.

Ermisch, J. (2008) 'Origins of social immobility and inequality: parenting and early child development', *National Institute Economic Review*, 205 (62–72). Available at: http://ner.sagepub.com/cgi/content/abstract/205/1/62 (accessed 18 June 2010).

Ermisch, J. and Francesconi, M. (2001) 'Family structure and children's achievements', *Journal of Population Economics*, 2 (14): 249–70.

Iacovou, M. (2001) 'Family composition and children's educational outcomes', ISER working paper 2001–12, University of Essex, available at: http://ideas.repec.org/p/ese/iserwp/2001-12.html (accessed 18 June 2010).

Iacovou, M. (2008) 'Family size, birth order and educational attainment', *Marriage and Family Review*, 42 (3): 35–57.

Jenkins, J., Rasbash, J. and O'Connor, T. (2003) 'The role of the shared family context in differential parenting', *Developmental Psychology,* 39 (1): 99–113. Available at: http://www.cmm.bristol.ac.uk/team/rsfcdp.pdf

Lampard, R. (2007) 'Is social mobility an echo of educational mobility? Parents' educations and occupations and their children's occupational attainment', *Sociological Research Online*, 12 (5). Available at: http://www.socresonline.org.uk/12/5/16.html (accessed 18 June 2010).

SECTION II

Researching Place

What is place?

The authors in this section give us very different ideas about how place is envisaged; whether it is a fixed location or a constantly changing construction.

While traditionally anthropologists locate ethnographic studies in a specific place, here Harvey and Knox conceive place not as a fixed location or as a firm physical concept but as a process that is dynamic and constantly changing.

> We are interested in how places are constantly in the process of becoming otherwise and elsewhere as people come and go, as environments evolve, as plans are enacted, and unplanned consequences unfold. (Harvey and Knox, Chapter 7, this volume, p. 107)

By choosing to study a road they were able to get away from traditional notion of place as a fixed location:

> the roads offered us an interesting challenge, and an opportunity to think about how traditional ethnographic practice limits our descriptions of 'place'. (Harvey and Knox, p. 110)

Although 'the road' is the central focus of their work, Harvey and Knox challenge the traditional concept of 'place' and essentially they explore the ways in which a road is both a place and a process, nonetheless 'the road' is the central focus of their work.

Guy and Karvonen locate their analysis of socio-technical processes in cities, in part because the city provides an ideal location for studying the processes of interest and thus the two become intertwined:

> The city is a frequent starting point for these studies because it has well-defined material and social boundaries that serve to delineate the stage upon which humans and technologies interact. It serves as a manageable starting point to study an infrastructure network, an urban development policy, a new building design, and so on. (Guy and Karvonen, Chapter 8, this volume, pp. 125–6)

However, the research is not 'just' about the city, just as Harvey and Knox's is not 'just' about the road, but each uses the city or the road as places where the processes of interest are played out and can therefore be readily studied and observed.

While Guy and Karvonen's interest is with the technologies that people use and that impact on them, Ballas and Dorling are concerned with the characteristics of the people who are living in particular places – local authorities, regions or countries. Their maps are based on places with grid-referenced boundaries, and use data from traditional sources such as censuses and surveys to summarize the characteristics of individuals in the areas of interest. However, their methods distort the traditional map-based understanding of place by changing its proportions to reflect variables of interest in population rather than its land mass. A conventional cartogram is also a distortion of land mass (for example, the traditional projection makes polar regions disproportionately larger than equatorial regions) but what Ballas and Dorling show us as a visualization of a place is a further distortion – land mass distorted by the additional layer of the size of the population with particular characteristics – thus giving layers of distortion.

The impact of this distortion on the reader works because the reader holds a visual image of a map of the UK or of Europe, or the world, based on land mass and the population-based map subverts and challenges that traditional image. They state this very simply:

> .... mapping the distribution of a human population on a conventional map means that urban areas with large populations but small area size are virtually invisible to the viewer. Conversely, the large rural areas with small populations dominate the map. When mapping data about people, it is therefore sensible to use a different spatial metaphor, one that reflects population size. (Ballas and Dorling, Chapter 10, this volume, pp. 150–1)

Despite the move away from a traditional land-mass cartogram, Ballas and Dorling are nonetheless concerned that populations can be identified as 'belonging' to a particular country or region that has a firm reality and clear boundaries. Although they make no claims for what place does, they are making a story; choosing variables to make an impact and to highlight inequalities in new and dramatic ways. Place is thus an integral part of the story.

Salway, Harriss and Chowbey's study of 'the links between long-term ill-health and dimensions of poverty' focused on four specific localities, but the importance of these was as communities, rather than as clearly delineated geographical areas. Their study of four different ethnic groups – in one of four different localities – focused on the way that these ethno-geographic communities had different implications for the health and well-being of the individuals who were the focus of their study. Thus ethnicity and geography interact to shape the opportunities available to individuals:

> ... having a particular ethnic identity and residing within a particular geographical area can have significant implications for the options available to individuals (particularly if disadvantaged by poverty and poor health). (Salway, Harriss and Chowbey, Chapter 9, this volume, p. 136)

How has place been chosen? Why one place rather than another?

Harvey and Knox have explicitly chosen a road because they want to break away from the traditional notion of ethnography taking place within a fixed location. However, we want to ask, why Peru? Why these roads in particular? They explain that Peru was chosen because of Harvey's familiarity with the country, but the specific road construction was chosen because it would raise issues of interest, for example, how technological developments would be played out; how decision making at many different levels would take place; how struggles over power would be enacted. There is a sense of serendipity in how they came to be in that particular place, and how it intersected with their theoretical interests. Although the road might appear to be a geographical 'place' they were more interested in the way in which it was constituted in relations through which things were made to happen and effects drawn forth. In that sense, their choice of place was also produced by prior relations, rather than conforming to apparently objective criteria of assessment.

In a rather similar way, Guy and Karvonen's choice of Tokyo allowed them to uncover non-traditional ways of understanding Japanese architecture:

> Taking a more ethnographic approach to the study of Tokyo, Guy discovers a seemingly chaotic built environment that belies the conventional Western perspective of Japanese architecture in serene harmony with nature. Rather than seeking out the remnants of ancient Japan or contemporary expressions of high Japanese architectural culture, Guy instead widens his analytical focus to acknowledge the sights, sounds, and smells of contemporary Tokyo. (Guy and Karvonen, Chapter 8, this volume, p. 129)

Salway, Harriss and Chowbey's choice of four communities was also an integral part of their research design.

> ... while exercising caution in using the term 'community', we nevertheless chose to identify four geographic localities, each within London, that were home to significant concentrations of people who self-identify as: Pakistani, Bangladeshi, Ghanaian or White English. (Salway, Harriss and Chowbey, Chapter 9, this volume, p. 136)

The fieldwork methods used, for example, an intensive seven-day study involving transect walks, observation and informal discussions also had implications for the size of the area that was appropriate and manageable.

Ballas and Dorling's mapping methods do not so much select specific places to study as focus attention on particular places through the non-traditional methods used. In one of their most graphic figures they make the researcher see how underweight children are very disproportionately located in parts of Africa and India. Their mapping methods draw attention to the inequalities associated with different geographical areas.

Methods of research

Harvey and Knox use ethnographic methods to study a very wide range of processes and interactions – all the stages of road construction and all the various people involved (either directly or indirectly) come within their remit as ethnographers. Having once selected their 'place' they keep an open mind – they are open to whatever presents itself. This involves immersing themselves in the 'road' and its social, cultural and material relations, and spending long periods of time living in the area, moving around with different sets of actors, making very detailed field notes.

By contrast, Salway, Harriss and Chowbey's research was conducted over a shorter time-span – a large part of the data generation took place within an intensive seven-day period and they discuss how fruitful this approach can be. They drew on information from many different kinds of sources, for example, observation, informal discussions, interviews, and their data was gathered not just by the researchers themselves but other university researchers and also community researchers. We should note, however, that although the fieldwork itself was speedy, this was only possible after a great deal of preparation, including training the community researchers, making local contacts and setting up a range of activities. Of particular interest was their desire to avoid over-reliance on in-depth interviews for respondents who may have had difficulty in 'telling a story' and hence their use of many different sources of information.

Guy and Karvonen's case study research also uses a very broad range of information and a range of methods.

> Similar to conventional case study research, socio-technical scholars employ methods of archival document review, semi-structured interviews, and various forms of ethnographic data collection. Archival reports, books, maps, and photographs provide an historical record of debates over technologies and the contextual and contingent factors involved in their success or failure. (Guy and Karvonen, Chapter 8, this volume, p. 125)

Both Salway, Harriss and Chowbey, and Guy and Karvonen have the challenge of bringing together and 'making sense' of very disparate kinds of data. As we suggested in Chapter 1, many researchers will not want to be limited to a particular ontological view of the world but will embrace a more complex view of the world that can encompass multiple ontologies.

Ballas and Dorling use conventional data sources that are widely available from archives and surveys for conventional geographical areas, but their mapping methods subvert our taken-for-granted assumptions places and place, centre stage, the human factors that are their concern.

These chapters contrast with others in this book by making place of central concern. While all research is located in space and time, other chapters do not make any claim to the role of place, and place is not centre stage in the way it is in this section. However, it is noteworthy that all these chapters have a very strong sense of time as well – the focus of our final section – whether in the sense of developing technologies, the process of building a road, or reflections on changing communities.

SEVEN

Ethnographies of Place

Researching the Road

Penny Harvey and Hannah Knox

Introduction

In this chapter we discuss our ethnographic explorations of the elusive qualities of place. We are interested in how places are constantly in the process of becoming otherwise and elsewhere as people come and go, as environments evolve, as plans are enacted and unplanned consequences unfold. Our interest in 'places in process' raises questions about description. As anthropologists we are particularly interested in how other people describe place and our work thus requires us to address the intrinsic multiplicity of place.[1] Attention to multiplicity alerts us to the ways in which descriptive practices entail epistemological and ontological claims. Ontologically, description requires some notion of what it is that is being described, the relevant entities and their relational fields. Epistemologically, descriptive claims are claims that reveal choices about how best to know and to persuade others of the relevance and credibility of one's own description. Descriptive accounts are in this sense claims on reality that, in their multiplicity, are constantly set against alternatives. In some contexts these alternatives become explicit sites of tension and negotiation. We chart a course through this complex politics of description by focusing on the notion of 'adequate description', hoping thereby to maintain awareness of description as an oriented practice, a purposeful activity.

Our interests in the ethnography of place emerged within the context of a collaborative research project which we carried out in Peru from 2005–2006.[2] The research, which focused on two road construction projects, critically explored the promise of technological development projects to deliver social change. Living on the road, and accompanying the road construction process, we quickly discovered that the imagination, design and construction of a road involve a complex process of reiteration. Descriptions are generated from many perspectives, and the construction company has to draw these together,

Figure 7.1 Constructing the interoceanic highway
Source: Thomas Grisaffi.

or to choose some over others, as they create the basis from which to produce their design. The designs are produced as singular descriptions of what the road will become, but they are multiple in the sense that they will be re-drawn, modified, and adapted throughout the life of the construction project. Furthermore the designs have to be sensitive to the changes that they themselves provoke. The building of the road is intended to modify the material and the social landscape; it is an intervention that generates effects before the construction even starts. Description in the context of such projects is thus on-going as construction companies seek to anticipate and register the effects of their intervention.[3]

A central focus of our project was to consider the knowledge practices on which construction work depends, and we were thus attentive to assumptions about knowledge and evidence, credibility, and communication. We wanted to explore ethnographically how expert knowledges are distinguished in practice from other ways of knowing. We were interested in Mitchell's (2002) analysis of the 'locationless logics' of experts and his argument that it is precisely the capacity to claim independence from the particular conditions of knowledge production that renders expert knowledges mobile, and transferable from one context to another. The capacity to deploy generic knowledges in order to transform particular places drew us to explore engineering practice, to see how it was done, and to try to understand how the very diverse expertises at work across a major construction project are co-ordinated such that they end up producing a single finished road.

As ethnographers this process had the added interest of representing a quite different form of expertise than that which we were exercising in our work. Ethnographers begin with local, place-based relations, and while we seek to identify the patterns, dispositions and forces that shape social life, these are never conceptualized as generic, but rather as the specific outcomes of previous relational processes. The aim is to get beyond how we, and others like us, habitually understand the world. We thus seek out alternatives and try to learn how other people know the world, and we are also interested in how disparate ways of knowing cohere, or not, across domains of practice. Ethnography in this vein is a practice that is based on participation and long-term co-habitation. During what is commonly referred to as the fieldwork period, ethnographers move to live elsewhere and otherwise, and through the disjuncture (and often discomfort) that such adjustments provoke, we try to identify the interests and passions of the people we encounter. In this way ethnographers try to allow the experiences of the fieldwork period to shape their research agendas, for what really matters to us are the things we know we cannot know in advance. Ethnography is a slow practice and requires patience. It entails a process of experimental engagement with others in which our experimental devices are our embodied selves, and the relationships that we form with others over time. We learn through a kind of attentive not knowing as we try to understand what participation involves, what it would be like to know the world in a different way. For this reason our research designs are necessarily open-ended and flexible. And while the ethnographer will always begin a research project with a specific focus and a sense of why their project is worth doing, we would also always expect things to happen along the way that would reveal the limitations of prior understandings and suggest alternatives.

In this sense we think of ethnography as a 'knowledge practice'. This orientation allows us to focus on how all knowledge practices (including our own) shape or give form to that which we come to know. Our approach builds on the important reflexive work in anthropology that interrogated the established ways of describing 'cultures'. *Writing Culture* (Clifford and Marcus, 1986) was a key intervention, making people aware of the rhetorical genres that were habitually used to encapsulate a complex reality and persuade others of its integrity. Since that time anthropological research has become more comfortable with the idea of partiality and of process (Strathern, 1991; Tsing, 2005), and of the inevitability of a narrative voice, and even the desirability of more explicit discussion of the emotional entanglements, doubts, and decisions through which any descriptive account emerges (Cerwonka and Malkki, 2007; Das, 2007; Stewart, 2007; Stoller, 2009; Taussig, 2006). One of the ways in which these debates have been taken forward focuses on story-telling as a way of connecting up the disparate events and imaginings from which lives are constituted. The important point is the shift away from an attempt to get at 'the truth' as a singular and static end-point of descriptive practice, and to look instead at how accounts are fabricated, how they are put together, and how they are put to work. Descriptive accounts are relational and evolving, and at least partially shaped by the particular fields in which they circulate (Latour, 1999).

Given the importance of specificity to the ethnographic approach, it is perhaps not surprising that studies in this vein are most commonly undertaken in particular institutions or places. As an ethnographic site the roads offered us an interesting challenge, and an opportunity to think about how traditional ethnographic practice limits our descriptions of 'place'. Unlike the setting of most ethnographic work, our two roads were extensive places, one was just under 100 km long, the other just over 700 km.[4] Always by definition both at and beyond the location of the ethnographer, roads are simultaneously specific historical and material sites, and somewhat ephemeral entities, often taken for granted, treated as (empty) spaces between places, rather than places in and of themselves.[5] But the (relatively) smooth surfaces that allow the roads to be ignored as places in and of themselves, only partially cover over the complex relations through which specific starting points and destinations become what they are. The histories of roads are the histories of the places they connect, the places they bring into being, and the places that disappear in their wake. They are also the material outcome of the diverse knowledges, skills and labour practices that went into their construction, and of the markets and the conflicts that moved populations and investments around the planet in particular directions at particular times. And just as they are somewhat invisible, once attention is directed to them they are self-evidently there, constructed, open-ended, in process, and integral to modern economies. The fact that they are networked spaces, inherently invoking the beyond of their specific location makes them particularly fruitful sites for historical and ethnographic research. Designed as generic networks, built to connect pre-existing places, they are material forms that produce relational dynamics that were never planned. It is the combination of the planned and the unplanned dimensions of roads that characterizes our interest in their particular transformational force. In the following section of this chapter we discuss in more detail how we found the roads that we focused on, how we engaged the people we encountered there, and how we addressed the specificity of these places in our descriptive practice.

Gaining access to the road

The question of *where* to start is there at the beginning of all ethnographic projects. As you begin to enact the 'methods' that are neatly set out in research proposals, you find in the field that you are immediately confronted with the barriers of other people's daily lives, preoccupations and assumptions. Getting started involves making decisions about where to set about the task of building the relationships through which the research project can unfold. And, as with all ethnographies, we started with what we had, specifically Penny's prior relationships in Peru, where she had done fieldwork on and off since the 1980s and our joint experiences in the ethnographic study of technological development projects in Manchester, where Hannah had done her PhD research in the late 1990s.

We had based our project in Ocongate to start with, because we knew that the Brazilian and the Peruvian governments, with support from international development banks, were going to re-pave the existing road. There was to be a major construction process in which many people from Ocongate expected to be personally involved as labourers. And the road promised to transform the town. People from Ocongate were actively involved in campaigns to ensure that the road was routed via their town and in the early days of fieldwork we, like they, were together trying to find out from the construction company where the road would go, how the construction would be managed and what the effects of the road were likely to be.

These questions that preoccupied our friends in Ocongate made it clear that we needed to build relations with the construction company. Following other contacts in the city, we gradually made our way to the offices of the top management. Patience and persistence were key at this stage. We visited many offices, waited in lobbies, chatted to receptionists and every now and then spoke to those authorized to get us onto the construction site, gleaning lots of information and getting to know all sorts of people along the way. Most of the people we met were generous with their time, happy to drive us around, to talk to us and to let us watch them at work. In time we were able to live for short periods in the construction camps, to make friends and to find out what building a road involved from the perspective of the engineering profession. We learnt that the workforce was a highly differentiated 'team'; some of whom never even visited the road but worked remotely, from offices in Eastern Brazil. Furthermore, the road construction process involved a complex network that spread far beyond the core construction company. Much of our early work was thus spent in identifying the key players and their relationships. To give a very brief overview these included national, regional and local government officials, the military and the police, an extremely diverse group of 'experts' and 'professionals' some employed by the construction company (itself a consortium), some employed by the state (the client and supervisor of the works), some sub-contracted by the state and/or the construction consortium (engineers, lawyers, economists, planners, managers). There were journalists, NGOs (both secular and religious), design and construction companies (national and international), labourers, drivers, travellers and transport companies, migrants, 'frontier colonists', Andean and Amazonian indigenous communities, urban and semi-urban populations. In addition we found it crucial to consider key non-human agents – particularly the materials (stone, earth/mud/dust, water), the inscriptions (numbers, images and written documents), the instruments and machines, the 'environment' (imagined and implicated in diverse registers) and an animate spirit world.

Writing is a key aspect of ethnographic research. Every day we each wrote extensive field notes, describing what we had done and the people we had met, detailing the conversations we had been party to, and noting down anything and everything that seemed relevant to our project. If we recorded interviews the field notes would detail the context of the conversation, who else was there, the atmosphere, the hints and suggestions of things that might not have been said and the reactions of others. Field notes are the basis from which subsequent accounts are distilled and elaborated, they shape and supplement memory, and they direct attention in the on-going process of research. As you write you become aware of things you feel unsure about, questions you forgot to ask, details you failed to notice. They are thus not simply a record of what happened, for a reflexive anthropologist will always assume that they are only aware of some of what is going on. As narratives they shape the trajectory of the research, and they also constitute an initial analysis of the mass of small encounters and events that constitute daily life in the field. Field notes are analytical from the start, and we do not draw a strong distinction between data collection and analysis. Understandings from one set of encounters can of course be modified by future encounters, including the encounters with other kinds of information in books and seminar rooms. All analyses are provisional. What our understandings add up to at any point in time are relative to the task in hand, to the question or problem that we seek to address in the presentation of the ethnographic work. Collaborative work is very enriching in this regard. We were able to compare notes from the start because of our mutual involvement in the project. We brought very different experiences and different perspectives to this project. Penny had worked in the Andes on and off for over 25 years, while it was Hannah's first visit. And there was an age difference of 20 years between us as well. Part of the research process was finding out what such differences implied, exploring our different perspectives and opportunities. Sometimes we remembered or interpreted things differently, we often noticed different things. We had our own opinions and interests, and sometimes we disagreed with each other, but on the whole we learnt from each other, as each of us extended the relations through which we could work to understand how the road was being shaped, and how it was in turn shaping people's lives.

Ethnographic work is not primarily directed to the discovery of 'facts-in-waiting'. It is a way of working that highlight ideas of process and the specificity of relational dynamics. Each researcher works through their relations with others, and while such work clearly allows the researcher to notice that some things are more stable, some ideas more common and some configurations more predictable, the focus on how things make sense, makes the question of relative value more significant than the question of relative truth. Building strong relational networks and gaining awareness of one's own influence within such networks is the core methodological concern.

It was with these ideas in mind that we attempted to keep our ethnographic perspective on the roads as mobile as possible. We travelled in different ways and in different company. With the engineers we often moved at speed in luxury 4×4s. The roads are different places when you are perched on top of a lorry, or lurching along inside a rickety bus. On two occasions we rented our own 4×4 and set off with a couple of experienced long-distance drivers. These were unusual journeys that we could make at our own pace, stopping at places that we or they thought interesting. These trips allowed us to engage the drivers in what were for them familiar journeys, as we stopped and talked to people they knew along the way. Most importantly we talked with them, and they also tried to fathom how to relate to us. They were always very keen to produce the first pioneers who had built the original road, having latched onto our interest in the history of the region. Whenever we stopped they would look for old people to talk to us. They were also constantly finding and talking with old friends and relatives. Working with them involved working with the encounters that their presence produced. Similarly the engineers who took us along to visit the road combined attempts to show us things they thought we would be interested in, with simply getting on with what they needed to do. We simply followed, trying as far as we were able, to understand where we were in their terms, rather than trying to lead our companions in particular directions. The road thus emerged piecemeal through the diverse modes of attention that we have described, and through the different kinds of engagement that our journeys produced.

Describing the road

One of the ways in which we came to know the road that we found most compelling and challenging, was through the stories that others told of their journeys. Our most prolonged narratives came from the drivers who we contracted to drive the 700+ kilometres from Cusco to the Brazilian border. Their accounts exemplified the diverse ways in which individual narratives connect up specific aspects of the trajectory, each forming a subtly distinct version of the place we were travelling through. At times their versions would coincide; at times they would differ, as with the accounts in our field notes. One of the men had, for 30 years or so, been fascinated by the artisanal gold-mining in the region. As we drove he would read the landscape with these interests in mind telling us how to identify where others are working from the state of the rivers, how the colour of the earth offers an indication of the minerals it contains. He was fascinated by the stories of those who had made and lost fortunes from their search for gold, and from the compulsions to spend the money that the gold produced. His stories offered glimpses of frontier economies where gold extraction was linked to potent and dangerous masculinities, where life was cheap and death common. Another driver had had little to do with the gold and had been more involved with working for government officials. He was an older man who sought to establish his connection with the spaces we were travelling through in terms of the people he had known and the positions they had held. As we stopped to interview people along the way he would often spend time trying to establish connections to those we met, offering them accounts of previous relationships with well-known public figures that would establish his credentials in their eyes. Both men had many stories of the dangers of long-distance travel in relation to the vulnerability of drivers who alone and exhausted struggled to fight off predatory spirits and to negotiate the shifting and unstable landscapes that led so many to die in accidents.

One of the powerful sensations that our travels with these men established for us related to the shifting quality of road-side settlements. The interoceanic highway in the Andean region connects a series of towns that have been settled for many centuries, but as we moved down into the Amazonian region the settlements became more provisional, more directly related to the arrival of the road, to the possibilities for trade and for extraction. These settlements were built by migrants who were in many cases still 'on the move'. The names of the settlements and the stories of their foundation introduced us to the histories of global population movements at the beginning of the 20th century. The mid-19th century saw struggles between rubber barons, which were characteristic of the early years of the Latin American republics in this region. These soon gave way to the interests in gold and timber and virgin farmland that provoked the arrival of Russian, Yugoslav, Polish and Japanese explorers, adventurers and entrepreneurs. Most of these early inhabitants were long gone – some leaving the trace of their presence in the name of settlements such as the Japanese 'Mazuko' and the Polish 'Malinowski'. Large numbers of Andean people arrived in the 1960s, looking for land, encouraged by the government to take advantage of colonization programmes. In subsequent decades the gold-rush drew more people still. Despite passing through an Amazonian lowland region, there are, with the exception of one small community, no native Amerindian forest peoples living alongside the road. This particular road has become an Andean space, peopled by colonists, many of whom maintain strong connections to their mountain communities of origin, but who have, nevertheless, made the lowland forest their home.

The methodological importance of these migration stories is related to the ways in which the very diverse accounts that we collected produced a sense of a place that people made through their own labour. People did not on the whole produce accounts of arrival in ready-made places. On the contrary they were stories of place-making in the process of living, of finding yourself in a specific situation looking to farm, to pan for gold, to extract timber or to trade, work that required people to establish relations with the land, and with each other. Places thus emerged through a complex process of alignment and realignment as each arrival brought possibilities, expectations and limits. These alignments and realignments mirror the social effects of the road itself which in practice – whatever the aspirations or understandings of planners and designers – also emerges through the relations between people and matter, humans and non-humans in the on-going process of life.

Learning about the road from the perspective of the construction company was a very different experience. The presence of the company in a particular place was both dramatic and explicitly transitory. Preparation for their arrival in local terms was certainly a scenario of active realignment as people made efforts to secure work, to rent land, to offer services of all kinds. Those well-placed to do so could secure substantial financial benefits by renting land to the company for the construction of their camps, or the location of an asphalt manufacturing plant. Others found their land-holdings became precarious as compensation rights produced regimes of explicit titling and ownership that delivered benefits for some, while dispossessing others. Desires for the potential transformation and modernization of particular places were matched by the fears of negative consequences. Many of these social expectations and threat focused on the location of the camps that accompanied the road construction, temporary residences for up to two thousand young male workers that threw a whole gamut of social and cultural values into turmoil. The promise of work drew people from all over the country to try their luck, but work was not always immediately available, so squatter camps grew up outside the perimeter fences. Despite legal agreements that had been put in place to guarantee that jobs were given to registered local people, the layers of sub-contraction and the company's need to be able to work fast and to react quickly meant jobs were sometimes available to these non-local migrants. This made such speculative place-building viable for some, not least those who appeared to service the chancers by providing food.

The reconfiguration of place around the activities of the construction company was not only visible in relation to population movements and their unsettling effects. The company engineers, designers and scientists, were themselves actively engaged in describing the areas through which they intended to move. Their descriptions were detailed and on-going. Soils were collected and analysed; the geological and hydraulic systems were mapped. Topographers traced possible routes in the landscape, negotiating the contours, the fault lines and the social demands, exciting local curiosity and anxiety as to where exactly the new road would be going. These physical, social and cultural topographies were all outlined in the various documents that public works of this scale require to secure the initial funding and the on-going political support required to keep such projects on track.

One of the things that interested us about the descriptions produced by the company was the ways in which they combined definitive statements as to the essential nature of a place (its history, material properties, legal status), and the recognition, in practice, that the places thus described were unstable, dynamic entities subject to change. The official documents on which such projects are originally based do not provide descriptions of what the engineers in fact encounter when they reach particular places, and far less what kind of place will emerge through such encounters. Engineers and local people knew equally well that the land itself was unstable. Earthquakes and landslides are common in the region, the numerous rivers and streams in the Amazonian basin are constantly changing course, and they swell and die down suddenly in relation to rainfall many miles away. Even with the benefits of the new road, journeys are constantly interrupted by contingent events – the weather, the state of the vehicle, other people or animals that block the road, or divert attention. Over time settlements and infrastructures move in relation to the wider circulations of which any specific road forms a part. We came across settlements that had, for example, been built in a moment of speculative optimism alongside rivers full of gold, but which had subsequently moved towards the road in order to effect a closer connection to the new trading opportunity it represented. We also found routes and bridges that had been abandoned as engineers and politicians from previous eras had decided to take a different route, had miscalculated or simply run out of money. As we watched the company lay down the new road it was clear that local people were highly attentive to their sense that while fixing a specific route, other previous relations and possibilities were simultaneously coming undone. The road provoked responses, it reformed what a place could be, that was its explicit purpose. What nobody could be sure of, and what excited the general air of speculation from the landless peasant to the venture capitalist, were the socio-economic contours of the future of these places.

Conclusion

One of the key outcomes of ethnographic research is the possibility of seeing the world in new ways, and of being able to ask questions and describe relations in ways that were not available to the researcher at the outset. Our travels on the roads of Peru taught us a great deal about the specific materiality of roads and, as importantly, about how the layering of materials through which a road appears in the environment as a specific and relatively stable structure also carried with it histories of skills, of trade, of hopes and of struggle. These histories leave their traces in the stories people tell, in the physical make up of a place, and in the daily practices of those we encountered along the way. We became more aware of the politics of place, the specific ways in which the tensions between national and trans-national spaces emerge and are negotiated, the investments and the withdrawals that offer and destroy the possibilities for people to stabilize relations with each other and with the world in which they live.

And here we return to the question of adequate description. Ethnography is a descriptive practice that tries to capture the affective dynamics of place and which attends specifically to the ways in which particular knowledges become credible and actionable, how they attain force and presence in the world. We had from the outset expected to find tensions between generic and specific knowledge practices, and our observations of the road construction process helped us to understand something of the techniques and the relational work through which some knowledge practices become more valued and more influential than others. We learnt that all accounts are subject to variation and modification whether we look at the metrics of the engineering professionals, or the stories of spectral forces that animate many an explanation of how places come to be the way they are. Now in the final stages of writing a monograph on the roads of Peru, nearly two years since we completed the fieldwork we have become more interested in the journeys that all descriptive accounts are launched on, the entities they are mobilized to connect and bring into being, and those that they leave to one side and designate as irrelevant. We have concluded that the narratives that connected a driver to an old acquaintance and that allowed them to talk meaningfully about a past event, were not different in kind to the accounts that circulated between a topographer and a designer sat at a computer terminal in a distant city. What was indeed different was the activity in which these people were engaged, and hence the elements that need to be assembled for effective engagement. It is this relational principle of orientation that is crucial to our understanding of descriptive adequacy. As ethnographers we seek to provide robust descriptions, by which we mean that our descriptions are recognizable and credible. Also, by putting our descriptions out into the world we become accountable for them in ways that differ from fictional writing, as we make claims that others can judge on the basis of their experience. The descriptions are specific to the relations through which they were formed, but they are oriented to a world beyond us. Ethnography is imaginative, creative work but its poetics are perhaps more akin to jazz than to fiction – there is no such thing as a wrong note, only more or less suggestive, imaginative or provocative interpretations.

As a facet of ethnographic methodology, we suggest that adequate description should expand the imagination rather than seek a singular truth. In relation to questions of space and mobility we have responded to the challenge of addressing how roads reconfigure social space by attending to the many dynamics in play and the specific conditions of the interactions that come to be revealed through description as multiplicity. Through the pursuit of a description adequate to the task of expanding our ethnographic imagination we have found ourselves able to reveal a common experience of contingency and experimentality towards shifting and unstable terrain among the diverse groups that have become entangled in the space that is the road. Acknowledging the possibility that through description people might be able to communicate something of how they intend to respond to this contingency (or not), be they engineers, drivers, gold prospectors or anthropologists, we have found ourselves able to describe a mode of sociality and relatedness which cuts across the seemingly immutable social divisions that get invoked by those who believe in the locationless logics of expertise.

Notes

1. Our discussions of multiplicity draw on Law (2004), Law and Mol (2002) and Mol (2003).
2. This research was supported by an ESRC research grant, and by CRESC the ESRC Centre for Research on Socio-Cultural Change.
3. Historical accounts of descriptive practices in relation to engineering work include: Carroll (2006), Joyce (2003) and Mukerji (2009); contemporary accounts of engineering practice include Latour (1996), Law (2002) and Suchman (2000).
4. One of the roads we studied is commonly referred to as the interoceanic highway and runs from the border with Brazil in the Peruvian Department of Madre de Dios to within 40 km of the Andean city of Cusco. The other road runs between the city of Iquitos and the town of Nauta in the Northern Peruvian Amazon.
5. See, for example, Augé (1995).

References

Augé, M. (1995) *Non-places: Introduction to An Anthropology of Super-Modernity*. Trans. J. Howe. London: Verso.

Carroll, P. (2006) *Science, Culture and Modern State Formation*. Berkeley, CA: University of California Press.

Cerwonka, A. and Malkki, L. (2007) *Improvizing Theory: Process and Temporality in Ethnographic Fieldwork*. Chicago, IL: University of Chicago Press.

Clifford, J. and Marcus, G. (eds) (1986) *Writing Culture: the Poetics and Politics of Ethnography*. Berkeley, CA: University of California Press.

Das, V. (2007) *Life and Words: Violence and the Descent into the Ordinary*. Berkeley, CA: University of California Press.

Joyce, P. (2003) *The Rule of Freedom: Liberalism and the Modern City*. London: Verso.

Latour, B. (1996) *Aramis or The Love of Technology*. Trans. C. Porter. Cambridge, MA: Harvard University Press.

Latour, B. (1999) *Pandora's Hope: Essays on the Reality of Science Studies*. Cambridge, MA: Harvard University Press.

Law, J. (2002) *Aircraft Stories: Decentering the Object in Technoscience*. Durham, NC: Duke University Press.

Law, J. (2004) *After Method: Mess in Social Science Research*. London: Routledge.

Law, J. and A. Mol. (2002) *Complexities: Social Studies of Knowledge Practices*, Durham, NC: Duke University Press.

Mitchell, T. (2002) *Rule of Experts: Egypt, Techo-politics, Modernity*. Berkeley, CA: University of California Press.

Mol, A. (2003) *The Body Multiple: Ontology in Medical Practice*. Durham, NC: Duke University Press.

Mukerji, C. (2009) *Impossible Engineering: Technology and Territoriality on the Canal du Midi*. Princeton, NJ: Princeton University Press.

Stewart, K. (2007) *Ordinary Affects*. Durham, NC: Duke University Press.

Stoller, P. (2009) *The Power of the Between: An Anthropological Odyssey*. Chicago, IL: University of Chicago Press.

Strathern, M. (1991) *Partial Connections*. Savage, MD: Rowman and Littlefield.

Suchman, L. (2000) 'Organizing alignment: a case of bridge-building', *Organization*, 7 (2): 311–27.

Taussig. M. (2006) *Walter Benjamin's Grave*. Chicago, IL: University of Chicago Press.

Tsing, A. (2005) *Friction: an Ethnography of Global Connection*. Princeton, NJ: Princeton University Press.

EIGHT

Using Sociotechnical Methods

Researching Human-Technological Dynamics in the City

Simon Guy and Andrew Karvonen

Introduction

You are roused from a deep slumber by the buzzing of your digital alarm clock. It's 6 a.m., time to get up. You begrudgingly comply, reach for the light switch, and stagger to the bathroom to use the toilet. After getting a drink of water from the tap, you head to the kitchen to switch on the kettle. Outside your window and four stories down, automated photosensors switch off the streetlights in anticipation of the sunrise, while the sidewalks and streets gradually fill with daily commuters travelling in cars and on bus, bicycle and foot. Back inside your flat, you settle into your favourite chair with a cup of hot tea and open your laptop to scan the day's headlines as the city gradually comes to life.

Technology saturates the city. From the most basic acts of sustenance and shelter to the most cutting edge forms of digital communication, city residents engage with a wide variety of technologies on a daily basis. Routinely, we pay little attention to these interactions; they are simply the taken-for-granted infrastructures of life in the contemporary age. We only recognize our reliance on technologies when they break down or act in unexpected ways – when a bridge collapses under too much weight, a heat wave causes a citywide black-out, an antiquated water main finally exceeds its service life or a hacker successfully disrupts the Internet. But what if we made an explicit attempt to understand the relationship between urban technologies and everyday life? What if we recognized that technologies have cultural, social and political implications that are intimately tied to our existence as urban residents?

In this chapter, we summarize what it means to study cities from a socio-technical perspective. We use the compound term 'sociotechnical' to describe the indelible link between humans and technologies; in other words, one cannot be considered in isolation of the other. We begin with a brief review of the origins of the sociotechnical perspective and its scholarly implications when investigating urban development processes. We then provide a brief summary of four sociotechnical studies of cities to understand the methodology and methods employed as well as the types of knowledge produced. In conclusion, we argue that the sociotechnical perspective allows us to embrace the messiness of contemporary cities and imagine alternative futures by reworking the relations between humans and their material surroundings.

Conceptualizing technology in the city

The sociotechnical study of cities is rooted in two distinct but related academic discourses, urban history and science and technology studies (STS). Urban historians have long been interested in the technologies that are central to the development and function of cities, particularly the large infrastructure networks built in Europe and North America beginning in the 18th century to sustain rapidly industrializing societies. These studies demonstrate that the success of cities is highly dependent upon large-scale technological networks that can funnel natural resources, waste products, information, goods and people into and out of cities (Tarr, 2005). 'Urban infrastructure provides what may be called the vital technological sinews of the modern city: its road, bridge and transit networks; its water and sewer lines and waste disposal facilities; and its power and communication systems. These sinews permit urban functioning and facilitate urban economic development' (Tarr and Konvitz, 1987: 195).

A second inspiration to the sociotechnical study of cities is the interdisciplinary field of STS. STS emerged as a discipline in the 1970s as scholars in the social sciences and humanities began to formalize the social study of scientific and technological development. An early touchstone for these scholars was Thomas Kuhn's seminal 1962 book *The Structure of Scientific Revolutions*. STS was also influenced by the social movements of the late 1960s and early 1970s in North America and Europe, and the contentious scientific and technological issues of nuclear weapons and power, environmental pollution, reproductive technologies, biotechnology and genetic research and so on. Today, STS includes a heterogeneous mix of philosophers, sociologists, anthropologists, political scientists and other social scientists who are interested in opening the 'blackbox' of scientific and technological development processes to reveal their origins, dynamics and consequences (Hackett et al., 2008; Hess, 1997; Sismondo, 2004).

STS scholars and urban historians argue that technological development does not occur in a vacuum; rather, it is inseparable from and implicated by, developments in the social sphere. These scholars reject the technological determinist perspective that sees technological development as an exogenous, linear and inevitable process of innovation. Instead, technologies are understood to be shaped by a wide variety of social actors, not only scientists, engineers and policymakers, but also politicians, activists, artists and even users. However, rejection of a technological determinist perspective does not entail the wholehearted embrace of social constructivism. Social forces are not the sole determinant of technological development, either, because non-human influences – physical and chemical properties, natural disasters, ecological and biological forces and so on – also shape and drive technological development.

In place of social constructivist and technological determinist perspectives, many STS scholars and urban historians embrace what is referred to as a 'co-constructivist' approach. The co-construction of technology rejects the essentialist tendencies of technological determinism and social constructivism in favour of more nuanced positions where mutual shaping occurs between the two (Bijker et al., 1987; Bijker and Law, 1992; Feenberg, 1999; Latour, 1993; MacKenzie and Wacjman, 1999b; Misa et al., 2003). 'It is mistaken to think of technology and society as separate spheres influencing each other: technology and society are mutually constitutive' (MacKenzie and Wacjman, 1999a: 23). There is an explicit attempt to look beyond conventional definitions and dualistic typologies that divide the world into humans and nonhumans, objects and subjects, and facts and values, while also avoiding a relativistic account of the world that has no point of reference (see Latour, 1993; Law, 2004). There is significant and heated disagreement among these scholars as to how the various processes of co-construction occur, but, in general, they tend to emphasize the relations between society and technology rather than focus on one or the other independently.

In the past decade, the sociotechnical study of cities has broadened beyond urban history and STS to include research in the spatial disciplines of architecture, urban planning and geography. The result has been an expanded view of technology that includes not only the artefacts produced through technological development but also 'the knowledge required to construct and use these artefacts, as well as the practices that engage them' (Guy, 2009: 232). Sociotechnical scholars examine topics such as the design, construction, maintenance and occupation of buildings; urban planning and policy activities; the relationship between infrastructure networks and metropolitan governance; the intertwining of nature, technology, and humans in the urban landscape; and the introduction and evolution of municipal regulations and codes (Graham and Marvin, 2001; Guy and Moore, 2005; Guy and Shove, 2000; Guy et al., 2001; Hård and Misa, 2008; Moore, 2007). The city is interpreted as a sociotechnical artefact in which technology and humans interact through the political, cultural and economic dramas of daily life (Aibar and Bijker, 1997; Brand, 2008; Hommels, 2005). Technical experts such as engineers, architects, planners and policymakers play a large part in these studies but there is an explicit attempt to understand how other, seemingly 'non-technical' actors also influence the development and management of technologies.

Sociotechnical scholars share at least four common perspectives on urban technologies. First, technological development processes are *contextually based*. While it is possible to transfer techniques, skills and knowledge between different places, processes of translation and interpretation dictate the success or failure of technologies in a particular locale. An example of the contextual nature of technological development is the skyscraper, a building type that has dominated North American skylines for over a century. The skyscraper has been slow to catch on in other developed countries, particularly northern Europe where the existing urban fabric and cultural expectations are not receptive to these modernist monuments to capitalism. The aversion to the skyscraper building type is due to its aesthetic and financial implications, and more broadly, to how the technological artefact resonates with specific cultural and material conditions.

Second, related to context, sociotechnical scholars also interpret technological development as a *contingent* process. While it is tempting to view seemingly mundane technologies such as road and water infrastructure networks as inevitable products of human progress, we can frequently identify alternative pathways of development that could have been taken. In other words, "interpretive flexibility" is attached to any artefact: it might be designed in another way' (Moore, 1997: 25). Again, this refers to the wide variety of actors and contextual factors that shape technologies, and, in the process, create multiple pathways or alternative routes by which technologies are realized (Evans et al., 2001; Guy and Marvin, 1999; Guy and Marvin, 2001; Guy and Moore, 2005; Moore, 2001; Moore, 2007; Moore and Brand, 2003). This is not to suggest that there are an infinite number of ways a technology could have been deployed in a particular context but rather that the resulting way was not the only one.

An historic example of the contingent nature of technological development is the adoption of combined and separated sewer systems in North America and Europe beginning in the late 19th century (Tarr, 1979). Sanitary engineers, public health officers and municipal officials engaged in heated debates to decide whether liquid wastes (stormwater and sanitary wastes) should be conveyed in one pipe or two, and argued for their positions on economics, physical and bacteriological grounds. Each technology had specific advantages and disadvantages and the final decision in each city depended upon influential technical actors, the availability of scientific and empirical data, past experiences with sewer technologies, climatic conditions, financial resources, user habits and preferences, and estimates of future urban growth. Today, both types of systems exist, demonstrating the multiple pathways upon which urban technologies can be developed.

The continued use of combined and separated sewer systems suggests a third theme of the sociotechnical study of cities: *obduracy*. This is simply to state that urban technologies are long lived and they are embedded in a complex array of material realities, social habits and institutional standards.

Indeed, many cities in North America and Europe continue to rely on 19th-century infrastructure networks because replacing them with newer, more cost effective and environmentally friendly systems would be too costly and disruptive. Of course, these infrastructure networks were designed to be long lived, but their obstinacy is also due to their embeddedness in their cultural and material contexts, making the introduction of a new technology a highly contentious process (Hommels, 2005).

Finally, processes of sociotechnical development are often *uneven*. Megacities in developing countries provide some of the starkest examples of unequal infrastructure service provision, with peripheral slums lacking the water, wastewater and electricity services (not to mention zoning, building codes, paved streets and so on) that are ubiquitous in the central city. And this tendency is not restricted to developing countries; the notion of the 'digital divide' in the global north belies the rhetoric of the Internet as a neutral and readily available communication network. Technologies can replicate and exacerbate existing social hierarchies and class distinctions, creating interstices and recesses of partial or no service rather than a level playing field for all urban residents (Graham and Marvin, 2001; Swyngedouw, 2004).

These four themes – contextuality, contingency, obduracy, and unevenness – permeate the sociotechnical studies of cities. They encourage the researcher to ask: How and why did a technology develop in a particular place and time? Who was included in development processes and who was excluded? How did processes of negotiation over competing technologies occur and how was a decision reached? What geographic and material conditions influenced the adoption or rejection of a technology? What were the political, cultural, environmental, and economic consequences? The overarching aim of these questions is to interrogate the multivalent character of sociotechnical development processes in cities.

Studying the sociotechnical city

Researchers who adopt a sociotechnical approach to study cities come from a wide range of disciplines and thus their research methods vary to some degree. However, there is a general tendency to apply qualitative methods to unpack the various meanings and implications of technological development. The case study methodology is prevalent in the sociotechnical study of cities because it allows the researcher to analyse the concrete, context-dependent interactions between humans and technology. In place of a single pathway, these researchers explore the multiple pathways and different meanings of technologies to urban actors. Macro characterizations of the city as a massive economic engine, a concentrated zone of human settlement, or a complex web of technological networks, are rejected in favour of fine-grained investigations of human–technology interaction. The research tends to be grounded, both theoretically and physically, with the researcher engaged in processes of tracing the relations or connections through multiple narratives and transects.

Similar to conventional case study research, sociotechnical scholars employ methods of archival document review, semi-structured interviews and various forms of ethnographic data collection. Archival reports, books, maps and photographs provide an historical record of debates over technologies and the contextual and contingent factors involved in their success or failure. When studying a particular technology, there is a tendency for the researcher to assume that the existing technology was the 'correct choice'. However, the historical record frequently reveals a palette of options that were weighed and contested by various social actors and material conditions, resulting in the success of one particular technology over others (Bijker, 1997). Exploring these processes of contestation can help the researcher uncover particular influences of culture and materiality embedded in the topic of study.

In addition to the review of archival materials, sociotechnical researchers frequently seek to 'follow the actors' by conducting structured or semi-structured interviews with technical experts, policymakers, political actors and users. The intent of these interviews is to gain insight from key actors who were involved in the design and development of a particular technology, what types of social conflicts and controversies occurred, how changing contexts informed the process and how the final design of the technical artefact eventually came into being. These interviews can provide some of the most illuminating data, particularly when the respondents provide conflicting interpretations of the subject at hand, revealing the multivalent character of technological development.

Finally, sociotechnical researchers often perform site visits to gain firsthand 'participative' experience as to how a particular technology is embedded in its material and cultural surroundings, and how its final shape emerges through design, dialogue, and dispute. It is here where the researcher becomes intimate with the subject of study and discovers details and issues that are not addressed explicitly in the historical record or through interviews with key actors. The site visit also offers the researcher a chance to engage directly in the study, rather than through representations in books or from secondary accounts by various stakeholders. These ethnographies also produce different forms of data, such as photographs, maps, calculations, models, even sensory experiences, that help to color and shade the textual data of interviews and archival research. Through these alternative datasets new 'voices' are added to the process of interpretation, allowing more actors to 'join the story' and provide the narrative of technological change with 'more voices, vantage points and concerns' (Yaneva, 2009: 7).

A particular challenge for sociotechnical researchers involves scale. The city is a frequent starting point for these studies because it has well-defined material and social boundaries that serve to delineate the stage upon which humans and technologies interact. It serves as a manageable starting point to study an infrastructure network, an urban development policy, a new building design, and so on. However, even the smallest technologies have a tendency to transgress these boundaries and circulate in regional, national and global flows of knowledge, capital and natural resources. A good example is historian Ruth Schwartz Cowan's (1987) study of the diffusion of American cast-iron stoves and gas cooking ranges through which she traces the networks of interests and influences on the consumer and their choices. By following influential actors and drawing network diagrams, Cowan identifies the site of consumer choice as the 'consumption junction', the interface where technological diffusion occurs and the place where technologies begin to reorganize societal practices and structures.

Like Cowan, the sociotechnical researcher is often faced with the challenge of tracing networks and jumping scales to connect the micro and macro implications of technological development. The city serves as a meso-scale and the sociotechnical scholar scales up and down to make connections between the global and the local. Critically, this requires the researcher to decide which connections to trace, how far to trace them spatially and temporally, and when to stop, thereby becoming another 'actor' in the network of assembly that surrounds the technical object.

A second challenge of the sociotechnical researcher is to interrogate the nonhuman and material aspects of technologies. This follows a more general trend in the qualitative social sciences to go beyond the human aspects of the world and engage with its material aspects (Dant, 2005; Thrift, 2007). From a co-constructivist perspective, it is not sufficient to follow the social actors who shape technological development because this only tells half of the story (Latour, 1992). Rather, there is a need to understand how the materiality of technologies is related to their development. This is a particularly tricky task for qualitative social scientists that tend to leave the characterization of the nonhuman world to the natural sciences and continues to be a contentious and emerging approach for sociotechnical researchers.

Examples of urban sociotechnical research

To illustrate the range of urban sociotechnical study, we briefly summarize four case studies in the following paragraphs. These examples illustrate how scholars in geography, architecture, planning and sociology have interpreted technological development as it relates to the introduction of water supply infrastructure, the politics of architectural design, the reform of urban transportation policies and the latent opportunities in modest building practices. The examples suggest some of the different types of knowledge and insights produced by examining cities through a sociotechnical lens.

In *City of Flows: Modernity, Nature, and the City*, geographer Maria Kaika examines how technological networks of water infrastructure are bound up in notions of human progress by tracing the development of water supply networks in Athens, Greece. The purpose of her study is to understand how nature, technology and urban development are embedded in messy sociotechnical configurations and to understand how the network logic of urban infrastructure is related to Western notions of progress and modernity. On the importance of technology to the city, she writes:

> The material mediators, the carriers of the flows that constitute the urban are technological networks: water, gas, electricity, information, and so on. Given their central role in the production of modern cities, technology networks are integral parts of the urban fabric and of the process of transformation of nature into the city and vice versa. (Kaika, 2005: 28)

Kaika argues that while the goal of societal progress and modernization was to separate humans from nature, the introduction of new technological networks does just the opposite, creating new hybrid human–nature configurations. She illustrates this by tracing water flows from the household scale (where nature, technology and humans interact face-to-face) to the neighbourhood, city and regional scales (where water supply networks are planned and built), and finally, to national and global scales (where ideas of capitalism and modernity are shaped). Engineers, planners, policymakers and politicians use infrastructure networks to define particular configurations of nature and society through narratives of technological progress and societal improvement, which have important implications for defining cities as centres of accumulation, capitalization, and the consumption of nature.

A second example of the sociotechnical study of cities is architect Steven Moore's analysis of the design and construction of the Commerzbank Tower in Frankfurt, Germany (Moore, 2007; Moore and Brand, 2003). The project, completed in 1997, is a well-known example of a sustainable skyscraper that simultaneously satisfies stringent economic and environmental criteria when compared to a conventional building. Here, Moore unpacks the history of the project to understand how the influence of competing actors is embodied in the technical artefact that now dominates the Frankfurt skyline. He argues that:

> This project was central to the city's growth pains in the 1980s and 1990s because it focused the attention of citizens, bankers and city officials on the future of the banking industry in the city. As a result, it serves as a concrete laboratory for more conceptual planning issues. (Moore, 2007: 125)

Through semi-structured interviews with key actors, archival research, site visits and mapping, Moore identifies dominant and counter storylines that had significant influence on the final design of the building. The Commerzbank Tower study demonstrates how a single technical artefact, a building, is related to particular forms of democratic politics that involve negotiations between the various vested interests of urban development. The process of creating an architectural icon was not merely one of balancing aesthetic preference with functional necessity; design is a contested process that involves complex negotiations between powerful social actors and material flows. Through processes of coalition building and conflict resolution, the building owners and design team were successful in bringing on board the banking community, environmentalists, political actors, municipal officials and residents to devise a project that would, for the most part, satisfy their competing visions of Frankfurt's future.

In a third case study, urban planning scholar Ralf Brand (2005, 2008) examines the Belgian city of Hasselt and the attempts by the municipality to implement transportation reforms in the 1990s. The city had been plagued for several decades by mobility issues including congestion, accidents, air pollution and poor accessibility and the municipality considered implementing a technical fix approach (building a third ring road) or a behavioural fix approach (persuading residents to use non-automobile forms of transport). In the end, the municipal government chose to adopt neither strategy and instead embarked on a redevelopment programme 'to make the built environment and other elements within its political remit more conducive to alternative forms of mobility through an integrated set of institutional, infrastructural and urban design interventions' (Brand, 2008: 183). The redevelopment included renovation of infrastructure services to facilitate mass transit, bicycling and walking, as well as significant changes to existing transportation, land use and parking policies.

Brand is particularly interested in the rhetoric of sustainable urban development and how integrated strategies to reorient urban metabolic processes are related to technological development. He describes the transportation reforms in Hasselt as a 'co-evolution of technical and social change' where the synergies between humans and technical networks are identified and exploited to produce a more livable and environmentally friendly city. Expanding upon the co-constructivist position described above, he argues that artefacts of the built environment such as bicycle lanes and convenient bus routes have inherent 'agendas' that facilitate particular forms of human activity. This is not to prescribe a social engineering approach to urban development but rather to recognize that technological design offers opportunities to encourage different habits and behaviours by urban residents.

Finally, sociologist Simon Guy (2009, 2010) explores sustainable architecture practices in Japan to understand how different cultural contexts enable particular arrangements of technology, nature, and humans. Guy's research goes beyond the textbook visions of Japanese architectural culture that, he argues, serve to fix and essentialize particular typologies of Japanese urbanism. This traditional form of architectural research relies on an interpretive mode of analysis that assumes cultural norms and values can be simply read from urban surfaces through photographing, drawing and memorializing. Faced with the scale, density, dynamism and heterogeneity of Tokyo, Guy suggests that this form of architectural research is unable to make sense of contemporary Japan.

Taking a more ethnographic approach to the study of Tokyo, Guy discovers a seemingly chaotic built environment that belies the conventional Western perspective of Japanese architecture in serene harmony with nature. Rather than seeking out the remnants of ancient Japan or contemporary expressions of high Japanese architectural culture, Guy instead widens his analytical focus to acknowledge the sights, sounds and smells of contemporary Tokyo. Widening his reading beyond architectural histories to include novels, anthropology field notes, diaries and newspaper columns, he moves between interviews with architects, developers, planners and academics, and his own ethnographic explorations of the city to explore how particular ideas of nature are being preserved, celebrated, exploited, ignored, discarded and damaged through processes of urbanization.

Case studies of individual developments are complimented by studies of the work of different architectural practices, notably the work of a small architecture practice, Atelier Bow-Wow. At this firm, the members take inspiration from what they call 'pet architecture', or monstrous buildings that embrace and celebrate wild juxtapositions of use, from temples and shops to laundries, saunas, restaurants, pachinko parlors and golf driving ranges. Writing of their own research approach, principal architect Yoshiharu Tsukamoto states, 'One could say that this research was to show that the vital, animate order of Tokyo's urban space, which joins together its disparate parts, is something that stands in opposition to existing modes of architectural criticism' (2008: 60).

Inspired by the 'rhythmanalysis' approach of Henri Lefebvre, Atelier Bow-Wow follow the unfolding of the city over time and through space, with buildings growing and shrinking and the use of spaces and places shifting between pubic and private, individual and collective, and document these processes with ethnographic field notes. Drawing on this research, the designers apply the lessons from these hybrid buildings to inspire their residential and commercial micro-projects that reinvent the 'non-standard spaces, the leftover, awkward spaces of urban development' that are abundant in Tokyo (Guy, 2010: 126). Rather than emphasize the artefacts produced, Guy is interested in their novel form of design practice that responds flexibly to the restless flux of humans, technology and nature bound up in the dynamism of the contemporary urban metropolis.

Guy's study focuses on the less glamorous side of architectural production, namely the incremental shaping of the urban fabric. Here, he discovers an alternative and inspiring approach to engage with and reorder the messy relations of the city. Using a sociotechnical lens, he identifies the unfamiliar and strange practices of Atelier Bow-Wow as an instructive way to understand the intertwined processes of urban development. Reflecting on the artefacts they produce, he writes, 'These are buildings as infrastructures of everyday life and demonstrate a remarkable fluidity of programme and purpose which presents the city as rather less obdurate than is often portrayed in urban studies' (Guy, 2010: 126). His emphasis is on the opportunities to change the relations between technology, humans and nature in urban contexts through tactical interventions that can respond to the rhythms of the contemporary city. Describing the objective of Bow-Wow's research work, Tsukamoto writes:

> The goal of our 'void metabolism' research is to find a way to counter-act the haphazard fashion in which single-family houses and small buildings are generally executed by presenting a framework in which buildings may develop contextual consistency. (2008: 61)

In this way, urban research escapes the objectifying distance of cultural criticism that seeks to define, historicize and evaluate Japanese design. Instead they engage in an action research project that contributes to processes of 'architectural production' that are capable of 'enriching people's lives' (Tsukamoto, 2008: 61).

The four studies described above provide examples of the knowledge produced by studying the sociotechnical aspects of urban development and change. Kaika's study of Athens focuses on the development of a new infrastructure network and how the flows of nature, namely water, are reoriented in the face of modernity and progress. Moore's study of the Commerzbank Tower in Frankfurt demonstrates how the design of a building influences the flows of capital and the politics of urban development in a globally connected metropolis. Meanwhile, the reordering of Hasselt's transportation network, as described by Brand, is a study of the flow of people and the simultaneous change of material and cultural conditions. And finally, Guy's study of pragmatic architectural practices in Tokyo recognizes opportunities for intervention in the ever-changing flux of the city. The connection between the four studies is an emphasis on technological development as central to urban culture, whether through infrastructure networks, politics, policies or practices. The researchers resist the tendency to carve these activities off from other aspects of urban development and instead, see them as an integral part of how cities evolve and change over time. Thus, they consider not only what was built but under what specific temporal and geographic circumstances these technical artefacts came into being.

Conclusion

> If we want to think about the messes of reality at all then we're going to have to teach ourselves to think, to practice, to relate, and to know in new ways. We will need to teach ourselves to know some of the realities of the world using methods unusual to or unknown in social science. (Law, 2004: 2)

The objective of sociotechnical research in urban design and development is twofold. First, there is a desire to open up analysis to the critical importance of technological artefacts, networks and practices as they relate to the social, economic and ecological life of cities. And second, as illustrated by the vignette at the beginning of this chapter, the approach is an attempt to explore the city as a site of dense and complex co-evolution of humans, technologies and ecologies. The aim is to understand the city as a sociotechnical artefact, thereby opening up research to the connections and interactions between society and technologies, and inviting new voices to reinterpret and reshape how cities develop and change over time.

The sociotechnical approach suggests, and even depends upon, novel implications for research methodology. Understanding the city as a heterogeneous mix of humans, technology and nature requires the researcher to embrace the messiness of urban change and then develop research approaches to unravel these complexities. However, as Law has argued, messiness is not something to fear methodologically or recoil from analytically; rather, it is in the messiness of the city where we can find its vitality. This means that, as researchers, we need to look beyond our routine methodological expectations, our 'desire for certainty', our search for 'more or less stable conclusions', our belief that as researchers we have 'special insights' and our tendencies to generalize or 'universalize' our findings. In other words, the sociotechnical perspective encourages us to 'unmake many of our methodological habits' and explore the ebbs and flows of urban change, the subtleties and ambiguities of human choice, and the plasticity and obduracy of urban form (Law 2004: 9). Such a perspective is a productive way to engage with the messiness of the city, to interpret the vitality and realness of the present urban moment, and ultimately, to imagine alternative futures.

References

Aibar, E. and Bijker, W.E. (1997) 'Constructing a city: the Cerda Plan for the extension of Barcelona', *Science, Technology, & Human Values*, 22 (1): 3–30.

Bijker, W.E. (1997) *Of Bicycles, Bakelites, and Bulbs: Toward a Theory of Sociotechnical Change*. London: MIT Press.

Bijker, Wiebe E., Hughes, T.P. and Pinch, T.J. (eds) (1987) *The Social Construction of Technological Systems: New Directions in the Sociology and History of Technology*. London: MIT Press.

Bijker, W.E. and Law, J. (eds) (1992) *Shaping Technology/Building Society: Studies in Sociotechnical Change*. London: MIT Press.

Brand, R. (2005) *Synchronizing Science and Technology with Human Behaviour*. London: Earthscan.

Brand, R. (2008) 'Co-evolution of technical and social change in action: Hasselt's approach to urban mobility', *Built Environment*, 34 (2): 182–99.

Cowan, R.S. (1987) 'The consumption junction: a proposal for research strategies in the sociology of technology', in W.E. Bijker, T.P. Hughes and T.J. Pinch (eds), *The Social Construction of Technological Systems: New Directions in the Sociology and History of Technology.* London: MIT Press. pp. 261–80.

Dant, T. (2005) *Materiality and Society.* Maidenhead: Open University Press.

Evans, R., Guy, S. and Marvin, S. (2001) 'Views of the city: multiple pathways to sustainable transport futures', *Local Environment*, 6 (2): 122–33.

Feenberg, A. (1999) *Questioning Technology.* London: Routledge.

Graham, S. and Marvin, S. (2001) *Splintering Urbanism: Networked Infrastructures, Technological Mobilities and the Urban Condition.* London: Routledge.

Guy, S. (2009) 'Fluid architectures: ecologies of hybrid urbanism', in D.F. White and C. Wilbert (eds), *Technonatures: Environments, Spaces and Places in the Twenty-First Century.* Waterloo, Ontario: Wilfrid Laurier University Press. pp. 219–41.

Guy, S. (2010) 'Beyond Japonisme: the adaptive pragmatism of Japanese urbanism', in S.A. Moore (ed.), *Pragmatic Sustainability.* London: Routledge. pp. 117–31.

Guy, S. and Marvin, S. (1999) 'Understanding sustainable cities: competing urban futures', *European Urban and Regional Studies,* 6 (3): 268–75.

Guy, S. and Marvin, S. (2001) 'Constructing sustainable urban futures: from models to competing pathways', *Impact Assessment and Project Appraisal,* 19 (2): 131–9.

Guy, S. and Moore, S.A. (eds) (2005) *Sustainable Architectures: Natures and Cultures in Europe and North America.* London: Spon Press.

Guy, S. and Shove, E. (2000) *A Sociology of Energy, Buildings and the Environment: Constructing Knowledge, Designing Practice.* London: Routledge.

Guy, S., Marvin, S. and Moss, T. (eds) (2001) *Urban Infrastructure in Transition: Networks, Buildings, Plans.* London: Earthscan.

Hård, M. and Misa, T. (eds) (2008) *Urban Machinery: Inside Modern European Cities.* London: MIT Press.

Hackett, E.J., Amsterdamska, O., Lynch, M. and Wajcman, J. (eds) (2008) *The Handbook of Science and Technology Studies.* London: MIT Press.

Hess, D.J. (1997) *Science Studies: An Advanced Introduction.* New York: New York University Press.

Hommels, A. (2005) *Unbuilding Cities: Obduracy in Urban Socio-Technical Change.* London: MIT Press.

Kaika, M. (2005) *City of Flows: Modernity, Nature, and the City.* London: Routledge.

Kuhn, T.S. (1962) *The Structure of Scientific Revolutions.* Chicago, IL: University of Chicago Press.

Latour, B. (1992) 'Where at the missing masses? The sociology of a few mundane artefacts', in W.E. Bijker and J. Law (eds), *Shaping Technology/Building Society: Studies in Sociotechnical Change.* London: MIT Press. pp. 225–64.

Latour, Bruno (1993) *We Have Never Been Modern.* Cambridge, MA: Harvard University Press.

Law, J. (2004) *After Method: Mess in Social Science Research.* London: Routledge.

MacKenzie, D. and Wacjman, J. (1999a) 'Introductory essay: the social shaping of technology', in D. MacKenzie and J. Wacjman (eds), *The Social Shaping of Technology, Second Edition.* Buckingham: Open University Press. pp. 3–27.

MacKenzie, D. and Wacjman, J. (eds) (1999b) *The Social Shaping of Technology, Second Edition.* Buckingham: Open University Press.

Misa, T., Brey, P. and Feenberg, A. (eds) (2003) *Modernity and Technology*. London: MIT Press.

Moore, S.A. (1997) 'Technology and the politics of sustainability at Blueprint Demonstration Farm', *Journal of Architectural Education*, 51 (1): 23–31.

Moore, S.A. (2001) 'Technology, place, and the nonmodern thesis', *Journal of Architectural Education*, 54 (3): 130–9.

Moore, S.A. (2007) *Alternative Routes to the Sustainable City*. Plymouth: Rowman & Littlefield.

Moore, S.A. and Brand, R. (2003) 'The banks of Frankfurt and the sustainable city', *The Journal of Architecture*, 8 (1): 3–24.

Sismondo, S. (2004) *An Introduction to Science and Technology Studies*. Oxford: Blackwell.

Swyngedouw, E. (2004) *Social Power and the Urbanization of Water: Flows of Power.* Oxford: Oxford University Press.

Tarr, J.A. (1979) 'The separate vs. combined sewer problem: a case study in urban technology design choice', *Journal of Urban History*, 5 (3): 308–39.

Tarr, J.A. (2005) 'The city and technology', in Carroll Pursell (ed.), *A Companion to American Technology*. Oxford: Blackwell Publishing. pp. 97–112.

Tarr, J.A. and Konvitz, J.W. (1987) 'Patterns in the development of the urban infrastructure', in Howard Gillette, Jr and Zane L. Miller (eds), *American Urbanism: A Historiographical Review*. New York: Greenwood Press. pp. 195–226.

Thrift, N. (2007) *Non-Representational Theory*. London: Routledge.

Tsukamoto, Y. (2008) 'Void metabolism', *The Japan Architect*, 71: 60–1.

Yaneva, A. (2009) *The Making of a Building: A Pragmatist Approach to Architecture*. Bern: Peter Lang.

NINE

Using Participatory, Observational and 'Rapid Appraisal' Methods

Researching Health and Illness

Sarah Salway, Kaveri Harriss and Punita Chowbey

Introduction

The past 50 years have seen a burgeoning volume of sociological studies examining the implications of living with long-term ill health for individuals and their families (Anderson and Bury, 1988; Bury, 1991). The rising prevalence of chronic illness makes this work ever more important as those responsible for health and welfare policy seeks solutions to the growing numbers of people requiring support and care (DH, 2004, 2006; DWP, 2006). The predominant methodological approach to researching the experience and implications of long-term ill-health has been face-to-face in-depth interviews, with a noted bias towards middle-class, White respondents who tend to be readily accessible and offer articulate, reflexive interviews (Charmaz, 2000; Williams, 2000). Influenced by social interactionist and phenomenological traditions, sociologists have sought to elicit introspective description from chronically ill people and their carers in order to construct an interpretive analysis of illness trajectories and their management (see, for example, seminal papers by Bury [1982], Charmaz [1983] and Williams [1984]).

This body of work has produced invaluable insights into the subjective, psychological processes of adjustment to chronic ill health (Bury, 1991; Lawton, 2003). However, we suggest that the dominant reliance on narrative interviews has meant limited attention to the social, structural and cultural conditions that articulate with individual responses to chronic illness. The study we describe here was concerned to counter this tendency. Thus, while we recognized the importance of listening to the personal testimonies of individuals living with long-term illness, we also aimed to understand wider contexts and processes that are commonly taken-for-granted and less open to investigation through interviews.

Seeking these insights was particularly important for the current study. The overall aim was to understand the links between long-term ill health and dimensions of poverty. The study looked particularly at access to employment, sickness benefits and social participation and sought to identify ways in which the marginalizing effects of chronic illness might be mitigated by policy and practice interventions (Salway et al., 2007). Our interest in minority ethnic disadvantage also suggested the need for tools that could grapple with underlying structural and cultural contexts. Given the disproportionately high levels of chronic illness among certain minority ethnic groups, the study included an ethnically diverse sample: Pakistani, Bangladeshi, Ghanaian and White English groups were chosen to allow contrasting, comparative analysis. We wanted to find ways of illuminating racialized processes of inclusion and exclusion that shape the experiences of minoritized individuals but which can be subtle and elusive, escaping attention in more traditional approaches to data generation (Gunaratnam, 2001; Pollack, 2003). A further objective was to understand more about the significance of place as associated with material, social and cultural value. We knew that residential locality was likely to be highly significant for people who are poor and marginalized, particularly those whose movement is potentially limited by chronic ill health (Bentham et al., 1995; Haynes and Gale, 1999; Jordan et al., 2000; Young et al., 2005). This desire to learn about place again demanded additional tools. A final reason for using data generation methods that did not rely exclusively on extended verbal descriptions was the recognition that chronically ill people vary greatly in articulacy and in the extent to which personal reflection has prepared them to offer their story.

We therefore sought to complement in-depth interviews with a package of other data generation methods that relied less on the verbal responses of individuals living with chronic illness.

Methodology and methods

Our methodological approach had three distinguishing features. First, we took a locality-focused approach, identifying four geographically delineable 'communities' or 'localities' and exploring their characteristics. Second, we worked in collaboration with a team of community researchers (CRs) drawing on their local networks and 'insider' perspectives. Third, we employed a range of data generation methods combining participatory techniques, observation and naturalistic interaction with individuals and groups. These three elements were combined in a period of 'rapid appraisal' lasting around seven days and involving four to six researchers in each location. The total time period for the rapid appraisal across all four localities was around eight weeks. A further design decision that proved invaluable was basing ourselves in the heart of the fieldwork areas. This was possible through our collaborative partnership with Social Action for Health (http://www.safh. org.uk) who gave office space to the project as well as providing additional insights into local issues.

Identifying 'communities'

The notion of 'community' can tend to suggest homogeneity and clearly delineated social and geographical boundaries, while in practice 'community' means different things to different people and individuals are active in creating networks of support (Alexander et al., 2004). Nevertheless, having a particular ethnic identity and residing within a particular geographical area can have significant implications for the options available to individuals (particularly if disadvantaged by poverty and poor health). Processes of inclusion and exclusion, which can have both ethnic and geographic dimensions, can shape entitlements in important ways. This may be particularly true for some UK minority ethnic 'communities' since there has been significant 'building of community' in many urban areas across the country in recent years (Alam and Husband, 2006). Therefore, while exercising caution in using the term 'community', we nevertheless chose to identify four geographic localities, each within London, that were home to significant concentrations of people who self-identify as Pakistani, Bangladeshi, Ghanaian or White English. Exploring the meaning and implications of these ethnogeographic 'communities' was then part-and-parcel of our research endeavour. In practice, this approach proved relatively unproblematic for the Bangladeshi and Pakistani 'communities' since, by and large, local residents strongly identified with these ethnic categories, there were many ethnically based community organizations that served as points of contact, and people also strongly identified with the local area that had been chosen. In contrast, though the notion of a Ghanaian 'community' was meaningful to many respondents, it was much less visible and more geographically dispersed. Varied waves of migration and a diverse linguistic and socio-economic profile meant significant intra-group divisions so that, despite large numbers of voluntary organizations and associations, these often did not cater to an overarching 'Ghanaian' community. Finally, identifying a White English ethno-geographic community was also challenging. Though a meaningful geographical area was identified with little difficulty, individuals often did not readily self-identify on the basis of ethnicity and no community organizations were overtly for White English people. Indeed, the idea that our research should seek to identify such a social grouping was greeted with hostility from some community-level workers. Nevertheless, as fieldwork progressed, the salience of the White English ethnic identity did become apparent both in terms of people's self-identification in opposition to perceived 'others' and its relevance for access to local resources.

Working with community researchers

Recent years have witnessed a rise in health and social research that aims, and claims, to engage 'the researched' as active partners. Terms such as 'user involvement', 'participatory approaches', 'community consultation' and 'inclusive research' are frequently used. Arguments in favour of such approaches usually centre on (1) a belief that research itself should be an empowering tool, particularly for people who are marginalized within society, and/or (2) a desire for more authentic and useful accounts. In practice, a wide variety of research approaches have been labelled as 'user involvement' or 'participatory'. Here we adopted a model of working in partnership with a team of community researchers. A CR is usually an individual who is a member, and has a detailed understanding of, a particular 'community' and uses this knowledge to facilitate the gathering and interpretation of information.[1] Though some researchers have made strong claims relating to the transformatory power of such research approaches (Fletcher, 2003), our focus was on the contribution to knowledge that the CRs could facilitate. Limited resources meant that aspirations for an empowering effect at local level were unrealistic, but we believed that CRs could build successful relationships within the communities.

A total of 12 CRs, at least two representing each 'community', were recruited through a variety of local networks. These were individuals who self-identified with one of the ethnic 'groups' of focus and who had strong links within the localities. A mix of ages, gender and experience was achieved. The CRs generally had no prior research experience, though most had worked for their 'community', for instance as health trainers or volunteers. A key criterion for recruitment was that they should be confident interacting with the public, be able to develop trust and explain the research in a positive way. As illustrated in Box 9.1, the CRs were provided with training and support at regular intervals throughout the project. CRs were remunerated at a fixed daily rate for their contribution. Owing to different skill levels, experience, availability and interest, the nature and degree of involvement varied between individual CRs. Nevertheless, all were involved in publicizing the research, identifying suitable locations and informants, guiding the university researchers in and around the local communities, and some direct collection and interpretation of data. Training was designed to be fun and interactive but also to ensure ethical and professional standards were maintained during the research.

Box 9.1   Recruiting, training and supporting community researchers (CRs)

1. Preparation of job description and person specification.

    ▼

2. Advertisements in local media and word-of-mouth recruitment drive (a total of 16 responses).

    ▼

3. Informal half-day briefing with potential community researchers (two-way discussion regarding role and expectations).

    ▼

4. Offers given and accepted/rejected by applications (12 CRs recruited).

    ▼

5. Two-day training programme (generic skills, project focus and specific data generation activities).

    ▼

6. Phase One: rapid appraisal planning (CRs and university researchers brainstorm and develop fieldwork strategy).

    ▼

7. Phase One: rapid appraisal fieldwork (seven days each location) (daily feedback and debriefing with university researchers).

    ▼

8. Half-day debriefing and analysis workshop (participatory exercise on theme identification, gaps, alternative perspectives).

    ▼

9. One-day training programme (interview techniques, four CRs continued to this phase).

    ▼

10. Phase Two: in-depth interviews (regular debriefing and support from university researchers).

    ▼

11. Analysis, interpretation and write-up (lead by university researchers in consultation with CRs).

    ▼

12. Explicit reflection on CR experiences (individual exercise, group reflection, interviews with independent party).

Though working with CRs added complexity to the management of the research project and raised a number of ethical and methodological issues discussed below, they brought unique perspectives and skills. In particular, the CRs contributed to the research process by: articulating the experience of the research participants in their own language; alerting the university researchers to issues that might have been overlooked; introducing the researchers to the physical and social geography of the communities; providing a link between the researchers and community members to increase trust and confidence; advising the researchers of appropriate ways of carrying out the research; offering alternative interpretations and counter-examples to the data emerging, and guiding the ways in which the research findings represented the communities.

A package of data generation tools

As illustrated in Box 9.1, the research project involved two main phases of data generation. Our focus here is on Phase One, the intensive seven-day period of rapid appraisal fieldwork that was conducted in each of our four localities. Following completion of the two-day training programme, each CR worked individually, and with support from a university researcher, to brainstorm ideas regarding suitable locations and useful informants for inclusion in the fieldwork. The team of three/four CRs for each locality then worked with the researchers to develop a fieldwork strategy for the seven days, usually beginning with a transect walk and proceeding on to a package of data generation activities designed to elicit insights from a wide variety of perspectives (see Box 9.2). The broad aim of this phase was to gain an overview of the patterns of social, material and cultural resources available to members of the four 'communities' as well as an understanding of how chronic ill health is perceived and its prominence in people's everyday lives. Box 9.3 provides an example of a planning sheet illustrating the package of tools used in one locality. CRs and university researchers were each provided with a custom-made, hard-cover field note diary which included guides for all the data generation activities and templates for recording information and observations. Shortly after the completion of each of the fieldwork periods, a half-day debriefing and analysis workshop was held.

Box 9.2   Data generation methods

Following a number of preparatory visits and meetings with numerous people living and working in the selected localities, a seven-day period of assessment was conducted by a team of four to six researchers. Six distinct data collection tools were employed by the team in each of the four geo-ethnic 'communities'.

Transect walk (x2 per locality): Pre-planned, purposive walks through the selected areas with the aim of identifying key features of the local community and observing local people going about their everyday business. CRs identified suitable routes and in some cases other local residents accompanied the research

(Continued)

---

team pointing out places of significance. Researchers actively engaged the CRs and local people in discussion about the local area. Detailed notes were taken. These walks yielded information on both current and past physical and social geography of the areas.

Observation and informal discussions (x4–6 each locality): The research team spent time chatting with people informally in places where they normally go. We visited numerous locations including: mosques, churches, shops, job centres, travel agents, cafes and restaurants, hairdressers, community centres, work places, leisure centres and parks. A list of topics and questions was used to guide the discussions. These observational exercises provided insights into people's daily lives, networks of interaction and support as well as relevant local terminology.

Community resource inventory: Utilizing information gained through the transect walk, observations and informal discussions with community members and the CRs, an inventory of local resources available to community members was prepared. A structured template was prepared for CRs to complete and this enabled the listing of items under the following broad headings: work and training; information and advice; support and care; cultural/religious; leisure/socializing; healthcare; and other facilities/resources.

Small group exercises at community venues (x2+ each locality): Facilitated exercises with small groups of men and women using two tools: an employment matrix which explored local job opportunities and preferences; and a problem tree which explored the knock-on implications of long-term health conditions for families and the wider community. These group exercises were arranged in mosques, churches, schools, community centres, workplaces and residents' homes and involved free-flowing discussion and debate. These exercises gave insights into the salience and implications of long-term illness at individual, family and community level.

Key informant discussions (x4–10 each locality): Semi-structured conversations were held with individuals who we identified as having particular knowledge about the community, and in particular some understanding of how long-standing health problems may affect families. We talked to a wide variety of individuals including community workers, job agency staff, employers, shop keepers, pharmacists, long-term residents, a police officer, religious teachers and school teachers.

Ethnographic interviews (x2 each locality): Detailed, open-ended interviews were conducted with a small number of people in each of the four locations who were identified as having a long-term health condition. The focus of these interviews was on understanding the personal experiences of respondents. These interviews were tape-recorded and shaped the form and content of later individual interviews.

Box 9.3 Illustrative example of rapid appraisal planning sheet

Day	Day & date	am/ pm	Data gathering tool	Location details/ informant details	Team members & roles	Comments
1	Mon 23rd	11:30 – 1:00	Problem tree	Women's group	KH, MM, PC	*arrange refreshments*
		3:00 – 5:00	Transect walk	Local area start: neighbourhood centre	All	
2	Tue 24th	10:00 – 12:00	Informal observation	Dressmaking ESOL class	KH, SA, PC	
		3:30 – 5:30	Problem tree	Community centre 50+ group	MS, KH, PC	*arrange refreshments*
3	Wed 25th	10:00 – 12:00	Key Informant (Development Worker)	Mr X, Address/ phone	KH (SY – note-taking)	
		1:30 – 4:30	Key Informant (Carer) Key Informant (Local business person)	Mrs Y, address/ phone Mr Z, address/ phone	KH (SY – note-taking)	
		7:00 – 9:00 pm	Informal observation	Park	KH	
4	Thu 26th	10:00 – 12:00	Informal observation	Drop in (women)	PC, KH, MM	
		1:30 – 3:30	Employment matrix Key informant (Imam)	Mosque	MS, PC, KH	
5	Fri 27th	10:00 – 1:00	Informal observation	Henna class community centre Chemists/Market	KH, SA, PC	
		1:30 – 3:30	Employment matrix	High street new mosque (women)	KH, SA, PC	
		7:00 – 9:00 pm	Informal observation	Parents group at school	KH, MS, SY	

(Continued)

(Continued)

Day	Day & Date	am/ pm	Data gathering tool	Location details/ informant details	Team members & roles	Comments
6	Sat 28th	10:00 – 12:00	Ethnographic interviews	Mr Q, address/ phone Mrs J, address/phone	SA, SY	
7	Mon 29th	11:00 – 1:00	Transect walk	Local area start: mosque	All	
		2:00 – 5:00	Community inventory	Local office	All	

Note: The names of individuals and places have been anonymized to maintain confidentiality.

Gaining insight and understanding

We now consider some of the ways in which our methodological approach offered additional insight that might not have been gained from an exclusive reliance on in-depth interviews. We first identify a number of general advantages that accrued and then describe in more detail three areas that were significant for our particular research focus.

The combination of working with CRs and employing a range of data generation tools that facilitated engagement with a diverse range of social actors had the advantage of encouraging broad and holistic thinking, of recognizing the interconnections between dimensions of people's lives and of the ways in which community-level factors influence the options open for individuals. Being out-and-about within the neighbourhoods with the CRs meant that physical landmarks and places prompted discussion, in turn revealing relevant structures and processes. For instance, when meeting at an underground station within the Pakistani locality the researchers were offered fliers from a man specializing in traditional African spirit healing, which the CRs contextualized locally by offering their opinions about the usefulness and authenticity of spirit healing for chronically ill people; recounting stories of people they knew who had used these services; giving further information about other places where spiritual services are advertised; and hinting at the types of cultural cross-overs that Pakistani Muslims might experience when they receive 'African' spirit healing. Similarly, the presence of large numbers of hairdressing salons and nail bars in the Ghanaian locality prompted discussion about UK Ghanaian women's behaviour patterns and how these might reflect broader changes in gender relations and marital instability in the Ghanaian community.

Another important advantage of the approach was its potential to alert the research team to the distance between norms and practice, and also between private and public enactments. Observing people in the public realm doing things (or not doing things) prompted discussion and further clarification. For instance, among the Ghanaian community we observed that individuals whom we knew to be suffering from long-term ill health maintained a veil of secrecy in public and this prompted us to investigate in greater depth what turned out to be a complex of factors relating to stigma and vulnerability that discouraged people from identifying themselves as 'chronically ill'. Finally, the naturalistic observation and interaction with community members provided researchers with the opportunity to hear local language and gather context-related information. When terms were used or references made the researchers could readily seek clarification from CRs and incorporate this understanding into subsequent interactions and data generation making them more sensitive and more productive. For instance, researchers witnessed a 'tally man' in action on a housing estate and were able to find out more about the operation of these unregulated lenders through discussion with the White English CRs and subsequently to incorporate sensitive questioning around debt and access to loans into in-depth interviews.

We now illustrate the usefulness of our approach further by highlighting three areas of understanding that were of particular relevance to our research topic.

Significance of 'invisible resources' to marginalized individuals

As well as providing an opportunity for researchers to observe physical landmarks and infrastructure within the communities of focus, our locality-based approach was successful in revealing less immediately visible resources. Furthermore, discussion about transformation over time and the loss of resources was prompted, as the CRs recounted stories from their own lives and those of their close family about the salience and meanings of local places. For instance, in the White English area the presence of many boarded-up pubs prompted discussion about social networks, identity and sense of belonging. Informants identified many places where pubs had been in the past. Further investigation revealed that socializing in local pubs within walking distance of home was an important manifestation of identity for many local White English people and that their demise had had a significant impact on their sense of well-being, particularly among men. The loss of this local resource was associated with the changing demographic make-up of the local area, which people perceived as increasingly populated by 'outsiders' distinguished by their affluence or minority ethnicity. In another example, one of our transect walks with our Bangladeshi CRs revealed the employment agencies that specialized in placing Bangladeshi men within the Asian restaurant sector. While this local resource was relatively visible (as were the many shops and community centres serving the needs of the Bangladeshi community) the observation of these agencies and related conversations with CRs and visitors gradually revealed the existence of similar resources catering specifically to the needs of those in vulnerable positions due to debt, complex legal situations or without permission to work in the UK. Though such resources are well known to community members, they are not openly discussed and the existence of these 'invisible' resources only became known to us due to the informal chatting with users and degree of trust engendered by the CRs. Similarly, the transect walk and informal observations within the Ghanaian locality revealed that several shops doubled up as regular meeting places for associations and groups often with regional affiliations and social support functions.

Complexities and contingencies in ethnic identities

Observing interactions between individuals in the community setting, the space that they shared or did not share, hearing local taxonomies, observing exchanges and, importantly, having the opportunity to seek clarification in discussion with the CRs, allowed us to uncover complexities and contingencies in the boundaries and content of ethnic and gender identities that would not have been possible in one-to-one interviews. In carrying out the transect walk within the Pakistani locality, for example, we observed the CRs negotiating skilfully between a number of different languages, dialects, accents and registers of interaction, emphasizing different parts of their complex identities in relation to different spatial contexts and social relationships. In the market, the CRs chatted in broad cockney accents with White English and Black Caribbean traders, asking about their children, their state of heath or how they had been getting on since their last meeting in the hospital. In the residential streets, the CRs conversed with relatives about extended family and village micro-politics in the Mirpuri dialect. Outside the mosque, they exchanged Urdu greetings with Pakistanis from urban migratory origins and with Bangladeshis. This kaleidoscope of social interactions illustrated our CRs' ability to draw simultaneously on diverse identities.

Similarly, observing the interactions between our Ghanaian CRs and various community members revealed complexities in their ethnic identities. Our two CRs spoke different languages and identified themselves as belonging to different lineages within Ghana. They also occupied different positions in terms of socio-economic status. These markers of difference alerted us to the multiple processes of inclusion and exclusion that operated within the Ghanaian 'community' that were further illustrated through the CRs' interactions at community level. For instance, while one CR was able to draw on professional and alma mater networks that spread across London, he was less able to call on his Ghanaian identity to seek cooperation from working class individuals living on council estates. However, a different incident illustrated how a broader Ghanaian identity can be meaningful at times and be drawn upon to demarcate difference from other West African communities. Here we observed a heated argument between one of the Ghanaian CRs and the director of a local organization who herself had migrated to the UK from Nigeria. The exchange revolved around the two women identifying and denigrating various cultural practices that they felt were not shared by, and indeed confirmed fundamental differences between, 'Ghanaians' and 'Nigerians'.

Our locality-based approach also revealed racialized associations with places. For instance, despite the sheer ethnic diversity of Newham, the Pakistani CRs and local people referred to the area spontaneously as 'our area' as compared with nearby Barking and Dagenham, which was the 'English people's area'. Similarly, in the White English locality the significance of place was very salient in people's ideas about identity and belonging. Such intuitive perceptions of un/comfortable spaces were found to influence people's willingness to move into new areas, which might present other opportunities, or to seek employment further a field.

These insights into the complex processes of ethnic identification greatly informed our subsequent fieldwork strategies, both in terms of guiding our questioning and prompting flexible use of our own identities.

Local economies and histories of industrial change

Observing and mapping out the local shops, businesses, factories and the infrastructures of administration, transport, health, school and leisure facilities provided by the local authority allowed us to understand how individual experiences and responses to chronic ill health are shaped by and embedded in local economies and histories of industrial change. For example, in the White English area the CRs pointed out dilapidated workshops and small factories that were used for the manufacturing of garments, furniture and electronic elements, and told stories about their previous owners and how they had closed down. They showed us the up-market restaurants, nightclubs and expensive new housing that was being converted out of old warehouses. Their negative and sometimes vitriolic reactions to the developments in the locality sensitized us to some the ways in which the old working-class White English population had been marginalized and excluded from the new economic opportunities that were opening up for those people they called 'yuppies' or 'outsiders'. The historical insights provided by our familiarization with the locality and the CRs' personal memories proved to be important contextual information alongside the later in-depth interviews, in which we found that for many of the informants local deindustrialization, economic decline and the slow transition to the service economy coincided with the onset of chronic ill health and left a cohort who had little alternative to long-term unemployment. However, comparisons between the four 'communities' indicated further important differences in the extent to which the lives of people with chronic ill health were constrained by the economic opportunities prevailing in their local areas. The localities differed with respect to the density of transport infrastructure allowing for rapid and easy commuting to areas with more job opportunities; a weighty consideration for people whose mobility is constrained by ill health. The 'communities' also differed with respect to the distances that people were prepared to travel for work. In particular, the Ghanaians seemed to be the most mobile and often travelled long distances across London to find work, articulating with their more geographically and socio-economically diverse 'community'.

Conclusion

The examples above illustrate some of the insights gained from our Phase One data generation activities. More generally, our approach allowed an understanding of the ways in which individual responses to chronic ill health were shaped by the socio-cultural and geo-physical context of people's residential neighbourhood. These insights shaped our recommendations to policymakers and practitioners across the health and welfare arenas. For instance, exploring contextual factors as well as individual experiences alerted us to the limitations of ethnic-specific support networks and the need for statutory agencies to provide a range of modes through which those with chronic illness can enhance their coping skills.

The advantages of our methodological approach to researching the experiences and implications of chronic ill-health seem to have resulted from the combination of the three elements: a locality-based focus, partnership with CRs and a package of varied, participatory methods of data generation. It seems likely that any one element alone would not have been so successful. For instance, without the active contributions of the CRs it seems unlikely that the limited amount of fieldwork could have yielded so many important insights. At the same time, however, working effectively with the CRs was greatly enhanced by the use of interesting and well-structured tools. We would, therefore, recommend the combination of elements to other researchers interested in addressing issues with a strong link to place. While our approach had many strengths, it is also important to highlight a number of challenges that presented themselves.

First, working with CRs raises both ethical and methodological challenges. The CRs' much longer standing knowledge of their communities offered authenticity to our analysis. However, being members of the local community inevitably meant that the CRs offered particular interpretations, emphasizing some dimensions and downplaying others. While all researchers shape the generation of data, bringing their own social and political position to the interpretation and presentation of findings, the insider status of the CRs meant that they had a particular stake in the emerging claims and accounts. We were concerned to draw on the CRs' insights while not privileging particular representations. We therefore adopted an approach to the co-production of knowledge that involved the use of carefully structured and facilitated analysis workshops. CRs and university researchers participated side-by-side and the workshop environment encouraged critical reflection and debate. Participants were prompted to both consider and challenge each others' interpretations, as well as gaps and silences, in arriving at a set of preliminary claims and issues to be explored in the second phase of fieldwork. In addition, the CRs' insider status made it difficult for some of them to undertake certain tasks, such as interviewing across gender, for fear of contravening social codes. Furthermore, it was clear that CRs could become indebted to local people as they sought opportunities to gain information and negotiated access (Salway et al., 2005). These ethical issues persisted long after the university researchers had left the field sites and deserve careful consideration in future work.

Second, our rapid, locality-based approach could risk the production of partial understanding, since chance and limited time may mean that only certain aspects are observed and noted.

This problem was minimized by the use of multiple methods in multiple locations by a team of several researchers. In addition, the team was alert to that which was not visible and sought to combine incisive questioning along with careful observation, constantly asking 'who is not here?', 'what is not happening?' and so on, as well as seeking interpretations of that which was observed directly. Furthermore, the approach is quite heavily dependent on note-taking skills and effective debriefing without which there is the potential for data to be lost. We found that university researchers working side-by-side with CRs to capture their insights and observations was a useful approach. The area-based approach can also suffer from being too locally-specific, highlighting local specificities to the exclusion of (1) elements of community that transcend geography and (2) commonalities across settings and communities. It was therefore important to consider the body of data across all four localities and to provide opportunities for the CRs representing the different communities to interact and share their findings.

Finally, weaving an argument and presenting evidence derived from these methods can be challenging. The heavy dependence on direct quotation in much sociological work on chronic ill health does not suit these methods and alternative ways of conveying findings, perhaps drawing more on anthropological traditions, are needed. In practice, we found that combining the Phase One data with the Phase Two in-depth interview material was productive in generating detailed understanding that could be conveyed effectively to those beyond the research team. Bearing these challenges in mind, we would encourage other researchers to experiment with these fieldwork approaches which can be both enjoyable and insightful.

Note

The study on which this chapter is based was funded by the Joseph Rowntree Foundation. We acknowledge the valuable contribution of the community researchers to the study.

1. 'Peer researchers', 'lay researchers' and other terms are also used to describe individuals who contribute to research studies in this way.

References

Alam, M.Y. and Husband, C. (2006) *British-Pakistani Men from Bradford: Linking Narratives to Policy*. York: Joseph Rowntree Foundation.

Alexander, C., Edwards, R. and Temple, B. (2004) *Access to Services with Interpreters*. York: York Publishing Services.

Anderson, R. and Bury, M. (1988) *Living with Chronic Illness: The Experience of Patients and their Families*. London: Umin Myman.

Bentham, G., Eimermann, J., Haynes, R., Lovett, A. and Brainard, J. (1995) 'Limiting long term illness and its associations with mortality and indicators of social deprivation', *Journal of Epidemiology and Community Health* 49 (Suppl.2): S57–S64.

Bury, M. (1982) 'Chronic illness as disruption', *Sociology of Health & Illness*, 4 (2): 167–82.

Bury, M. (1991) 'The sociology of chronic illness: a review of research and prospects'. *Sociology of Health & Illness*, 13 (4): 451–68.

Charmaz, K. (1983) 'Loss of self: a fundamental form of suffering in the chronically ill', *Sociology of Health & Illness*, 5: 168–95.

Charmaz, K. (2000) 'Experiencing chronic illness', in G.L. Albreght, R. Fitzpatrick and S.C. Scrimshaw (eds), *Handbook of Social Studies in Health and Medicine*. London: Sage. pp. 279–92.

Department of Health (DH) (2004) *Choosing Health: Making Healthy Choices Easier*. London: HMSO.

Department of Health (DH) (2006) *Our Health, Our Care, Our Say: a New Direction for Community Services*. London: HMSO.

Department for Work and Pensions (DWP) (2006) *A New Deal for Welfare: Empowering People to Work*. London: HMSO.

Fletcher, C. (2003) 'Community based participatory research relationship with aboriginal communities in Canada: an overview of context and process', *Pimatziwin*, 1910: 32–61.

Gunaratnam Y. (2001) 'Eating into multiculutralism: hospice staff and service users talk food, "race", ethnicity, culture and identity', *Critical Social Policy*, 21: 287–310.

Haynes, R. and Gale, S. (1999) 'Mortality, long-term illness and deprivation in rural and metropolitan wards of England and Wales', *Health & Place*, 5 (4): 301–12.

Jordan, K., Ong, B.N. and Croft, P.. (2000) 'Researching limiting long-term illness', *Social Science & Medicine*, 50 (3): 397–405.

Lawton, J. (2003) 'Lay experience of health and illness: past research and future agendas', *Sociology of Health & Illness,* 25: 23–40.

Pollack, S. (2003) 'Focus-group methodology in research with incarcerated women: race, power, and collective experience', *Affilia*, 18 (4): 461–72.

Salway S., Chowbey, P., Akhter, S., Amponsah, S., Laryea, E. and Harriss, K. (2005) 'Conducting health and social research with community researchers: methodological, theoretical and ethical challenges', paper presented at Race and Social Research Conference, York, 8 November.

Salway, S., Platt, L., Chowbey, P., Harriss, K. and Bayliss, E. (2007) *Long-term Ill-health, Poverty and Ethnicity*. Bristol: Policy Press.

Williams, G. (1984) 'The genesis of chronic illness: narrative construction', *Sociology of Health & Illness*, 6 (2): 175–200.

Williams, S. (2000) 'Chronic illness as biographical disruption or biographical disruption as chronic illness? Reflections on a core concept', *Sociology of Health & Illness*, 22: 40–67.

Young, H., Grundy, E. and Kalogirou, S. (2005) 'Who cares? Geographic variation in unpaid caregiving in England and Wales: Evidence from the 2001 census', *Population Trends*, 120: 23–34.

TEN

Innovative Ways of Mapping Data About Places

Danny Dorling and Dimitris Ballas

Introduction

Spatial information about the world and its people has always been at the forefront of visualization. Most people are used to conventional maps of their regions, countries and the world. Such conventional maps appear on television every evening in the weather reports, showing geographical regions and countries as they appear from space. Conventional maps are very good for showing where oceans lie and rivers run. Their projections are calculated to aid navigation by compass or depict the quantity of land under crops. These maps are typically based on area projections such as that of Gerardus Mercator, developed in 1569, which was and is suitable as an aid for ships to sail across the oceans because it maintains all compass directions as straight lines.

All projections inevitably result in a degree of distortion as they transfer the area of the Earth being mapped (or the whole globe) onto a flat surface such as a piece of paper or a display unit; most usually today a computer screen. For instance, the Mercator projection stretches the Earth's surface to the most extreme of extents and hence introduces considerable visual bias. Areas are drawn in ever expanding proportions to how near territory is to the poles and this results in areas such as India appearing much smaller than Greenland (when in reality India has an area more than seven times the size of Greenland). The degree to which such a distortion may be acceptable depends on the intended use of the map. There are a number of alternative projections that correspond to the actual land area size and these are much more suitable for the visualization and mapping of environmental variables and for pinpointing the location of physical geographical features of interest than Mercator's map ever was.

However, looking at a city, region or country from space is not the best way to see their human geography. For instance, mapping the distribution of a human population on a conventional map means that urban areas with large populations but small area size are virtually invisible to the viewer. Conversely, the large rural areas with small populations dominate the map. When mapping data about people, it is therefore sensible to use a different spatial metaphor, one that reflects population size.

This chapter presents alternative ways of mapping human societies and demonstrates that these alternatives are more suitable for human-scale visualization than conventional maps. In particular, the chapter argues that it is 'human cartograms' that should be used conventionally to visualize societies instead of conventional thematic mapping. We begin by providing a brief history of environmental and human mapping, arguing when it is good to employ conventional mapping techniques to visualize places and why human cartographical approaches are more appropriate in a social science context. We then give illustrative examples of how the innovative methods of mapping data can be used to create maps of the areas within a city (taking London's parliamentary constituencies as an example) with each spatial unit re-sized and re-shaped according to a particular variable. Similarly, it shows how the method can be applied for larger areas such as regions and countries to create new knowledge about the extent of geographical divides at different levels. We conclude by offering some concluding comments and outline possible new areas of research that could extend existing approaches and ways of thinking.

Visualizing data about people and places

The term 'human cartography' is credited to Swedish cartographer Janos Szegö (1984, 1987) who criticized the use of conventional mapping to depict people. Human cartography pertains to mapping in which the focus is on people, where they live, where they go and what they do. Human cartograms were based on the development of ideas that underpin traditional cartograms, focusing on human variables. In this section we provide a brief history of conventional cartograms and show how human cartograms have been developed on the basis that we should focus on people, not on land and sea, when we are studying the geography of people.

Conventional cartograms tend to focus on people and can be thought of as maps in which at least one scalar aspect, such as distance or area, is deliberately distorted to be drawn in proportion to a variable of interest. Many conventional maps are cartograms, but few cartograms appear like conventional maps. An equal area conventional map is a type of area cartogram, as is the Mercator projection briefly described in the introduction. The Mercator projection is just one of many that draws land areas in proportion (albeit non-linear and descending) to their distance from the poles. This definition of cartograms sees them as a particular group of map projections.

The map projection definition is just one of a plethora of definitions that have been offered for cartograms. The cartography of cartograms during the 20th century has been so multifaceted that no solid definition could emerge – and the multiple meanings of the word continue to evolve. The heterogeneous development of cartograms into the 21st century is partly reflected in the many names that exist for cartograms. For instance, the area distorting kind alone have been termed: *anamorphosis*; diagrammatic maps; map-like diagrams; *varivalent* projections; density equivalized maps; isodensity maps; value-by-area maps; and even mass distributing (*pycnomirastic*) map projections. The sub-category of those where area is drawn in proportion to population have gone under many names also, including: political map; demographic map; population scale map; and many very specific titles such as 'a map for health officers'.

There are non-continuous (Olson, 1976) as well as contiguous (Tobler, 1973) varieties, and – as an infinite number of correct continuous area cartograms can be produced (Sen, 1975) for any given variable – very many different cartograms have been drawn scaled to the same quantity, usually population. However, by the end of the 20th century, it became clear that only one area cartogram will approximate the best, least distorting solution (Tobler, 2004) and a practical means to achieving that solution became available shortly after (given in Gastner and Newman [2004] and discussed below). These examples are, of course, just part of the story of cartograms. Tobler's (2004) review is an excellent place to start for a fuller story – for work since then see Henriques (2005), Keim et al. (2002, 2004, 2005) or Dorling (2006; Dorling et al., 2007a, 2007b) and for a more detailed discussion of relevant literature see Ballas and Dorling (2011).

Recently there have been significant developments in cartographic methodologies aided by increasing computational power and sophisticated graphics capabilities leading to alternative maps and visualizations of societies that were not based on physical geography. These cartogram-based visualizations differ considerably from traditional thematic maps. The latter drastically distort the reality they purport to contain, at worst reversing the patterns that exist. People who study people, who are interested in societies, politics, history, economics and increasingly even human geography, usually do not use these maps. They usually do not use any maps at all. A topographic map base allows, at most, the depiction of human land use. People have created maps based on human geography in the past, but only with the advent of sophisticated image and graphics software has it become possible to do this on an easily replicable basis.

Human cartography concentrates on the human experience of space and portrays the human encounters with 'reality', rejecting the view that behaviour (and, therefore, features such as population distribution and the location of industrial activity) is governed totally by the framework of the earth and the 'tyranny of distance'. During the 19th century, as interest in population statistics grew and as people who had been peasants became consumers, the relative value of land to human life fell, and human rather than physical geography began to matter more. The emergence of detailed census cartography after the Second World War grew out of these shifting priorities. However, most of the thematic maps of census variables were still governed by the logic of physical geography. For instance, choropleth maps of population data typically shade regions with boundaries defined on the basis of their area size in proportion to the measurement of a variable of interest. It can be argued however, that such maps, apart from often being bad examples of physical geography's cartography, are bad social science. They make concentrations appear where they are not, and dissolve existing patterns.

Human cartography can address these issues by redrawing the locations of boundaries and size of territories on the basis of a population variable of interest. In this way the relative values of objects on a map are reflected by the size of the area. This is much easier for the human eye-brain system to assess than trying to translate the shades of colour into rates and then to imagine what they imply. Rescaling area to show the variation in particular variables is very effective in terms of visual communication and a good example of this is the traditional homunculus used in medical science to portray the human body in terms of the degree of sensitivity: the skin and the whole human body is rescaled in proportion to the number of nerve endings in all areas[1] (also see Dorling, 2007a, 2007b).

There are several types and methodological approaches to human cartography, but it can be argued that all approaches generally attempt to address a number of key challenges:

- Develop a method which is as simple and easy to understand and implement as possible.
- Generate 'readable' maps by minimizing the distortion of the shape of the geographical areas being mapped, while at the same time preserving accuracy and maintaining topological features.
- Determine the cartogram or other distorting projection to be unambiguous.
- Minimize computational speed for the construction of new visualizations.
- Make the end result independent of the initial projection being used.
- Make the end result look aesthetically acceptable.
- Have no overlapping regions or other more complex portrayal.

The problems of distortion and projection-dependence have been successfully addressed by Gastner and Newman (2004) who developed computer software that creates unique cartograms that minimize distortion on the surface of the sphere while still scaling areas correctly. The process is essentially one of allowing population to flow out from high-density to lower-density areas. They used the linear diffusion method from elementary physics to model this process. The computer algorithm re-projects the boundaries of territories on the surface of the sphere – rather than on the plane using a diffusion equation from the physics of heat transfer and molecular mixing (for a detailed formal discussion see Gastner and Newman [2004]). The resulting maps remain recognizable and incorporate the striking re-sizing used previously in 'rectangular maps'. Furthermore, unlike its predecessor projections, Gastner and Newman's method does not reflect the arbitrary choice of initial projection (for instance, Newman has adopted it for the Worldmapper project so that it joins East–West unlike any other equal population projection) and produces an image that approximates a unique least distorting solution. This means that the cartogram reader has only one new projection to learn should they wish to map upon population rather than land. The next section of this chapter shows how this projection method can be used to map cities, regions, nations and the world.

Human mapping of the city, region, nation and world

In this section we show how the Gastner and Newman diffusion cartogram method can be employed to visualize human variables at different geographical levels. First we show how the method can be applied at sub-regional and sub-city level, drawing on recent research on poverty, wealth and place in Britain (Dorling et al., 2007) and focusing on the city of London.

The Greater London metropolitan area, which is used as an example here, comprised, up until 2009, 74 parliamentary constituencies which are shown in Figure 10.1.

Figure 10.1   Map of Greater London parliamentary constituencies, 2009

As can be seen the shapes and the size of each area vary considerably and this variation introduces undesirable visual bias, given that all areas have roughly the same population. As it was the case with regions and countries, such bias can be corrected by using cartogram methods. In the case of UK parliamentary constituencies a population cartogram would result in all areas having roughly the same size (Dorling and Thomas, 2004). However, cartogram methods can also be used to distort the size of each constituency on the basis of a socio-economic variable that pertains to the political agenda of national and local government authorities. A policy-relevant theme in this context is the spatial distribution of poverty and wealth, which according to recent research has been characterized by high degrees of spatial polarization at regional and local levels (Dorling and Ballas, 2008; Dorling et al., 2007). In particular, the highest wealth and lowest poverty rates in Britain tend to be clustered in the South East of England, with the exception of some areas in inner London (Dorling et al., 2007). The geographical patterns of social and spatial inequalities can be explored further with the use of human cartograms. For instance, Figures 10.2 and 10.3 show an alternative human scale visualization of the geography of poverty and wealth in London. In particular, they show how the London parliamentary constituencies can be distorted on the

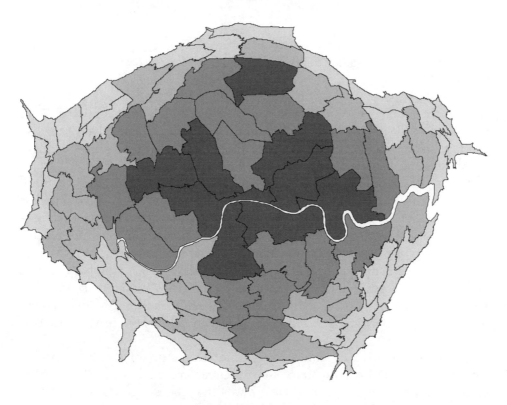

Figure 10.2   'Core poor' cartogram of Greater London parliamentary constituencies

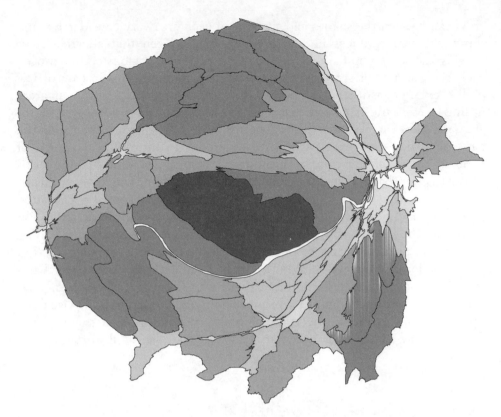

Figure 10.3 'Exclusive wealthy' cartogram of Greater London parliamentary constituencies

basis of the number of households living in them which are classified as 'core poor' and 'exclusive wealthy' respectively. In both maps darker shades are also used to colour larger areas (areas with more poor and rich people) so help emphasize the distortions.

As can be seen in Figure 10.2, the 'core poor' map is dominated by inner city areas and areas in the South East of London. 'Core poor' are defined as those who are simultaneously income poor, materially deprived and subjectively poor and who thus have very little money coming in, very few possessions and resources and they also perceive themselves as poor (Dorling et al., 2007). The parliamentary constituencies with the largest numbers of this group of households that dominate the map (and also with darker shades) are Poplar and Canning Town, Vauxall, Hackney South and Shoreditch, North Southward and Bermondsey and Bethnal Green, all located in the East End of London.

In contrast, Figure 10.3 shows a very different picture of London, as it distorts the size of all parliamentary constituencies on the basis of the number of households classified as 'exclusively wealthy'. These are households that have sufficient wealth to exclude themselves from the norms of society, if they so wish (Dorling et al., 2007). As can be seen, the west end of London dominates the map, but also some of the wealthy suburbs in the outskirts of the city, whereas the size of most of the areas in the east end of London has shrunk. Kensington and Chelsea (the largest dark shaded area in the middle of the cartogram) is the parliamentary constituency with the highest number of exclusive wealthy households, which is nearly double that of Richmond Park which comes second, followed by Finchley and Golders Green and Twickenham (all areas in the west end of London). Conversely, most of the areas in the shrinking (in Figure 10.3) East End of London have very few households that could exclude themselves from the norms of society if they wished to do so.

The power of cartogram technologies for human-scale visualizations can be further demonstrated by mapping regions within a country, resizing the areas of the regions on the basis of a variable which is increasingly used in the social sciences: subjective happiness. In particular, we use data from the British Household Panel Survey (BHPS) which is one of the most comprehensive social surveys in Britain draw from a representative sample of over 5000 households and which includes a number of questions pertaining to subjective happiness and well-being, such as: 'Have you recently been feeling reasonably happy, all things considered?'

It has often been argued that responses to such questions may not be readily comparable between countries due to various kinds of cultural bias (Diener et al., 1995). For instance, it has been suggested that Americans tend to claim that they are very happy because the term 'happiness' is positively valued in their society whereas in other countries such as Japan and France, there is the exact opposite tendency (Frey and Stutzer, 2002). It can be argued therefore that the subjective happiness variable is more suitable for analysis and visualization at the national and sub-national level, when such data is available. Figure 10.4 is based on data from the BHPS and represents the 'mirror image' of happiness and unhappiness in Britain. The cartogram on the left hand side was created using the Gastner and Newman diffusion method to rescale the sizes of all areas according to the number of the 'unhappy' respondents in the survey. Likewise, the same method was used to create the cartogram on the right hand side of Figure 10.4, in which the sizes of all areas are rescaled on the basis of the number of 'happy' respondents.

These human cartograms are very different from conventional maps of Britain. They give more prominence to regions with large concentrations of a human variable of interest, which in this case is the number of 'happy' and 'unhappy' people. Taking a closer look at these cartograms, we observe similarities in terms of the shape and size of most regions. For instance, the region 'Rest of South East', shaded in black in both cartograms, has very similar numbers of both 'happy' and 'unhappy' people. Nevertheless, there are also

Unhappy
- ☐ 22–24
- 25–44
- 45–64
- 65–107
- 108–201

Happy
- ☐ 23–39
- 40–54
- 55–71
- 72–105
- 106–224

Figure 10.4 Mirror image of happiness/unhappiness in Britain. Both figures are scaled by the numbers of people saying they are less or more happy. The figures look very similar as geographical variations are not huge, but look closely, or at the shading, and they become evident.

some notable differences. In particular, the sizes of Scotland and Wales are slightly larger in the cartogram of 'unhappy' people. In contrast, the regions of Inner and Outer London have considerably larger sizes in the cartogram of 'happy people' (for a more detailed discussion of the happiness data used to create Figure 10.4 see Ballas et al. [2007]).

The Gastner and Newman diffusion technique has also been used extensivly to generate a series of world cartograms in the context of Worldmapper,[2] which is a collaborative project between researchers at the Social and Spatial Inequalities Research Group of the University of Sheffield, UK, and Mark Newman, from the Center for the Study of Complex Systems at the University of Michigan in the USA. The project has so far produced nearly 700 world maps where territories[3] are re-sized on each map on the basis of a number of subjects, ranging from health, life and death to income, poverty

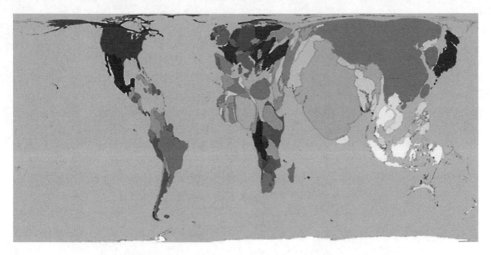

Figure 10.5 Total population (Worldmapper map 002), the size of each territory shows the relative proportion of the world's population living there
Source: United Nations Development Programme, 2004, Human Development Report.

and wealth (Barford and Dorling, 2007a, 2007b; Dorling, 2006). Figure 10.5 shows a Worldmapper cartogram of the world population distribution across territories.

It is noteworthy that, unlike conventional choropleth maps of population data, the Worldmapper cartogram shown in Figure 10.5 reveals more of the real pattern of population distribution by showing where the highest population concentrations are and therefore how human population can more revealingly be mapped by social scientists. China and India, which account for about one-third of the world population, are the largest territories on the map. In contrast, the size of territories of countries with large land sizes but low population densities such as Russia, Canada and Australia are diminished when compared with conventional land-based choropleth maps.

It is also interesting to see how the sizes of the territories change in relation to the population cartogram when mapping other socio-economic variables and to think about the societal impacts of such a cartogram on collective imaginations. Using a cartogram instead of a conventional map has a very different impact upon the public's perception regarding the World's progress in achieving the United Nations Millennium Development Goals. One of these goals is the eradication of extreme poverty and hunger and a more specific target in relation to this goal is to halve between 1990 and 2015 the number of people who suffer from hunger (UNICEF, 2007). A useful indicator pertaining to this target is the prevalence of underweight children under five years of age (UNICEF, 2007). According to data collected and calculations made by the Worldmapper project, between 1995 and 2002 almost one-quarter of all children aged under 15 years old were estimated to be underweight,

Figure 10.6 Total population (Worldmapper map 182), territory size shows the proportion of all underweight children in the world that live there
Source: United Nations Development Programme, 2004, Human Development Report

which was then approximately equivalent to a total number of about 439 million.[4] Figure 10.6 shows a world map where area is drawn in proportion to this number.

It is interesting to consider at this stage the impact that Figure 10.6 may have on the public's perception of progress regarding the achievement of Millennium Goals, when compared to conventional maps. Figure 10.6 is a much better representation of the spatial inequality and in particular it highlights that half of all underweight children under the age of 5 years live in Southern Asia, whereas Southeastern Africa, Asia Pacific, Northern Africa and Eastern Asia also have very large numbers of underweight children, and especially in Ethiopia, Indonesia, Nigeria and China. In contrast, it is very difficult to distinguish the shapes of most countries in Europe and the Americas. When compared with conventional maps a human-scale visualization as shown in Figure 10.6 is possibly presenting a much more accurate, appropriate and powerful depiction of the magnitude of issues such as child poverty as well as the associated social and spatial inequalities. Apart from the statistical human population data that this map communicates, it can be argued that it also has a very effective and emotionally powerful visual impact. Cartograms have been around for many years and thus it is perhaps surprising that human cartograms have not been used so far by organizations such as UNICEF and other non-governmental organizations to increase awareness and improve the quality of information that the public have about global issues. In very recent years the number of children going hungry in the world has been rising as food prices rose due to financial speculators.

The cartograms presented in this chapter are just a few examples of how new innovative cartogram methodologies can be used to draw alternative human-scale visualizations by keeping the shape of intra-city areas, regions and nation-states familiar, while at the same time showing clearly striking patterns of inequalities. There are of course numerous other examples of variables that can be and have been mapped in a similar way. The methods presented here are very relevant not only to human geographers and cartographers but to any social scientist with an interest in the spatial dimension of human variables. For instance, the examples that were briefly discussed in this chapter may be of interest to people working in a number of social science disciplines ranging from sociology, economics and social policy to psychology. Perhaps the best example of the diversity of social science fields to which the cartogram methods are relevant is the list of variables that were mapped in the Worldmapper project (currently 696 variables pertaining to a different social science fields).[5]

Due to the recent availability of new algorithms it is increasingly easy to create such cartograms. For instance, freely available web-based software such as the online 'Cartogram Generator' developed by Frank Hardisty at the University of South Carolina are very simple and easy to use by any social scientist who has a minimal knowledge of geographical information systems.[6] All that is required to run this free online software is a file containing the digital boundaries of a conventional polygon map (for example, in the digital boundaries of the parliamentary constituencies of London as shown in Figure 10.1) together with a metric statistical variable (for example, the number of 'core poor' households) for each area. The data needs to be in ESRI shapefile format, one of the most common formats for geographical data used in the social sciences.[7] This data can then be uploaded by the software with the use of any Internet browser that is supported by the Java Virtual Machine (version 1.4 or later, also freely available from: http.//java.com). The software then asks for the variable of interest that should be used to rescale the polygons of the conventional map and proceeds to convert the map into a cartogram on the basis of this variable by applying the Gastner and Newman diffusion algorithm that was discussed above. A more recent software development that allows the creation of cartograms is 'Scapetoad'[8] (Andrieu et al., 2008), which is also freely available, but does not run online. As with the 'Cartogram Generator', 'Scapetoad' just needs a digital polygon boundary file with a statistical variable of interest in shapefile format and applies the Gastner and Newman diffusion technique. It also enables the user to set their own 'cartogram quality' settings (for more details see Andrieu et al., 2008).

In principle, such software can be used to create human cartograms of any variable pertaining to human populations. It is also user-friendly and simple enough to be used by any social scientist with an interest in the spatial distribution of socio-economic data.

Conclusion

This chapter provides an overview of the state of the art in human area population cartogram creation and also gives a number of examples at different geographical levels in order to illuminate issues and problems that are inherent in visualizing human populations. We have argued that conventional maps that show how cities, regions and countries appear from space, are not an appropriate way to show the spatial distributions of humans and their characteristics, other than simple location. A more human cartography begins to provide a more appropriate set of methods and tools for the depiction of the spatial distribution of variables pertaining to human societies rather than projections designed to illuminate environmental, geological or meteorological problems.

Undoubtedly there has been much progress in human cartography over the past 20 years. The new developments in human cartogram technologies reviewed here provide just a small glimpse of the tools and the enabling environment for social scientists across disciplines to map their data using methods that are appropriate for human scale visualizations. The new methods are relatively easy to understand and use and the resulting cartograms can be extremely powerful tools to support the arguments of social science researchers.

Nevertheless, it should be noted that one of the potential drawbacks of the methods presented here is the difficulty in recognizing the regions that are being mapped. This is perhaps less of a problem when creating cartograms of nation states, as generally people are more likely to be familiar with their physical shapes as opposed to smaller sub-regional or intra-urban areas. In addition, caution is needed when comparing trends through time, given that the shapes and sizes of geographical units being mapped change through time and therefore the temporal analysis that can be conducted is very different (and more powerful) than conventional maps.

One of the ways in which human cartography can be improved is the enhancement of the visual impact of human cartograms through the use of computer animation showing the changing shape and size of neighbourhoods, cities, regions and countries on the basis of different variables. It would also be useful to link the new, more human, cartography to other new mapping technologies such as 'Google Earth' in order to allow viewers to spin around the sphere, to zoom in and out of the globe, to find out more about each place more quickly, and even to see one image morph into another. This is one of the immediate priorities of projects such as the Worldmapper, and by the time you read this chapter, the Worldmapper or other web sites may well have enhanced three-dimensional human cartograms, showing not just human geography but also our history when people are put at the visual centre. Animations are already there.

Acknowledgements

The British Household Panel Survey data that were used to create Figure 10.4 were made available through the UK Data Archive. The data were originally collected by the ESRC Research Centre on Micro-social Change at the University of Essex, now incorporated within the Institute for Social and Economic Research. Danny Dorling was funded by the British Academy (British Academy Research Leave Fellowship) while writing this chapter and by the Leverhulme Trust for developing Worldmapper further. Dimitris Ballas would like to gratefully acknowledge funding from the UK Economic and Social Research Council (research fellowship grant number RES-163–27–1013). This chapter draws on a longer paper that will be published in Nyerges, Couclelis and McMaster (eds) (2011), *Handbook of GIS & Society Research*, Sage (forthcoming in February 2011; ISBN: 978-1-4129-4645-2)

Notes

1. Also see: http://en.wikipedia.org/wiki/Homunculus
2. See http://www.worldmapper.org/
3. The Worldmapper maps and data files cover 200 territories, mainly United Nation Member States plus a few others to include at least 99.95 per cent of the world's population.
4. See: http://www.worldmapper.org/display.php?selected=182#
5. See http://www.worldmapper.org/textindex/text_index.html
6. See http://people.cas.sc.edu/hardistf/cartograms/
7. See http://en.wikipedia.org/wiki/Shapefile
8. See http://scapetoad.choros.ch/

References

Andrieu, D., Kaizer, C. and Ourednik, A (2008) 'ScapeToad: not just one metric, on-line document'. Available at: http://scapetoad.choros.ch (accessed 20 August 2009).

Ballas, D. and Dorling, D. (2011) 'Human scaled visualizations and society', in T. Nyerges, H. Couclelis and R. McMaster (eds), *Handbook of GIS & Society Research*. London: Sage (forthcoming in February 2011)

Ballas, D., Dorling, D. and Shaw, M. (2007) 'Social inequality, health, and well-being', in J. Hawroth and G. Hart (eds), *Well-Being: Individual, Community, and Social Perspectives*. Basingstoke: Palgrave. pp. 163–86.

Barford, A. and Dorling, D. (2007a) 'Re-ordering the world', *Geography Review*, 20 (5): 8–11.

Barford, A. and Dorling, D. (2007b) 'A map a day, for every day of the year: a new view of the world', *GeoInformatics*, April/May: 14–16. Available at: http://www.worldmapper.org/articles/Worldmapper-GeoInformatics.pdf (accessed 17 June 2010).

Diener, E, Diener, M. and Diener, C, (1995) 'Factors predicting the subjective well-being of nations', *Journal of Personality and Social Psychology*, 69 (5): 851–64

Dorling, D. (2006) 'New maps of the world, its people and their lives', *Society of Cartographers Bulletin*, 39 (1–2): 35–40.

Dorling, D. (2007a) 'Worldmapper: the human anatomy of a small planet', PLoS *Medicine*, 4 (1): 13–18.

Dorling, D. (2007b) 'Anamorphosis: the geography of physicians, and mortality', *International Journal of Epidemiology*, 36 (4): 745–50.

Dorling, D. and Ballas, D. (2008) 'Spatial divisions of poverty and wealth', in T. Ridge and S. Wright (eds), *Understanding Poverty, Wealth and Inequality: Policies and Prospects*. Bristol: Policy Press. pp. 103–34

Dorling, D., Rigby, J., Wheeler, B., Ballas, D., Thomas, B., Fahmy, E., Gordon, D. and Lupton, R. (2007) *Poverty, Wealth and Place in Britain, 1968 to 2005*. Bristol: Policy Press.

Dorling, D. and Thomas, B. (2004) *People and Places: a Census Atlas of the UK*. Bristol: Policy Press.

Frey, B. and Stutzer, A. (2002) *Happiness and Economics*. Princeton, NJ: Princeton University Press.

Gastner M.T. and Newman, M.E.J. (2004) 'Diffusion-based method for producing density equalizing maps', *Proc. Natl. Acad. Sci. USA*, 101: 7499–504.

Henriques, R.A.P. (2005) 'CARTO_SOM: cartogram creation using self-organizing maps', masters dissertation, Instituto Superior de Estatistica e Gestao de Informacao, Universidade Nova de Lisboa. Available at: http://www.izegi.unl.pt/servicos/documentos/TSIG010.pdf (accessed 5 February 2008).

Keim, D.A., North, S.C. and Panse, C. (2004) 'CartoDraw: a fast algorithm for generating contiguous cartograms', *IEEE Transactions on Visualization and Computer Graphics*, 10 (1): 95–110.

Keim, D.A., North, S.C. and Panse, C. (2005) 'Medial-axes based cartograms', *IEEE Computer Graphics and Applications*, 25 (3): 60–8.

Keim, D.A., North, S.C., Panse, C. and Schneidewind, J.O. (2002) 'Efficient cartogram generation: a comparison', *Proceedings of the IEEE Symposium on Information Visualization*, 33:1–4. Available at: http://www.computer.org/portal/web/csdl/doi?doc=doi/10.1109/INFVIS.2002.1173144 (accessed 18 June 2010).

Olson, J.M. (1976) 'Noncontiguous area cartograms', *Professional Geographer*, 28: 371–80.

Sen, A.K. (1975) 'A theorem related to cartograms', *American Mathematics Monthly*, 82: 382–5.

Szegö, J. (1984) *A Census Atlas of Sweden*. Stockholm: Statistics Sweden, Central Board of Real Estate Data, Swedish Council for Building Research and The University of Lund.

Szegö, J. (1987) *Human Cartography: Mapping the World of Man*. Stockholm: Swedish Council for Building Research.

Tobler, W.R. (1973) 'A continuous transformation useful for districting', *Annals of the New York Academy of Sciences*, 219: 215–20.

Tobler, W. (2004) 'Thirty five years of computer cartograms', *Annals of the Association of American Geographers*, 94 (1): 58–73.

UNICEF (2007) *The State of the World's Children 2008: Child Survival*. New York: UNICEF. Available online: http://www.unicef.org/publications/files/The_State_of_the_Worlds_Children_2008.pdf (accessed 18 February 2009).

SECTION III

Researching Change

What is change?

While all research has a temporal dimension and change is implied in most, if not all of the chapters of this book, the chapters in this section have a much more explicit focus on change as a process. 'Change' is not itself an entity in the same way as 'relationships' or 'place' but, nonetheless, may be seen in very different ways – for example, change may be measured through standardized survey instruments or constructed on the basis of documentary and archival evidence. A focus on change allows us to consider the range of evidence and methods used to make claims about change over time.

The kinds of change covered in this section vary widely, in terms of the time-span involved, whether it is individual, societal or even 'epochal' change and what constitutes change. Different methods are needed to capture different kinds of change. Savage draws a distinction, which is played out in these chapters, when he asks:

> Do we emphasize the messiness of the historical record, the unevenness, complexity and incompleteness of change, or do we use standardised sources to delineate secular trends and even the possibility of epochal shifts. (Savage, Chapter 11, this volume, p. 171)

Savage (Chapter 11) and Weeks (Chapter 12) both look at long-run societal change – over the last 50 years or so. Savage champions the use of archived qualitative interviews, the 'messy data' he refers to, above, to show change in the way that people talk about social class while Weeks engages with the politics of change in seeking explanations for the processes that have produced such profound changes in sexual life since the 1970s. In both chapters there is a sense of change as a contested concept – different versions of history, for example, can compete with each other, and both suggest that this is not value neutral.

Elliot (Chapter 14) and Nazroo (Chapter 15) both examine change over a long time-span but with an explicit focus on change which is part of the individual's life-course or ageing process. Both use longitudinal individual-level survey data to identify individual change and use statistical methods of analysis that allow results to be generalized to the wider population. Although using survey data, Elliott conceptualizes individual life-course transitions as having narrative features whereby respondents answer pre-defined questions about events such a childbirth, partnership or employment. By contrast, Nazroo is concerned with using individual longitudinal survey data to show how the causal factors that lie behind an observed change can be established. He stresses that, while causality lies at the heart of much social science, it is very difficult to be sure that a relationship is causal, even when using longitudinal data.

Rogers (Chapter 13) is also concerned with individuals, but her focus in on the role of health-related interventions in producing short-term change in people's behaviour. Her interest is on the way in which qualitative interviews can be used in tandem with a randomized control trial (RCT) to give greater insights into the processes that influence behavioural change. In her study, an RCT was used to establish the relative benefits of two different interventions, by comparison with a control group, in a health setting. The interventions designed took the form of complex face-to-face discussions with patients who were taking narcoleptic medication. She shows how qualitative methods can be used, first, to improve the design of a complex intervention so that it corresponds more closely to the patients' perceptions and encompasses a more complex understanding of how change occurs and, second, to provide a greater understanding of the processes by which patients responded to the interventions given.

What evidence is used to identify change?

Unsurprisingly, given some major differences in perspective on what change is, the authors in this section use very different methods to understand it, and provide interesting contrasts in terms of the basis on which they make claims about change, what kinds of change occur, and the factors that explain these.

Savage contrasts the value of historical survey data with non-standardized data sources, including Mass-Observation correspondence dating from the 1930s, and more recently archived qualitative interviews from a range of studies. He makes a strong argument for the power of these forms of 'messy' data notwithstanding their unsystematic and unstandardized nature (in fact, sometimes, precisely because of it). Although recognizing the strengths of standardized survey sources, he argues that our repertoire of approaches should be extended to include non-standardised archival data which can provide more 'telling detail', including 'rich, personalized and evocative accounts of social change' and a 'feel for particular interviewees, locations or issues of the day' (Chapter 11, this volume 174). He argues that the non-standardized data he uses can yield new and surprising insights into how experiences of social class have changed over the decades, and that these data can provide insights into the lives of people whose accounts would not otherwise have been recorded or become part of bigger historical narratives.

Both Savage and Weeks make claims for change based on an analysis of historical records and interviews for which there is no sampling frame, no desire to standardise one's measures, and where the researchers play a key role in deciding not just what material to include but also how to 'read' it. Both discuss the basis on which arguments about change can be substantiated when using data that are not collected in any sort of systematic way but represent 'what is available'. While there is the risk that textual data such as Mass-Observation interviews can be 'cherry-picked' rather than analysed systematically, Savage argues that standardized data cannot yield all the contextual and evocative material that is needed to appreciate a more complex view of social change.

However, survey data increasingly allow complexity and context to be captured and modelled. This is apparent in Nazroo's discussion of causality, in Elliott's discussion of 'analysis as narrative' in relation to event history modelling, and also in some of the examples given in Dale's earlier chapter on relationships. Of course many researchers seeking to understand change will combine multiple sources and ways of conceptualizing change, and thus gain the richness of qualitative sources while benefiting from the standardization offered by surveys.

Weeks explains how, as an historical sociologist (or sociological historian) he seeks to challenge existing 'truth' (Chapter 12, this volume, p. 184). His sources of evidence allow the inclusion of voices hidden from most historical accounts and thus produce new readings of events that may challenge traditional power structures. He also emphasizes the need for reflexivity to interrogate his own assumptions and his own lived experience. Weeks' explains that the narrative constructed by the researcher, and supported by empirical evidence, is presented as a persuasive 'true history'. However, it is then open to challenge by other researchers and thus its credibility is based not only on the published work but also on the extent to which other researchers critique the narrative or offer alternatives.

This process of constructing a narrative, which is then open to challenge to others, has parallels with the much more formal analysis of change discussed by both Elliott and Nazroo using survey data. While their data are drawn from a sample which is representative of the population, nonetheless, the topics covered in the survey and the questions asked reflect the assumption and interests of the researchers who compiled the questionnaire. Similarly, the models used to conduct an analysis of change over time are largely based on theory and prior evidence although the final step of establishing what factors explain change – or whether or not change has occurred – rests on formal statistical tests which are outside the influence of the researcher and may, in that sense, be seen as 'objective'.

For research based on statistical analysis of surveys there is a large body of methodological work that addresses many of the issues of selection (where data are only available for some respondents and this is on a non-random basis); incomplete or missing data and methods to allow the strength of different influences to be assessed. Elliott describes event-history methods that allow the analyst to overcome the problem of 'censored data' – where some respondents have not yet experienced the outcome of interest. Although technically challenging, this is important because those respondents who have experienced the event of interest (for example a birth) may be systematically different from those who have not. Event history methods also allow the analysis to establish the relative importance of explanatory variables (covariates) in explaining the outcome.

Nazroo's focus is on the design of analyses that can identify those causal factors or variables that directly influence the outcome – for example, whether social class has a causal effect on health outcomes. Nazroo highlights many of the difficulties of attempting this kind of analysis. For example, causality may not run in one direction only – health may be affected by unemployment but unemployment also affects health; key factors may not be included in a model. Although economists and statisticians have developed methods to deal with these well-established issues they are tricky to use and it is not always possible to be certain that answers are correct. Rather akin to Weeks, who uses narrative methods to explain changes in sexual life since the 1970s, causal analysis also depends on a narrative – although this is usually in the form of theory that proposes the process by which social class, for example, affects health. Although not couched in the terminology of causal analysis, Weeks is also seeking to find explanations that account for the changes he identifies.

Causal analysis methods are of great value to those formulating policy interventions who need to know, for example, whether retirement has a direct causal effect on health or whether an apparent relationship can be explained by other factors such as income levels after retirement. However, it is usually wise to build up a body of evidence based on a number of studies which, if all pointing in the same direction, can provide a more robust basis for decision making than a single study.

The difficulty of establishing causality – and controlling for all the intervening or 'nuisance' factors – lies behind the use of RCTs. As Rogers explains, the use of random allocation to a particular intervention or regime should mean that all the other factors that might influence the outcome have been randomly assigned between the trial group and the control group and thus they cancel each other out. This then makes analysis very straightforward as a direct comparison can be made between the two groups. However qualitative research has shown that some of the assumptions behind RCTs lack the methodological sophistication needed to understand social change, and in many areas of social science an RCT would be either impractical or unethical.

Of course, change features in many other chapters in this book. It lies at the heart of Harvey and Knox's (Chapter 7) ethnography of building a road. Change was invoked by the process of road-building and all those associated with the road were experiencing or anticipating change, or were instrumental in causing some kind of change. However, unlike the examples of change in this section, Harvey and Knox's aim was not to establish whether and how change had occurred but to use the upheaval of the road building to observe and understand more about the lives of the people involved. Change is also an important part of Thomson's (Chapter 4) longitudinal study of motherhood and, in a very different way, in Ballas and Dorling's chapter on mapping, where the aim is to initiate change through the stark presentation of particular messages about inequality (Chapter 10).

ELEVEN

Using Archived Qualitative Data

Researching Socio-cultural Change

Mike Savage

The challenge of social change

How do we render the past, now lost to us, so that we can delineate and comprehend the course of change? This challenging question can be addressed in two contrasting ways. Scholars from the humanities argue that historical residues – documentary sources, oral histories, literary narratives, archaeological remains, artefacts and so forth – need to be interrogated and ordered into historical narrative. Here the skilled historian, having inspected the relevant evidence, whatever form it might take, acts as a kind of judge, adjudicating on the nature and causes of change. Social scientists, by contrast, prefer to deploy standardized data sources to allow the systematic comparison of observations over sustained periods of time. This allows the delineation of trends, often through the deployment of quantitative indicators. For much of human history, the historians' perspective has dominated. This partly reflects the paucity of standardized data until the recent past. In the UK the first major standardized data source is probably the Census, administered on a decennial basis from 1801. However, it was only with the expansion of the social sciences themselves, especially from the second half of the 20th century, that the range and scope of such sources increased to permit the sustained deployment of quantitative data. Today, however, the amount of relevant data for the recent past is considerable and allows the systematic study of social trends over the course of the 20th century and especially since 1950. The authoritative edited collection of Halsey and Webb (2000), which surveys social trends in 20th-century Britain, thus contains 19 chapters covering diverse aspects of demographic, economic, social, political and cultural change over the course of the 20th century. Every one of these chapters relies upon data from documentary and official data, buttressed by sample surveys conducted in different time periods, as the bedrock of their analysis.

These are two very different perspectives. In the former, historians have to make do with whatever survives, inferring general patterns taking into account the biases of different sources. The historian's narrative thus acts as the device which unifies a huge array of possible sources into some kind of 'historical account' (see, famously, Carr's [1961] distinction between facts and historical facts). The social scientist, by contrast, typically seeks a different kind of guarantee, through the standardization of research instruments so that comparable data is collected over different periods of time, so permitting change to be measured by the careful inspection of observed differences at various time points. Yet we need to see this process of standardization as itself an historical process, involving three elements (see, more generally, Desrosieres, 1994; Mitchell, 2002; Porter, 1996):

- Ensuring that the research instrument is administered to a consistently defined sample at different, preferably regular, periods. We can trace the origins of this to the decennial census, but this process becomes much more systematic in the post second world war period when the annual repeat survey, using some kind of national sampling frame, becomes a key research device. A particularly interesting and powerful method here was the use of panel, or longitudinal, surveys, whereby the same units (people or organizations) were sampled at different points in time, so allowing changes to them to be measured. These panel studies can be traced to the 1930s, being incorporated into the early BBC audience research, before being taken up in cohort studies (notably the 1946 Birth Cohort Study and the 1958 National Child Development Study), and later in the British Household Panel Study from 1991.
- Ensuring that questions are asked in similar, preferably identical, ways. The use of regular repeat questions was used to trace changes in 'public opinion' and more especially to gauge shifts in voting intention, from the 1930s. Political opinion polling became highly influential from the 1960s. Similar concerns to ask regular questions on a range of socioeconomic and demographic indicators were also embedded in Government Surveys such as the Family Expenditure Survey (from 1957) or General Household Survey (from 1971).
- Ensuring that the resulting datasets are transportable, combinable and analysable using clearly defined procedures. Until the 1970s, when census and survey data had been analysed by hand or by simple mechanical methods, the prospects of being able to re-analyse survey and census material was impractical. The formation of the Social Science Research Council Data Archive (in 1966) which acted as a key depository of datasets was an important precondition in the British case. The large-scale deployment of computer technology (from the 1970s), and the development of standardized software (notably the Statistical Package for the Social Sciences, see Uprichard et al. [2008]) made the secondary analysis of survey data a realistic possibility (see also Agar, 2003). Dale, Arber and Proctor (1988) played a key role in the UK in popularizing the potential for 'secondary data analysis'.

This process of standardization depends on detaching research instruments from their immediate context so that both they, and the data collected, can be circulated autonomously (in the form of questionnaires, codebooks, procedures and software, on the one hand, and datasets and indicators, on the other). There is a contrast here with the data normally used by historians, and which has been deposited in leading archives (notably in the British case, the National Archive and in County Record Offices). This latter material is mostly derived as by-product of administrative processes, ranging from cabinet meetings to the operations of government departments, local authorities, businesses and voluntary organizations. Their survival is haphazard, their quality variable, their meaning often obscure. Interpretation of such varied documents often involves defining, and analysing, those sources in which the most important decisions were made. There is little alternative to the individual scrutiny of specific sources, though economic historians have sought a more systematic means of analysing large-scale datasets. In general, it is difficult to obtain information on relatively powerless and less visible groups, due to a persistent power bias in such documents. It is in contrast to these necessarily partial sources that social scientists often emphasize the value of their use of standardized data and the power of the survey method to discount the biases which historical sources entail (see Marsh's [1982] brilliant advocacy for the survey method).

We can see that around these two strategies for researching change, deep divisions are enmeshed: between humanities and social science disciplines, but also between qualitative and quantitative methods, between inductive and deductive perspectives, and between idiographic (particularizing) and nomethetic (generalizing) accounts. These distinctions underscore how our accounts of social change are contested. Do we emphasize the messiness of the historical record, the unevenness, complexity and incompleteness of change, or do we use standardized sources to delineate secular trends and even the possibility of epochal shifts (Savage, 2009)? This is an important point for indicating that there is no neutral platform from which we can interpret change, and that the very methods for delineating change are complicit with the kinds of accounts we tell.

It might appear that – in those places and periods where it exists – standardized social science data allows a much more rigorous account of change. There are indeed impressive examples of how such data can be used to provide subtle stories of change and stability. The American political scientist Ronald Inglehart (1997) has used attitude surveys from the 1960s, from 43 different nations, representing 70 per cent of the world's population, to show the steady rise of 'post-materialist' values across the globe. John Goldthorpe and his associates (Erikson and Goldthorpe, 1992; Goldthorpe et al., 1980) have similarly used a standardized class scheme to demonstrate the persistence of relative class inequalities in social mobility across time, even in periods of apparently abrupt economic change, and across leading industrial nations. In both cases, it is clear that standardization of data sources allows much discussed claims about life chances and cultural change to be analysed much more systematically than was previously the case.

While recognizing these strengths, we also need to note that the process of abstracting standardized data from its context so that it can be rendered in comparable form is not an innocent one. Abstraction involves stripping away detail, possibly telling detail. A good example comes from Inglehart's account of value change. His main argument is that since the Second World War people have become more likely to express 'post-materialist' values, for instance concerned with individual self-expression. This is developed on the basis that fewer people claim that fighting inflation (which he takes to be a materialist concern) is a major national priority. Yet, in a period when inflation falls (as it did in many nations in the 1980s) respondents become less likely to see it as a national priority to fight inflation. Inglehart, however, neglects such contextual detail and treats this shifting attitude as a sign that respondents have become less materialist. Thus, the kind of exogenous, contextual, economic factors, which may shape attitudes in important ways, may be neglected when standardized data sources are compared.[1]

A second example of the problems involved comes through Goldthorpe's (1980) celebrated studies of social mobility. While brilliant in its own terms, these standardized measures of occupational class are inevitably broad brush in aggregating occupational groups to only a small number of social classes, thereby making it difficult to assess mobility at a more fine grained level. It is difficult to obtain standardized comparative data on elites, for instance, or on different fractions of the middle class, even though such groups might be highly socially significant.[2]

In short, although there are unquestioned advantages, standardization involves losses as well as gains: making data comparable involves processes of abstraction entailing the removal of information.

What, then, is the value of working with more 'messy' data sources? Consider, for example, the case of Mass-Observation, set up in 1937 by the anthropologist, Tom Harrisson, the surrealist poet, Charles Madge, and the photographer Humphrey Jennings, to elicit the accounts of large numbers of observers about a range of everyday issues. The Mass-Observers wrote diaries, compiled long letters in response to 'directives' and became involved in collective ethnographic projects (Garfield, 2004; Hubble, 2006). Although being widely used during the Second World War to gauge civilian morale, during the later 1940s survey researchers (notably, Abrams, 1951) poured scorn on Mass-Observation. It had a hopelessly un-representative sample (since its writers were predominantly drawn from the literate members of the 'chattering classes'), used idiosyncratic methods and had no quality control over its data. By contrast, the national sample survey, increasingly being deployed by government, was held up as offering a much more rigorous and systematic account of social indicators and public opinion. Probably so. But today, 60 years later, the proliferation of data held at the Mass-Observation Archive at the University of Sussex is the subject of huge interest by historians who are able to exploit its contextual detail to provide rich, personalized and evocative accounts of social change in the middle years of the 20th century as they were articulated by the Mass-Observers themselves (for example, Addison [1975] on civilian morale in the Second World War; Summerfield [1988] on gender relations; Kynaston [2008] on the culture of post war austerity Britain). Precisely because much extraneous material is included in these sources, it is possible for later researchers to find material of value in them. By contrast, we usually only have the cell counts generated in response to the structured questions asked by market research surveys and these offer little scope for extensive re-analysis. The process of stripping out and making comparable limits the potential of later researchers to use the data in imaginative ways.[3]

Given this limitation of standardized data for analysing the complexities of social change, the last decade has seen an interesting third possibility emerge – the use of archived qualitative social science data. Mass-Observation is only one, well known, example of such archived data (for examples of the re-analysis of this data, see Stanley [1995] and Savage [2007, 2010]). During the course of the 20th century, increasing amounts of qualitative data collected by social scientists – field notes, interview transcripts, letters, drafts and the like – have been collected and archived. Some of this has been catalogued by the ESRC's Economic and Social Data Service Qualidata Archive (http://www.esds.ac.uk), including the field notes of 'classic' qualitative studies dating back to the 1950s, many of which are stored at the University of Essex, or at other sites such as the Modern Records Centre, University of Warwick. Other important sources remain largely un-catalogued, however, for instance the archives of The Sociological Society held at the University of Keele.

Until recently these documents were largely ignored: social scientists did not know how to use them since they did not conform to standardized norms from which trends could be inferred. Historians did not have the experience of using such sources and in many cases were ignorant about them. In short, these are 'troubling' forms of data which query the powerful binaries I have discussed above. Yet they have some remarkable features. The most interesting of these is that we often obtain the (more or less) verbatim accounts of people whose views would otherwise be unknown and allow unusual scope for capturing popular identities in earlier periods. They hence provide a very unusual window on previous periods. But what kinds of issues are posed by using this data?

De-contextualization?

One argument used by social scientists to emphasize the value of repeat studies is that re-analysis allows the original results to be validated through their re-testing. Is it possible to re-analyse the data collected by qualitative researchers and assess whether the published accounts of the projects are accurate representations of the material they collected? If so, it could be argued that this would allow qualitative research to be put on a firmer footing through correcting the biases of the original researchers themselves. In fact, this argument turns out to be mistaken. I myself have looked at several of these archived qualitative data sources, notably the interviews collected by Elizabeth Bott in the early 1950s which formed the source of her famous study *Family and Social Network* (Bott, 1971, see Savage, 2008), as well as the interview transcripts collected by Goldthorpe and Lockwood which were written up as *The Affluent Worker Study* (Goldthorpe et al., 1968a, 1968b, 1969; Savage, 2005). Even though these were both relatively structured projects, relying on standardized interview schedules to ensure certain common questions were asked to every respondent, only rarely is it possible to correct the readings of the researchers themselves. In part this is because their own analyses of the data are often lost, so it is not clear how they coded up interview transcripts. It also becomes clear from reading the actual publications of the researchers they were able to deploy a wealth of contextual information which is now lost: a 'feel' for particular interviewees, locations or issues of the day. Occasionally one glimpses this, as when Bott corresponds with her co-researcher Jim Robb and they both talk about which of the interviewees they personally identified with and liked as people (Savage, 2010). The researcher looking at the archived material becomes only too aware of what they do not know. This point is important in response to the view of some practicing qualitative researchers who have shown considerable suspicion in using archived qualitative sources. Noting that such sources are themselves abstracted from their original context and hence fail to adequately convey the subjectivities and identities of the research subjects, they doubt their value as resources. In this respect, they are neither standardized, nor are they adequately qualitative – the worst of both worlds.

There are, however, two important objections to this line of argument. First, experience can never be captured in its raw state by any research method and holding up that possibility is therefore a chimera. All research tools involve some process of objectifying data: this applies as much to research on current subjects as it does to that which is historically archived (see Silverman, 2000). Second, and relatedly, it follows that if social scientists are concerned with historical data, then there is considerable potential in re-using archived qualitative data compared to standardized quantitative data. The de-contextualization of qualitative sources, while undoubtedly evident, is nonetheless considerably less than that which exists for survey sources, and there is the potential of reading the material 'against the grain' to reveal key, perhaps underappreciated, aspects of the research context. Indeed, it might even be possible to reveal aspects of the research context which the researchers at the time might not be aware of, for instance class related condescension towards their respondents.

The real issue then, is that if we do want to examine change over time empirically, archived qualitative data offers certain advantages. How do we best go about this process of analysing archived data?

Research strategies

When one conducts secondary analysis of standardized survey data, one invariably gains access to some kind of codebook, usually listing the questions asked, and a data file. The researcher can thus gain ready access to an abstracted set of data collected at different points in time, aspects of which can be analysed very quickly, and quantitative measures of change can then be developed.[4] By contrast, records archived by qualitative researchers have no common standard governing their format (although this is becoming somewhat less true for more recent deposits archived in accordance with ESDS Qualidata procedures). Typically, there is considerable information on the conduct of the study itself, such as correspondence with sponsors, colleagues and respondents, alongside the actual 'data'. Various field notes, diaries, and papers are kept in differing states of organization. Where in-depth interviews have been conducted – even when these are systematically filed – they are not amenable to quick analysis in part because they are not machine-readable (although this situation may change as a result of initiatives towards the digitization of paper copy).[5] There is no easy way of producing 'aggregate' findings, in the way equivalent to the quantitative researcher who can, within seconds, run frequencies on their data. Each item of archived qualitative data usually needs to be read, one-by-one. Yet the sizes of some of the archives are enormous and make it very difficult to allow the researchers to read all the possible material comprehensively. The Mass-Observation Archive, for instance, contains around 200 diaries written at some point between 1937 and the 1960s, and some of them run for several decades. The directives, which began in 1939 and continued until 1955 (and have also been revived from 1981), ask panels of Mass-Observers to respond to issues of the day, and typically generate several hundred responses. Some of these letters extend to several thousand words (Savage, 2007). There is therefore a very real danger that such material can be 'cherry-picked' rather than analysed systematically.[6] Similarly, some of the datasets held at Qualidata are very large, for instance that collected as part of the Affluent Worker Study, which runs to 730 long interviews in seventeen large boxes.

How do we deal with this amount of data which by virtue of its qualitative nature does not lend itself to easy summary or codification? One response is nonetheless to read it all so that the researcher can present him or herself as the expert on all of it. On some occasions this is possible, as for instance with Elizabeth Bott's *Family and Social Network* material which is collected in one box (Savage, 2008). Yet, if this strategy is to be attempted on a large dataset, one has little choice other than to code up the material to simpler categories or sample cases from the complete dataset. Both strategies have their strengths and weaknesses. The former allows summary measures of the data to be derived and it is possible for such codes to be imaginatively constructed, for instance generated by phrases or terms in the material in the text so that they do not simply become standardized deductive categories. Because little archived qualitative data is digitized, it is difficult to use qualitative software packages such as NVivo® or ATLAS.ti, though this may change in the future. The second strategy recognizes that because the archive is itself not a representative sample, there is no particular virtue in reading all the material. Instead, it is possible to adapt strategies to read only a requisite amount of the archived material. One technique here, akin to the idea of saturation as advocated by Bertaux and Bertaux-Wiame (1981) is to stop reading additional material once one no longer feels that substantive new issues are being raised in the material. Even so, it remains important to report systematically differences within the sample.

This sampling issue is also related to whether one chooses to focus on the *content* or *form* of the archived material. If the researcher is interested in the extent to which particular terms are used, then it becomes more important to read large amounts of material so that systematic counts can be generated. Thus I was able to detail how many of the 227 responses to the Affluent Worker interview questions about class identities reported mentioning named classes such as the 'aristocracy', as groups that they were aware of (Savage 2005). However, in many cases researchers are less interested in the raw number of times that particular items are mentioned and more in the form in which they are talked about. Thus, when I was comparing how Mass-Observers talked about class in 1990, compared to the 1940s, I was interested in the kind of narrative which was deployed, rather than the number of references to particular social classes (Savage 2007). By using a few detailed examples, I was able to show that in 1990 Mass-Observers were more able to talk about class, and did so in the form of an individual life history, often concerning their social mobility. In general, it is this focus on form, rather than aggregate frequencies and counts which allows qualitative research to be used to best purpose and suggests the value of using extended case studies as a means of elaborating analytical points. Nonetheless, I think it is still advisable to sample a certain minimum number of cases to avoid relying on a few atypical cases.

The lack of representativeness of qualitative datasets is conventionally held up as one of their major problems. The samples chosen for study by qualitative research vary enormously, and rarely (if ever) approximate to the kind of representative sample that allows quantitative researchers to report national demographic trends. However, a defence can be mounted. Most qualitative datasets do contain the kind of contextual information which allows the extent of their bias to be recognized and hence taken into account. For instance, they usually contain information on where the data was collected and the kind of constituency that is being researched. By then comparing different qualitative datasets it is possible to build up some kind of composite picture. Thus, for instance, it would be problematic to use the data collected as part of The Affluent Worker Study to infer the nature of working-class life in England in the early 1960s: the interviews were only conducted with married men aged between 20 and 45, working in assembly line occupations in Luton. However, by comparing this study with other similar ones, for instance conducted by Richard Brown on Tyneside shipyard workers in the later 1960s, or by Brian Jackson with workers in Huddersfield, it might nonetheless be possible to tentatively recognize certain common features – for instance the extent to which workers in all these settings talked about class as linked to the inheritance of money.[7] The challenge here is to take advantage of the 'messy-ness' of archived qualitative data and build up a more composite picture from different (partial) inquiries, even when recognizing at every step the provisional and limited nature of this exercise. This can be linked to Jennifer Mason's suggestions about the possibility of developing 'cross-contextual generalities', where a more general picture is built up through the detailed analysis of specific cases (Mason, 2002).

Conclusion

As the social sciences age, so new opportunities for using archived social science sources arise. In this chapter I have argued that we should extend our repertoire, not only to conduct secondary analysis of survey data, but also to use archived qualitative social science data more extensively. The considerable range of sources available make this a realistic and attractive possibility, and is already producing interesting findings on changing social identities. But I have also emphasized that this exercise is one which has the additional value of making us rethink our views about the relationship between historical and social scientific research strategies themselves. Rather than worry unduly about the specific issue of 're-using' qualitative archived data, we might instead learn from historians who are much more concerned to get their hands dirty and work with whatever material is available. Recently, Niamh Moore (2006, 2007) has argued that we should focus less on how we 're-use' qualitative data, in terms of whether we are true or not to the original aims of the research, but we should construe the data as equivalent to that which historians use when confronted with disparate sources. Not the least challenge of archived qualitative social science data is therefore to make us reflect on the meaning of disciplinary divides and the way that we try to connect past, present and future.

Notes

1. The example here about inflation is a simple one, but there are also more complex issues regarding the process by which a range of attitude questions are 'reduced' to unitary indicators of values. Majima and Savage (2007) offer an introduction to this debate.
2. The issue of elites is discussed in Savage and Williams (2008), and see the 'debate on the middle class' in which critics of Goldthorpe have argued his use of the 'service class' category is too wide ranging to uncover important variation between its different fractions (Butler and Savage, 1995).
3. There is, however, great potential in returning to the archived raw questionnaires and possibly digitizing and re-analysing them since not all the material might have been coded up. However, this still largely entails examining in greater detail the issues which intrigued the original researchers. A good example is Gazeley and Newell's (2007) restudy of poverty on the basis of 1904 Board of Trade returns.
4. There is also often substantial material on contextual features of the research such as the sampling frame. However, the secondary researcher does not need to refer to such material and indeed rarely does, in order to carry out subsequent analysis.
5. Qualidata is currently digitizing some of its material and making it available for download, though this process is expensive and time consuming. Mass-Observation, by contrast are not pursuing digitization processes. There also ethical problems in reproducing testimony in digital format.
6. In my view this is a criticism which can be levelled at the way some historians have used such data, for instance in Kynaston's *Austerity Britain*.
7. I have attempted an exercise along these lines in Savage (2010: ch. 9).

References

Abrams, M. (1951) *Social Surveys and Social Action*. London, Heinmann.

Addison, P. (1975) *The Road to 1945: British Politics and the Second World War*. London: Cape.

Agar, J. (2003), *The Government Machine*. Boston, MA: MIT Press.

Carr, E.H. (1961) *What Is History?* London: Penguin.

Dale, A., Arber, S. and Procter, M. (1988) *Doing Secondary Analysis*. London: Unwin Hyman.

Bertaux, D. and Bertaux-Wiame, I. (1981) 'Life stories in the baker's trade', in D. Bertaux (ed.), *Biography and Society*. London: Sage.

Bott, E. (1971) *Family and Social Network*. London, Tavistock.

Butler, T. and Savage, M. (eds) (1995) *Social Change and the Middle Classes*. London: UCL Press.

Desrosieres, A. (1998) *The Politics of Large Numbers.* Cambridge: Cambridge University Press.

Erikson, R. and Goldthorpe, J.H. (1992) *The Constant Flux.* Oxford: Clarendon.

Garfield, S. (2004) *Our Hidden Lives: The Everyday Diaries of a Forgotten Britain, 1945–1948.* London: Ebury,

Gazeley, I. and Newell, A. (2007) 'Poverty in Britain in 1904: an early social survey re-discovered', IZA Discussion paper, number 3046, Bonn.

Goldthorpe, J.H. with Llewellyn, C. and Payne, C. (1980) *Social Mobility and the Class Structure in Modern Britain.* Oxford: Clarendon.

Goldthorpe, J.H., Lockwood, D., Bechhofer, F. and Platt, J. (1968a) *The Affluent Worker: Industrial Attitudes and Behaviour.* Cambridge: Cambridge University Press.

Goldthorpe, J.H., Lockwood, D., Bechhofer, F. and Platt, J. (1968b) *The Affluent Worker: Political Attitudes and Behaviour.* Cambridge: Cambridge University Press.

Goldthorpe, J.H., Lockwood, D., Bechhofer, F. and Platt, J. (1969) *The Affluent Worker in the Class Structure.* Cambridge: Cambridge University Press.

Halsey, A.H. and Webb, J. (2000) *Twentieth Century British Social Trends.* Basingstoke: Palgrave MacMillan.

Hubble, N. (2006) *Mass Observation and Everyday Life: Theory, Culture, History.* Basingstoke: Palgrave MacMillan.

Inglehart, R. (1990) *Culture Shift in Advanced Industrial Societies.* Princeton, NJ: Princeton University Press.

Inglehart, R. (1997) *Modernization and Post-Modernization: Cultural, Economic and Political Change in 43 Countries.* Princeton, NJ: Princeton University Press.

Kynaston, D. (2008) *Austerity Britain.* London: Bloomsbury.

Majima, S. and Savage, M. (2007) 'Have there been culture shifts in Britain?', *Cultural Sociology*, 1 (3): 293–315.

Marsh, C. (1982) *The Survey Method.* London: Allen and Unwin.

Mason, J. (2002) *Qualitative Researching.* London: Sage.

Mitchell, T. (2002) *The Rule of Experts.* Boston, MA: MIT Press.

Moore, N. (2006) 'The context of context: broadening perspectives in the reuse of qualitative data', *Methodological Innovations Online*, 1 (2). Available at: http://erdt.plymouth.ac.uk/mionline/public_html/viewarticle.php?id=27

Moore, N. (2007) '(Re)using qualitative data?', *Sociological Research Online*, 12 (3). Available at: http://www.socresonline.org.uk/12/3/1.html

Porter, T. (1996) *Trust in Numbers.* Princeton, NJ: Princeton University Press.

Savage, M. (2005) 'Working class identities in the 1960s: revisiting the affluent worker study', *Sociology*, 39 (5): 929–46.

Savage, M. (2007) 'Changing social class identities in post-war Britain: perspectives from mass-observation', *Sociological Research Online*, 12 (3).

Savage, M. (2008) 'Elizabeth Bott and the formation of modern British sociology', *The Sociological Review*, 56 (4): 579–605.

Savage, M. (2009) 'Against epochalism: numbers, narrative and social change', *Cultural Sociology*, 3 (1): 217–38.

Savage, M. (2010) *Identities and Social Change in Britain since 1940: The Politics of Method.* Oxford: Clarendon.

Savage, M. and Williams, K. (2008) *Remembering Elites.* Oxford: Blackwells.

Silverman, D. (2000) *Doing Qualitative Research.* London: Sage.

Stanley, L. (1995) *Sex Surveyed 1949–1994: From Mass-Observation's 'Little Kinsey' to the National Surveys and the Hite Reports.* London: Taylor and Francis.

Summerfield, P. (1984) *Women Workers in the Second World War: Production and Patriarchy in Conflict.* London: Routledge.

Szreter, S. (1996) *Fertility, Class and Gender in Britain, 1860–1914.* Cambridge: Cambridge University Press.

Uprichard, E., Burrows, R. and Byrne, D. (2008) 'SPSS as an inscription device', *Sociological Review,* 56 (4): 606–22.

TWELVE

What's History Got to Do With it?

Researching Sexual Histories

Jeffrey Weeks

... though I have tried to be fair ... I cannot pretend to have been unbiased. History is biased by definition. (Marquand, 2008: xii)

Making sexual history

The development of a serious history of sexuality can be traced back no further than the 1970s. Drawing on an eclectic set of influences, and deploying a range of methods, including oral history, archival research, discourse analysis and demographic reconstitution, it was stimulated above all by the efforts of scholars rooted in and influenced by the sexual dissidence of the period, both as writers and researchers, and as activists and theorists of the new sexual world (Weeks, 2000: 1). A great deal has changed since the 1970s, and there is now a vast and flourishing historiography about sexuality and intimate life, with younger as well as more established scholars enthusiastically involved, but many of its preoccupations can still be traced to its formative moment. I would pinpoint three key elements in the practice of historical understanding that are rooted in that founding moment, each of which poses major challenges to the process of historical research and analysis.

The first is the originating commitment to a more comprehensive, more inclusive history, both in terms of areas covered (especially gender, sexual and intimate life) and in people listened to. It is no accident that two key texts in feminist, and lesbian and gay history went by the title *Hidden from History* (Duberman et al., 1989; Rowbotham, 1973). This was essentially a work of recovery, of listening to those condemned, in E.P. Thompson's famous phrase, to the 'condescension of posterity'. It is not surprising that the new gender and sexual histories were closely associated with the development of a 'history from below' particularly associated with the History Workshop movement, which in turn fed into the growth of oral and life history methodologies: listening and trying to understand those forgotten or ignored by conventional history, or better understanding the gendered or sexual context of those histories remembered all too well.

However, it soon became clear that the practice of history was more than simply a rediscovery or reconstruction of the past – it was also, critically, helping to re-make our understanding of the present. The present is burdened with history, just as the past is fiercely contested and historians are often inclined to mount the barricades in defence of their own strong positions. This is the second key element in the new practice of sexual history: a recognition that history is political, not simply because 'the personal is political', but because sexual and intimate life is deeply implicated in power relations. So by challenging, through scholarly interventions, the structures of domination and exclusion that had shaped the moral and cultural climate, legal framework and institutional practices for generations, and by affirming the values of restricted, forbidden or tabooed activities and describing the emergence of identities, the new generation of historians were not only remaking the history of sexuality – they were helping to re-define what sexuality could or should be. Nor should this be surprising, because so were millions of people, in a vast range of 'everyday experiments', engaged in re-making their sexual lives in what I shall call the Great Transition between the 1950s and the 2000s (Weeks, 2007).

Writing about sexuality is constitutive: through the web of meaning that we writers on sexuality weave not only are beliefs and behaviours shaped, but the very definition of what sexuality is can be refined and then radically rethought. 'Social constructionism', pioneered in the 1970s and radically changing what was meant by the history of sexuality, rejected simple essentialisms and recognized that the sexual is invented in and through diverse histories by a variety of social forces, including language (Weeks, 2009). After Foucault (1979), a major influence on the new history, but far from being its *onlie begetter*, we have become accustomed to seeing sexuality as a discursive ensemble only contingently related to bodily needs. With Judith Butler we have learnt that gender and sexuality are performatively elaborated in power laden situations, simulacrum of simulacrum, a 'stylized repetition of acts' (1990: 140), rather than simply emanations of a biological sex. Through Plummer (1995, 2003), we have come to see the significance of sexual stories in voicing and giving meaning to sexual practices in various communities of meaning. Now it is commonplace to see identities as cultural phenomena, fictional unities that give meaning to personal and collective journeys (Weeks, 1995). Even embodiment is now seen as a complex social practice rather than the source and fountain of meaning, part of the reflexive project of the self (Giddens, 1991).

All this has profound implications for the practice of history, and is the third key element. Historical research on contemporary sexuality requires a complex set of research approaches, and has to be theoretically informed – using theory as a box of tools, as Foucault suggested (Weeks, 2005). It requires us to be aware of the diversity of sexual cultures within any given society, and of comparative, cross national perspectives. It follows from the constructionist and historical approaches that there are many sexualities. It also requires a high degree of self-awareness and sensitivity to one's own assumptions. The dense interconnection between the doing of historical work and the living of sexuality forces a form of reflexivity in which the author as historian and sociologist, observer and involved sexual citizen can bear witness to the transformations, and deploy his/her own lived experience as a form of provisional evidence in the making of historical narratives.

The practice of sexual history

My own experience as a gay man certainly structured my long standing preoccupation with sexual identity, sexual theory and the regulation of sexuality, and shaped the direction of my early research (Weeks, 1977). The impact of HIV/AIDS in the early 1980s, which impacted powerfully on the communities with which I identified, and on many of my friends, led towards a re-orientation of my research interests, particularly towards a preoccupation with changing relationships and values (Weeks, 1995). However, my own experience is not local and irrelevant because personal life and macro-historical trends are inextricably combined. As I wrote in an earlier work:

> In the contingencies of everyday life we can see the impact of world-historical events, and through our understanding of the long-term shifts in social and economic transformation we may grasp the limits and possibilities of change in the sphere of the intimate. The changes in our own private lives are part of wider, collective transformations. The challenge lies in teasing out the hidden connections, making sense of what seems incomprehensible, or merely idiosyncratic. (Weeks, 2000: 3)

In my own practice as a sociologically inclined historian, or a historically minded sociologist (identities vary and change), I have utilized a range of methodologies. In my early works, particularly concerned with the development of sexual categorizations (especially the heterosexual/homosexual binary divide from the 18th century), sexological interventions, and emerging gay and lesbian identities I used a wide range of sources: personal and institutional archives, sexological texts, medical journals and newspapers, police and court records, and oral history interviews (Weeks, 1977; Rowbotham and Weeks, 1977; Weeks and Porter, 1998). The latter proved especially important for later work, such as exploring the community based responses to HIV/AIDS in the 1980s and 1990s, and my more recent work, especially with Brian Heaphy and Catherine Donovan, on same-sex intimacies (Weeks et al., 2001).

In my most recent book, *The World We Have Won* (2007), which explores the re-making of sexual and intimate life since 1945, that is during my own life time, I begin by placing my own experiences, born into a working-class community in the South Wales mining valleys, with its very specific sexual and family culture, within a wider history of sexual and intimate change. By moving between the particular and the general, and back again, I hoped to illuminate the ways in which individual and collective agency, in sharply determined social and cultural milieux, shaped the ways in which the possibilities of intimate life were re-imagined during the Great Transition.

All this, I realize, poses the danger of seeing sexual history as like a patchwork quilt, building up the evidence from a range of sources bit by bit until a coherent pattern emerges. The reality, of course, is infinitely more complex. Truth does not emerge fully formed from hours in the archive, or from listening to those who lived their experiences, or even from serious reflection on one's own life and professional practices. Indeed, what is strikingly evident in any work on sexuality (but in this it is no different from any other area of research) is that 'truth' is highly contested. It is precisely the 'truth of sexuality' that the pioneering historical work from the 1970s sought to challenge.

In my own work on the history of homosexuality, for example, I sought to undermine the notion, readily assumed in all the existing studies of same-sex activities, that 'the homosexual' was a trans-historical personage, present through all cultures in more or less the same ways as the contemporary lesbian or gay. On the contrary, I argued, along with some other pioneering researchers, that the idea of 'the homosexual' as a person with a specific identity had a history, that could be traced – and in the case of England, could be traced no further back than the 18th century, and in a recognizable contemporary form had existed only since the late 19th century. I was influenced towards this position by sociological theorization about 'the homosexual role' (McIntosh, 1981) and about the malleability of sexuality (Gagnon and Simon, 1974; Plummer, 1975), and by reflecting on my own experiences of the changing nature of sexual identities. But whatever my new theoretical assumptions, the decisive evidence came from the archive, once I began to read it in a different way: not as confirmation of the traditional assumptions, but against the grain, as the product of new processes of categorization, regulation and resistance, especially at the end of the 19th century, a struggle between social definition and self-definition (Weeks, 1977). Subsequent historians have questioned some of my assumptions and produced a mass of new data that have challenged the time-frame and the detail of my account. I still believe, however, that the core of my argument stands: sexual identities have a history whose contours can be traced in concrete circumstances. They change as history changes, and it is both possible and necessary to understand those shifts and the key moments in which they occur, in order to understand the making of sexualities.

Narratives of change

Revision of historical interpretations is inevitable and desirable. But we should not deceive ourselves that it is a neutral activity. It is laden with epistemological and ideological assumptions that are rarely explicit but shape the story historians strive to unfold. Even 'experience', that apparently grounded source of the truth of what happened to us, is rarely a simple category. It is always mediated by a host of cultural practices and elaborated through different historical narratives, embodying a host of beliefs and political positions. All data has to be interpreted and framed within a historical account that has coherence and makes sense. Plummer (1995, 2003) has elaborated an account of 'sexual stories' that helps us to understand this further:

> Society itself may be seen as a textured but seamless web of stories emerging everywhere through interaction: holding people together, pulling people apart, making societies work ... [The] metaphor of the story ... has become recognized as one of the central roots we have into the continuing quest for understanding human meaning. Indeed culture itself has been defined as 'an ensemble of stories we tell about ourselves'. (Plummer, 1995: 5)

Historians also tell each other stories, which they easily assume tell the ultimate truth about the way things were, and are. However, we need to learn to understand these narratives better, especially how they structure meanings into a more or less coherent account of what is happening to us. Narratives or stories are examples of the ways in which 'reality' is constituted through sets of beliefs, assumptions and the appropriate selection of evidence. They are powerful because they carry the unconscious assumption that what is being elaborated for the reader is a 'true history'. But, I want to argue that the very act of selection can occlude a complex and more contested history. Four strong narratives of sexual change have been particularly powerful in shaping recent scholarship (developed from Weeks [2007: 4–7]) and understanding their often hidden assumptions can help us see what is missing.

The first is the progressive story. It is rooted in the optimism of the late 19th- and early 20th-century pioneering sexologists and sex reformers, expressed in Magnus Hirschfeld's famous slogan, 'through Science to Justice', that sexual change would come as a result of good will and rational thought (Weeks, 1985). A more muted and cautious sexual modernity arose in the 1950s and 1960s, which strongly influenced the modest, though vitally important, sex reforms of the late 1960s. At the same time, a stronger liberationist story emerged, which directly linked sexual freedom with social revolution. The spirit of this liberationist politics, associated most famously with Reich and Marcuse, but influential on the radical sexual movements of the 1970s, was quite different from the cautious liberalism that proclaimed sexual modernity, but there were important links. In the first place, they both partook of a theoretical assumption that sexuality was a powerful force that the social repressed. This was soon challenged by new theoretical approaches. As Michel Foucault (1979) pointed out more than a generation ago, you cannot 'liberate' sexuality as if you were taking the lid off a cauldron. Sexuality is not a property that can be repressed or released, but a historically shaped series of possibilities, actions, behaviours, desires, risks, identities, norms and values that can be reconfigured and recombined but cannot be simply unleashed.

The second problem with the narrative is the assumption of inevitable progress that propelled it. There is, of course, something to be said for that, at least if you live in large parts of the West. But to say that does not mean change to be either automatic or inevitable. And in many parts of the world radical change in intimate life has barely begun, or has been subjected to severe repression (Weeks, 2007).

The mirror image of the progressive narrative is the declinist story. Its characteristic note is a lament for the awful state of the present – the broken families, the high rate of divorce, the violence of young people, the incidence of mindless sexual promiscuity, the commercialization of love, the incidence of homosexuality, the explicitness of sex education and the media, the decline of values, the collapse of social capital, the rise of sexual diseases – and to compare that with some golden age of faith, stability and family values (see, among others, Himmelfarb, 1995). If the progressive mindset assumes that the erotic in itself is a positive force for good, the declinist or socially conservative view (a social conservatism, it has to be said, that transcends traditional party-political commitments) assumes that it is not so much bad as potentially dangerous, unless framed in specific contexts – usually heterosexual marriage.

It is a perspective that has had a powerful political impact in key parts of the world, especially those influenced by fundamentalist movements. In most of the West, America apart, it is a minority perspective; on a global scale it is possibly on the rise. If, as I argue, we live in an age of great moral and cultural uncertainty (Weeks, 1995), then a fundamentalist affirmation of the truth of the gendered body, heterosexual sex, the horrors of perversity and the sanctity of faith can seem an appealing antidote. That does not make it right or valid.

The third great narrative believes that despite superficial shifts, nothing has really changed. This is a story of continuity in terms of the underlying structures of power, despite apparently striking epiphenomenal changes. There is a feminist subset of this story, which acknowledges some changes, but stresses the continuities, especially in terms of the relations of power between men and women. A 'queer' subset of the story recognizes that there have been great changes in attitudes towards, for example, homosexuality and sexual diversity. Certainly western societies have seen a cultural revolution, with affirmative LGBTQ (Lesbian, Gay, Bisexual, Transgendered, Queer/Querying) identities everywhere, carrying massive cultural weight. But how much has really changed? Isn't a gay identity little more than a pseudo ethnic identity that is easily accommodated by late capitalist societies? Isn't same sex marriage simply an assimilation into heteronormative structures (for example, Warner, 1993, 1999)?

Finally, there's a political economy subset of this story. It acknowledges the continuing exploitation of women on a global scale, economic as well as sexual. The structural readjustment policies of the World Bank trap millions in poverty that inhibits the development of sexual freedoms and intimate life. It recognizes the power of individualizing tendencies, but sees them as accommodating to the necessities of the latest phase of capitalist expansion. Indeed, the legal reforms and institutional achievements of LGBTQ people that many have welcomed as the signs of greater toleration are seen as fully complicit with the strategic need of neo-liberalism (Richardson, 2004, and discussion in Weeks, 2007: chs 5 and 8).

I cannot deny that there are elements in all these positions which are at least plausible. None, however, convince me fully. The progressive story too readily forgets the contingencies of history, the tortuous routes that have brought us to the present. The declinist story celebrates a golden age that never was. The continuists want to stress the resilience of hidden structures of power and to embody an implicit determinism, suggesting that sexuality is a direct product of determining forces ('patriarchy', 'capitalism', 'heteronormativity', to name but the most popular). In doing this it is all too easy to forget the power of agency and of the real changes that individuals have been able to make in their everyday lives. In their various ways, all these narratives ignore what seems to me the reality: that there have been significant changes that have broken through the coils of power to enhance individual autonomy, freedom of choice and more egalitarian patterns of relationships. The journey has not been hazard free, nor straightforward. It has certainly not been inevitable. We are still in the midst of a long, unfinished revolution. But unless we start with this recognition of real and profound change we cannot really understand what happened in the past, where we are in the present and where we could go in the future.

In the 1950s Britain was widely regarded as having one of the most conservative sexual cultures in the world, with one of the most draconian penal codes. Today it has one of the most liberal and tolerant (Weeks, 2007). The pattern can be replicated in many other countries. That is not the result of a single change. Rather, it has been a process of millions of people remaking their own histories, though not necessarily in circumstances of their own choosing. In trying to understand how this has happened, rather than attempting to fix it in a single narrative of progress, decline or continuity, we need to attend to the complexity of forces at work: holding the long term structural changes (in terms, for example, of class formation, industrialization and urbanization, the rise of the welfare state, patterns of migration, settlement and race and ethnic change) in balance with changing forms of agency (the rise of feminism and lesbian and gay politics, for example, and the impact of individualizing forces). But given that these processes were not linear, we also need to balance a sense of perspective, of the *longue duree*, which can help us locate the significance of change with a conjunctural analysis, which explores the range of forces which made change possible (or impossible) at particular key periods or moments.

Fateful moments

At this stage I would like to introduce the concept of a 'fateful moment' which I think can guide us through the hazards of historical understanding. Fateful moments, according to Anthony Giddens, are:

> Times when events come together in such a way that an individual stands, as it were, at a crossroads in his [sic] existence ... *There are, of course, fateful moments in the history of collectives as well as in the lives of individuals. They are phases at which things are wrenched out of joint, where a given state of affairs is suddenly altered by a few key events.* (1991: 113, my emphasis)

It is that sense of a collective rather than individual moment I want to use here. Fateful moments disrupt conventional narratives, whether of individual or collectives lives, and force us to rethink the stories of our lives. They shake the kaleidoscope, so that new patterns emerge. These new patterns are, of course, heavily overdetermined, in the sense that they embody a variety of forces at play in any given situation, rather than a single causation. Their outcome is never pre-set, or even predictable. And yet they can deflect or re-shape what seems to be a determining pattern deeply embedded in historical processes.

So how do we decide what are 'the fateful moments'? And how do we research them?

Let me try to clarify what I mean by a concrete example. In *The World We Have Won* (2007) I develop the argument which I have already referred to, that there was a Great Transition between the 1950s and the present that re-made sexual and intimate life. A variety of factors have been mooted by historians to explain this. Characteristically, the 'sexual revolution' of the 1960s has been seen as the symbolic starting point and for many critics this has become a major causative explanation (Himmelfarb, 1995). It was then that traditional values were fatally eroded leading to a new emphasis on individual self-realization and hedonism. Individualization has been seen by others as a dominating social process which has fundamentally undermined traditional collective life (Beck and Beck-Gernsheim, 2002). There have been sharp critiques of the commercialization of everyday life and the colonization of the life world by late capitalism, especially in its neo-liberal guise (Bauman, 2003). We apparently live the illusion of freedom while remaining trapped within the coils of power, norms, regulation and commodification.

And yet when we look at the past 40 years since the 1960s the actual history seems more complex than all these theories suggest. Among the most important changes are: the separation of sex and reproduction; the separation of sex and marriage; the separation of marriage and parenting; the separation of heterosexuality and parenting; and the separation of heterosexuality and marriage (Weeks, 2007). Together they signal the effective demise of the traditional model of sexual restraint and opened the way to a new moral economy – one that was less hierarchical and more democratic, more hedonistic, more individualistic, but also one that was vastly more tolerant, experimental and open to diversity and choice in a way that had been inconceivable just a generation earlier. However, the path to this was never straightforward and was the result of struggle rather than inevitability, of agency as much as ineluctable forces.

I have found it useful in my own research to try to identify specific moments for analysis, moments when various forces at play do seem to shape the kaleidoscope, and re-order the narrative and constitute new possibilities. I have to confess that the selection of such fateful moments has a certain degree of arbitrariness. For example, in researching recent sexual change in Britain I would select three key periods which strike me as critical: the Wolfenden moment; the Thatcher moment; and the Blair moment, which I explain below. As the naming suggests, I have deliberately selected key players to symbolize a change. I am not arguing, however, that change can be explained solely or even at all by the actions, or non-actions of these historical actors. Rather, a range of forces were at play during these periods which condense or crystallize possibilities that together altered the trajectory of events. Other historians might well put an emphasis on other key periods – for example, as I have mentioned above, the 1960s has been seen as a critical moment (Marwick, 1998). I would not dispute that, but it seems to me we can better understand the real impact of the 1960s on sex reform if we see it as part of a reshaping of sexual discourses that began earlier. What I am not suggesting is that my own selection of fateful moments provides a conclusive answer to important historical debates. Rather, they are heuristic devices to aid analysis, or pragmatic choices of key events that offer the possibility of new perspectives on recent sexual change. They are, in a sense, working hypotheses. I want to illustrate this by examining in a little more detail the three key moments I have chosen here.

The report of the Wolfenden Committee on prostitution and male homosexuality, which was published in 1957, has been widely recognized as a key moment in the evolution of more liberal attitudes towards homosexuality and it set the framework for regulating sexuality more generally. It is thus a test case for the progressive narrative, but also for the other two major narrative structures. For declinists it could be seen as the moment when liberal/utilitarian principles concerning sexuality began to re-shape the legal system, replacing shared notions of morality with pragmatism. For continuists it has been read straightforwardly as a new and more effective form of regulation, substituting a limited concept of consent and self-regulation for punitive, unworkable and old-fashioned laws. The challenge for historians is to balance a recognition of the importance of the moment, with an understanding of its underlying effects.

The establishment by the UK government of the Wolfenden Committee in 1954 was a compromise, between the desire among more conservative elements to do something to control homosexuality and rid the streets of overt displays of prostitution, and a wish on the part of liberals to find more modern forms of regulation than prison or the law (Weeks, 2007). Wolfenden suggested that the purpose of criminal law was to preserve public order and decency, and to protect the weak from exploitation, while at the same time decriminalizing homosexual acts between 'consenting adults' in private (Waites, 2005; Weeks, 2007). The privatizing of homosexuality could thus be seen as a more effective way of controlling it, and this is what the continuist narrative has tended to argue.

But wider research, looking at both the socio-legal context and at grass roots shifts, indicates that it had more radical implications, pointing to a different story. For the reform proposals, socio-legal researchers suggest, bought the idea of a distinctive homosexual identity and way of life into the law for the first time (Moran, 1995). Prior to Wolfenden, homosexuality as such had had no presence within the law at all. The committee 'discovered', even invented, the meaning of homosexuality as sexual identity, sexual practices and forms of knowledge. A new form of sexual wrong was invented in order that it could be righted, through decriminalization. Wolfenden, the classic re-statement of legal liberalism in the 1950s, offered a framework for the expression of self identities that pointed forward to the new opportunities of the 1960s and beyond.

The Sexual Offences Act 1967 that turned this into law was concerned more about regulation than rights, about how to set in place a new balance between private consent and public acceptability and order. But what is more crucial is that from the late 1960s the real initiative for change shifted, away from the liberal moral reformers to the grassroots. This is what can too easily be missed by the researcher simply focusing on the new patterns of regulation. The emergence from 1969 of second-wave feminism and from 1970 of a gay-liberation movement ultimately changed the terms of the debate. Wolfenden deliberately avoided any endorsement of homosexuality as a valid life choice. The new social movements, however, positively affirmed the merits of lesbian and gay lives, and of the necessity of self-activity in defence of those lives (Weeks, 2007). In other words, under the surface of events, a new narrative of self-activity was emerging that was profoundly important for the future, and which researchers must take into account.

The liberal moment soon passed. As the 1970s faded into the 1980s the political climate apparently became more accommodating to moral conservatism. Margaret Thatcher more than anyone embodied the change in mood as she evoked the idea of a return to 'Victorian Values'. This was declinism at its most fervent. The 1980s saw a significant closing of space for sexual minorities, especially as the onset of the HIV/AIDS epidemic seemed at first to threaten an apocalypse (Weeks, 2000: 163–76). The rhetorical bias was towards the centrality of the family, the importance of bolstering marriage and a strong support of traditional moral standards. This implied a renewed assault on homosexual openness. Section 28, introduced in 1987/8 at the high water point of Thatcherism was widely seen as an attack on the gains of the previous 20 years. It sought to ban the 'promotion' by schools and their local authority funders of homosexuality as 'a pretended family relationship'.

Conservative triumphalism seemed absolute. And to a certain extent Section 28 was successful. For almost two decades it did undoubtedly inhibit any local government initiatives to advance lesbian and gay rights. In other ways, however, and from a rather different perspective, the impact was totally counter-productive. For what above all it did was to mobilize a lesbian and gay community that had been badly battered by the HIV/AIDS crisis. It is from this date that a new energy for coming out, community building and working towards legitimization manifested itself (Weeks, 2000: 149).

More generally, when measuring rhetoric against changes on the ground, the success of moral conservatism was very limited (Durham, 1991). Above all, the economic individualism at the heart of the Thatcherite project was already gnawing away at its social conservatism. It was increasingly difficult, in an increasingly individualized culture, to affirm the importance of individual self-assertion in economic advancement, and to deny yourself the right to choose your own sexuality and way of life.

The third moment, represented by the Blair government between 1997–2005, is more ambivalent than the Thatcher one. The legitimizing story is at first less distinct, and it perhaps can best be seen as representing 'liberalism by stealth' than a frontal attack on the declinist position, with which rhetorically at least it frequently flirted. Yet these years saw perhaps the most radical legislative changes concerning sexuality, and especially homosexuality, in British history. Despite a slow start, the post-1997 Labour government, prompted in part by European court decisions, moved to equalize the law and treatment of LGBTQ people: immigration rights, equal adoption and fostering rights, an equal age of consent at 16, repeal of Section 28 of the Local Government Act, abolition of the specifically gay offence of gross indecency in the Sexual Offences Act, protection against discrimination in the provision of goods and services, employment protection, the Gender Recognition Act, and the passing of the Civil Partnership Act (Holden, 2004; Weeks, 2007). The result has been a remarkable modernization of the law.

The direction of change was unmistakeable, but its meanings remain contested. For many queer critics the underlying story was of assimilation into the heteronormative status quo. For critics of neo-liberalism, liberal reforms simply reaffirmed the arrival of new forms of governmentality, in which self-surveillance replaced external regulation. But there is here, surely, another strong narrative. What is fundamentally different today is that LGBT people have the protection of the law, with recognized rights (and attendant responsibilities), and social recognition. The unexpected success of the Civil Partnership Act – in the first nine months of 2006, 15,000 same-sex couples took advantage of the opportunity – underlines the significance of the transformation over fifty years (Weeks, 2007).

The recommendations of Wolfenden and the reforms that followed in the 1960s, emanated from the political elite. They were done for people, and by and large were in advance of public opinion. Recent reforms, on the contrary, can largely be seen as a catching up with public opinion. In the long transition from the 1960s to the 1990s Britain had moved on significantly. When the Blair reforms came public opinion was to a large extent ready. In part this was the result of the impact of the new social movements of the 1970s. More importantly, the lives of millions of people in civil society, at the grassroots had changed. It has become increasingly difficult, in a culture where every family has been touched by sexual change, to sustain the old prejudices that characterised the Wolfenden era.

The Wolfenden proposals were based on the assumption of a normative family life and a normative sexuality. The current discourse is one of equality and citizenship. This is a fundamental shift. We live now in a post-Wolfenden era. LGBTQ people have moved from the extreme margins to the mainstream in barely half a century. Homosexuality has moved from being an unfortunate condition, through transgression, to ordinariness. This is the key story that historians need to focus on.

Conclusion

In all three case studies we can find a cohering logic that helps us understand why new directions in the regulating of sexuality seemed likely. Yet at the same time there were strong countervailing possibilities that in the event proved decisive. As a result, the narratives that historians have constructed – about new patterns of control (Wolfenden), about cultural reaction (Thatcher) and about the impermeability of heteronormative structures (in the Blair period) – do not actually account for the complexity of events. The reason for this, as I have suggested, is the strength of new forms of sexual agency, as individuals in their hundreds of thousands made their own 'life experiments' (Giddens, 1992; Weeks et al., 2001) and to greater or lesser degrees muddled through to different sexual choices from those of their parents, or even their younger selves. There are plentiful historical examples of the ways in which laws designed to restrict same sex activity invariably encourage it, how efforts to push people back into the closet inevitably enhance identity and the urge to openness, how the banning of birth control and abortion make people aware of the need for them and how the fervent advocates of sexual purity are often brought low by their own reckless promiscuity.

This takes us back to that democratizing impulse that gave birth to modern sexual history in the first place. The shift in the agency of sexuality, from the forces of regulation to the grass roots, has become the most important trend in human sexual relations. We are in the midst, in my interpretation, of a profound democratization of sexuality and intimate life, which is largely the result of grass roots transformations. That in turn produces fierce and prolonged opposition in many parts of the world, so that the outcome is never pre-ordained. But the important point is that today, after a generation of scholarship and dramatic social change, we can go much further in grasping that we make our own sexual histories. Historians need to be all the time alert to these grass root shifts, to research the interstices of social life as much as the great formal patterns.

That is not, of course, the end of the story for contemporary historians. Sexuality will continue to be the focus of division and conflict. Sexuality and intimacy readily become the focus for critical value debates: about relations between men and women, the future of marriage, the family, and relationships, on the meanings and implications of sexual, gender and ethnic/racial diversity, on the needs of children, on parenting, reproductive rights and new reproductive technologies and so on. These value debates translate into political conflict and to an unprecedented degree sexual issues have moved to the centre of the political stage. So those who are engaged in attempting to understand change in historical and intimate life are inevitably doing more than simply recording the truth of the past. By their interventions they are inevitably engaging in an attempt to assert a particular set of values not only about the past but about the present too. It is at this point that we need to reaffirm the significance of our own reflexivity as researchers. Unless we are alert to our own biases and assumptions, and unless we are prepared to listen to the same in our interlocutors, those we are engaged in researching, past and present, then we will never fully understand the ways in which we make our sexual histories, in complex and ever-changing circumstances, both as historians and citizens.

References

Bauman, Z. (2003) *Liquid Love: On the Frailty of Human Bonds*. Cambridge: Polity Press.

Beck, U. and Beck-Gernsheim, E. (2002) *Individualization: Institutionalized Individualism and its Social and Political Consequences*. London: Sage.

Butler, J. (1990) *Gender Trouble: Feminism and the Subversion of Identity*. London: Routledge.

Duberman, M.B., Vicinus, M. and Chauncey, G. (eds) (1989) *Hidden from History: Reclaiming the Gay and Lesbian Past*. New York: New American Library.

Durham, M. (1991) *Sex and Politics: The Family and Morality in the Thatcher Years*. Basingstoke: Macmillan.

Foucault, M. (1979) *The History of Sexuality: Volume 1: An Introduction*. Harmondsworth: Penguin.

Gagnon, J. and Simon, W. (1974) *Sexual Conduct: The Social Sources of Human Sexuality*. London: Hutchinson.

Giddens, A. (1991) *Modernity and Self-Identity*. Cambridge: Polity Press.

Giddens, A. (1992) *The Transformation of Intimacy: Sexuality, Love and Eroticism in Modern Societies*. Cambridge: Polity Press.

Himmelfarb, G. (1995) *The De-moralization of Society: From Victorian Values to Modern Values*. London: Institute of Economic Affairs.

Holden, A. (2004) *Makers and Manners: Politics and Morality in Post-war Britain*. London: Politico.

McIntosh, M. (1981) 'The homosexual role', in K. Plummer (ed.), *The Making of the Modern Homosexual*. London: Hutchinson. pp. 30–49.

Marquand, D. (2008) *Britain since 1918: The Strange Career of British Democracy*. London: Weidenfeld and Nicolson.

Marwick, A. (1998) *The Sixties: Cultural Revolution in Britain, France, Italy, and the United States, c.1958–c.1974*. Oxford: Oxford University Press.

Moran, L. (1995) 'The homosexualization of English law', in D. Herman and C. Stychin (eds), *Legal Inversions: Lesbians, Gay Men and the Politics of Law*. Philadelphia, PA: Temple University Press, 1995. pp. 3–28.

Plummer, K. (1975) *Sexual Stigma: An Interactionist Account*. London: Routledge and Kegan Paul.

Plummer, K. (1995) *Telling Sexual Stories: Power, Change and Social Worlds*. London: Routledge.

Plummer, K. (2003) *Intimate Citizenship: Private Decisions and Public Dialogues*. Seattle, WA: University of Washington Press.

Richardson, D. (2004) 'Locating sexualities: from here to normality', *Sexualities*, 7 (4): 391–411.

Rowbotham, S. (1973) *Hidden from History: 300 Years of Women's Oppression and the Fight Against It*. London: Pluto Press.

Rowbotham, S. and Weeks, J. (1977) *Socialism and the New Life*. London: Pluto Press.

Waites, M. (2005) *The Age of Consent: Young People, Sexuality and Citizenship*. Basingstoke: Palgrave Macmillan.

Warner, M. (ed.) (1993) *Fear of a Queer Planet: Queer Politics and Social Theory*. Minneapolis, MN: University of Minnesota Press.

Warner, M. (1999) *The Trouble with Normal: Sex, Politics and the Ethics of Queer Life*. New York: The Free Press.

Weeks, J. (1977) *Coming Out: Homosexual Politics in Britain from the Nineteenth Century to the Present*. London: Quartet Books.

Weeks, J. (1985) *Sexuality and its Discontents: Meanings, Myths and Modern Sexualities*. London: Routledge and Kegan Paul.

Weeks, J. (1995) *Invented Moralities: Sexual Values in an Age of Uncertainty*. Cambridge: Polity Press.

Weeks, J. (2000) *Making Sexual History*. Cambridge: Polity Press.

Weeks, J. (2005) 'Remembering Foucault', *Journal of the History of Sexuality*, 14 (1/2): 186–201.

Weeks, J. (2007) *The World We Have Won: The Remaking of Erotic and Intimate Life*. London and New York: Routledge.

Weeks, J. (2009) *Sexuality*, 3rd edn. London: Routledge.

Weeks, J. and Porter, K. (1998) *Between the Acts. Lives of Homosexual Men 1885–1967*. London: Rivers Oram Press.

Weeks, J., Heaphy, B. and Donovan, C. (2001) *Same Sex Intimacies: Families of Choice and other Life Experiments*. London: Routledge.

THIRTEEN

Using Qualitative Methods to Complement Randomized Controlled Trials

Researching Mental Health Interventions

Anne Rogers

Introduction

The aim of this chapter is to illuminate how the use of sociologically informed qualitative studies conducted prior to and alongside randomized controlled trials (RCTs) can add to knowledge about attempts to change peoples' behaviour which, in turn, gives us a more sophisticated and complex view of social change. The chapter draws on an example from health research involving a programme of research that included an RCT and nested qualitative studies relating to self-management of mental health. I shall argue that, by marrying trial interventions with qualitative studies, it is possible to take account of some of the complexity of the existing ways in which people manage their health. This can be used as a means of both designing interventions that are genuinely more person-centred and provide a broader understanding of the kinds of artificial attempts to change peoples' behaviour that currently form the basis of health and social policy initiatives.

In the health care field RCTs are seen as the most reliable way to evaluate the effect of an intervention, for example, a new drug. In an RCT patients will be invited to take part in the trial and they may be told that they may receive the standard treatment or a new form of treatment. It will be explained that allocation to one or other form of treatment will be made at random – and thus the patient's characteristics will not influence which treatment they receive. In some trials neither the patient nor the person administering the trial will know which group the patient is in – in other words they are both 'blind' to the treatment that is given. The reason for this is to ensure that knowledge of the treatment does not influence the outcome. It is then assumed that, by comparing the outcomes of the two treatments, it will be possible to assess which treatment was more effective or whether there was no difference.

Until relatively recently quantitative evaluation methods in the form of RCTs and qualitative methods were often characterized as traditions separated by a 'stale-mate over first principles' (Pawson and Tilley, 1997). Experimentalists were seen as crude positivists peddling simplistic realist preoccupations with causal connections and measures. This view was juxtaposed against a view of social constructionists as having empathy with, and understanding the fine grained negotiated reality of, personal relationships and interactions, which they discovered through the use of qualitative methods. While the latter have been of central utility to understanding the everyday nuances of social life, including in the realm of health and illness, they have less frequently been deployed in tracking what happens in experimental situations where change is artificially introduced into a setting. However, qualitative research has been used to a limited extent to explore previously hidden agendas and this has helped to produce more critical understandings of the social processes and practices implicated in trial design. For example, in four US trials of psychiatric treatment (Applebaum et al., 1987), informed consent processes were observed and patients were interviewed immediately afterwards. Contrary to the information that they had received, one-third of the patients believed that they had been allocated on the basis of their *individual* therapeutic needs rather than at random. The authors concluded that participants might agree to trials because they believed they were getting more personalized care. Similarly, in a qualitative study by Donovan et al. (2002), participants' narratives of their experiences revealed that while most individuals were able to recall key aspects of the trial design, including aspects of randomization such as the involvement of chance, respondents held co-existing alternative views about the ways they were allocated to treatment and viewed engagement as a struggle between the rationality of the trial as presented to them and their own lay knowledge, recall and framing of the study. Those responsible for recruiting to trials had difficulty discussing and presenting alternative treatments equally. They unknowingly used terminology that participants misinterpreted. This struggle between rationality and lay knowledge in turn impeded the development of trusting relationships with clinical staff. Both of these studies show the way in which qualitative research can demonstrate that what are often taken as 'simple' procedures in RCTs – for example, randomization – are problematic, and that prevailing assumptions of trial design are shown to be mistaken when narrative accounts of the understanding of individuals are taken into account.

In the fields of health and illness, interventions are increasingly orientated not only to bio-medicine but also to areas implicating behavioural change, people's participation in their own care and the delegation of work traditionally undertaken by health professionals. The growing 'burden' of ageing, chronic illness and disability within Western democracies has prompted responses targeted at the better management of long-term conditions. Attempts to control costs and also meet demands on health care services has led to pressure to reduce the professional labour involved in the management of chronic illness. Inevitably, changes made to medical management in the form of new routinized ways of working reduce tasks to simpler components, which are more easily delegated down to other workers and to patients. The idea of self-management as a set of skills that can be learned by the patient has increasingly taken hold, not least because it provides the possibility of a continuum with professionally delegated work. In particular, self-management interventions have been aimed at maximizing the capacity of individuals to manage their own mental and physical chronic conditions through behavioural change. These have been evaluated in the main through the use of the so called gold standard method of evaluation and the preferred evaluation tool of health policymakers – the RCT.

RCTs are widely accepted and increasingly used as a rigorous method to evaluate the effects of interventions designed to change behaviour in health and social care settings. The focus in this chapter is on describing the combination of two methods (RCTs and qualitative interviews) to produce a complimentary view of social change – in this case the way in which people do or do not respond to attempts to change attitudes and behaviour to self-medication with psychotropic drugs (neuroleptics). The combination of two strands of thinking influenced the process of research described in this chapter. These were, first, the combining of RCT methods with qualitative research and, second, knowledge from the sociology of chronic illness about the experience of, and adaptation to, living life with a long-term condition.

In the past RCTs have been viewed by social scientists with some ambivalence because of their perceived tendency to objectify social reality. Additionally, complex healthcare interventions (RCTs that involve a number of parts to the intervention) involve social processes that can be difficult or impossible to explore using quantitative or trial methods alone. RCTs are good at measuring whether an intervention changed a discrete behaviour or attitude. They are poor at exploring the social and personal context of behaviour and actions, values, beliefs and community norms that are central to understanding the process and outcomes of change.

By contrast, the sociology of health and illness literature suggests that adjusting to living with a chronic condition, together with broader contextual influences, are likely to be relevant to understanding responses to self-management initiatives and therefore to the acceptability and workability of complex interventions in patients' everyday lives. Thus the key focus of understanding change was to attempt to illuminate through two qualitative studies (one undertaken *prior* to designing the interventions used in the RCT and one at the *end* of the trial) whether or not a trial designed to change attitudes and behaviour to taking neuroleptic medication could also take into account and be informed by people's existing experience of managing medication for a long-term mental health problem.

My inquisitiveness and motivation for engaging in this field of research was fuelled by an interest in tracking the nuances of policy interventions that had been designed to bring about 'behavioural' incited change. It seemed to me that while sociology, and particularly interpretive sociology, had been both resourceful and resoundingly successful in illuminating the complexities and richness of everyday life, less attention had been given to its capacity to explore the nature and processes of 'outcomes' and reactions to deliberative change introduced from external sources. Thus, I was keen to take an approach that incorporated the ability to explore the underlying patterns, order and practices of everyday life in living with a mental health problem.

As a grant holder on a clinical trial funded by the Medical Research Council, and which aimed to evaluate how psychological interventions could be designed to influence neuroleptic adherence, I had the opportunity to join a multi-disciplinary research team of health services researchers with disciplinary backgrounds in statistics, clinical psychology, psychiatry, economics and statistics. This allowed me to look again at a traditional research dichotomy and to build on a nascent interest in examining the way in which qualitative research might contribute to the design of complex interventions. In bringing together qualitative methods with a randomized controlled trial we were attempting to bring fresh insights into how trials 'work' and what happens when change is artificially introduced into the life-worlds of people diagnosed with a chronic mental health condition.

Qualitative research meets randomized controlled trials

Randomized controlled trials: measurement of change and types of interventions

As discussed above, RCTs are the most rigorous way to evaluate the effectiveness of interventions including those that are complex.

Complex interventions are made up of a number of interacting practices, organizational or behavioural elements[1] and are most commonly used where policy and practice also involves complexity (as is the case here).

> Complex interventions in health care, whether therapeutic or preventative, comprise a number of separate elements which seem essential to the proper functioning of the interventions although the 'active ingredient' of the interventions that is effective is difficult to specify. ... Complex interventions are built up from a number of components, which may act both independently and interdependently. The components usually include behaviours, parameters of behaviours (e.g. frequency, timing), and methods of organizing and delivering those behaviours (e.g. type (s) of practitioner, setting and location). (Medical Research Council, 2000: 695)

With a focus on modelling and theory building stages, complex interventions (CIs) are designed to accommodate the nuances of everyday practice.

Outcomes in the evaluation of CIs extend beyond the type of 'outcome' used in pharmaceutical trials in the sense that they deal with broader areas of health care (for example, alternative medicine, policy evaluation) and see change as a result of the interaction between intervention, process and context over time (Patterson et al., 2009). Qualitative research is central to this because it is concerned with illuminating the taken for granted nuances and meaning of everyday life. The emergence of a genre in which the use of complex interventions is becoming normative offers greater opportunities for a meeting between qualitative and traditional trial methodologies. Qualitative research is able to make a contribution to complex trial methodology at all stages (before, during and after). In this particular instance qualitative studies were used at two different points: *before* the trial a study was undertaken to explore the context of the trial (how people took medication) and to develop and refine one of the two interventions to be tested. We needed to know the meaning attributed to medication taking so as to include this in a way which was likely to engage people in more active self-management (this turned out to be the ' therapeutic intervention' described in (Box 13.2, below). The second point at which another qualitative study was undertaken was *after* the trial was completed. The aim here was to unpack the processes of implementation and change and to identity how the recipients of the trial had responded to the intervention.

Sociology of chronic conditions: research into the life worlds of patients

Qualitative research, therefore, has the power to illuminate and disrupt dominant presumptions about patients' understandings of trials, but it can also reveal micro and personal social changes which result from being diagnosed with a chronic condition (Bury, 1991). A number of sociological studies using interview and observational methods have drawn attention to the way in which self-management of chronic conditions constitutes a ubiquitous, taken for granted, intuitive and routinized set of activities embedded in the everyday life of communities (Robinson, 1971). In-depth studies (Bury, 1982, 1991) suggest that people who are diagnosed with a chronic condition are required to change and adapt to the social world by re-defining their competencies as social actors (Gerhardt, 1989), by protecting their self-identity from the threat of stigma and by developing various 'new' coping mechanisms, strategies and styles of managing (Bury, 1991). From this vantage point, change and self-management are represented by the construction of novel practices, the mobilization of resources and the maintenance of normal activities and relationships (family, friends and occupations) in the face of an altered situation.

Sociologists of health and illness have produced a rich body of knowledge about the experience of illness that champions a patient's perspective by presenting an insider's view of living life with a long-term condition. Qualitative methods have been used to study a broad range of matters confronting individuals at different points in an illness career and in a variety of contexts: for example, experiences of stigmatization, discrimination, adjustments, and introduction to new and specialized technologies. Implicit in this literature are concepts and ideas relating to both continuity and change (Rogers et al., 2007). The diagnosis of a chronic condition brings to the fore the prospect of unwanted change not only to personal meaning, but also to pre-existing relationships and material and practical matters. Unexpected dependency on others creates breaches in prior norms of social reciprocity and mutual dependency resulting in a reformulation of a person's sense of self and biography. For example, the 'disruption' caused by the pain and suffering in physical illness or extremes of emotions, perceptions and feelings in the case of mental health problems, may bring shifts from a taken for granted notion of the body and mind to an embodied consciousness which is both insecure and contingent. People have to make personal alterations in how time and tasks are managed. However, sociologists of health and illness have also illuminated how those who already live with considerable adversity encounter illness more as a continuation in personal circumstances than a profound disruption or change. In the process of 'coping', a sense of coherence is re-invented through striving to maintain ordinary activities and relationships (Corbin and Strauss, 1991). The sociology of chronic conditions has a declared affinity with interpretive sociology, symbolic interactionism, phenomenology, and grounded theory. In the mental health field this relates particularly to analysing the management of social rejection (Wright et al., 2000) which is relevant in considering the research example I use here.

Use of qualitative research to inform an RCT of adherence to neuroleptic medication

The example involves a self medication neuroleptic trial, the aim of which was to determine whether quite simple, yet different, approaches to patients taking their medication had differential outcomes in terms of attitudes towards medication, adherence to treatment and avoidance of relapse. Neuroleptics (anti-psychotics) are drugs commonly prescribed to patients diagnosed as suffering from schizophrenia to control or diminish psychotic symptoms such as hallucinations, delusions and ideas of persecution. Continuing or changing the dosage of this medication is viewed as a primary method of managing psychosis, even though the outcome literature indicates that the response to neuroleptics is highly variable. Because these drugs are used to tranquillize patients who are seen to be a danger to themselves or others, failure to take medication has a different significance to not taking medication for other conditions. Thus, patients who are prescribed this medication and who fail to submit to medical authority by adhering to a regime are usually regarded as lacking 'insight' – a factor which is viewed as integral to the illness and linked with frequent readmissions to hospital.

The sequence of the research is presented in Table 13.1 and the interventions forming the bases of the RCT are presented in Boxes 13.1 and 13.2.

Table 13.1   Sequence of the qualitative studies and the trial

1. Qualitative study of the meaning and management of everyday neuroleptic medication taking 1994–1995

Setting:	Different points in the mental health system community, hospital and outpatient settings.
Participants:	34 people on long-term neuroleptic medication (22 men, 12 women aged between 18–65) interviewed over a one-year period 1994–1995, recruited from different social class backgrounds and living arrangements.
Outcomes:	Personal accounts of the reasons for taking medication and self–regulation practices on a day-to-day basis.

2. A cluster randomized controlled trial testing two approaches: alliance against compliance 'Nuero99' 1995–1998

Setting:	28 inpatient wards at 8 hospitals in North Wales/Northwest of England with inner-city and rural catchment areas.
Participants:	228 patients meeting diagnostic (*DSM-IV*) criteria for schizophrenia or schizoaffective disorder, assessed during acute admission over a three-year period 1995–1998 were recruited and randomly assigned to the alliance, compliance and treatment as usual 'condition' groups.
Outcomes:	Attitudes toward treatment and self-reported adherence to medication measured using a quantitative scale.

3. Pre and post trial qualitative study 1996–1998

Setting:	Community locations and hospital wards.
Participants:	An initial purposive sample of 16 people drawn from the two active arms of the trial. People were interviewed soon after they entered the trial and immediately after the final assessment at the end of the trial. We interviewed an additional 10 people (to the original 16) in the second post- trial interviews.
Outcomes:	Peoples' experience of the process and outcome of the trial which could not be observed or were additional to the quantitative assessment.

The two 'active' intervention groups described in Boxes 13.1 and 13.2 were compared with a third – a treatment as usual group (or control group) where patients continued to receive care as usual.

The trial was designed to detect change between the groups using scales of adherence and attitudes. The main outcome measures were attitudes to neuroleptic medication which were assessed using a questionnaire called the Drug Attitude Inventory (DAI),[2] the Van Putten dysphoria scale and the

Morisky Compliance Scale. The DAI, the primary outcome measure, is a 30-item attitudinal scale, on which respondents rate items true or false, with scores ranging from –30 to +30. Positive or negative ratings on this scale were used to select respondents for the third study identified in Table 13.1 – the pre- and post-trial qualitative studies.

The interventions forming the bases of the trial are presented in Boxes 13.1 and 13.2.

Box 13.1   Compliance intervention

The intervention was delivered in 8–12 half-hour sessions by two psychology gradu-ates, initially in hospital and then in the patients' own homes. The delivery style of the compliance intervention designed to persuade patients to take neuroleptic medication was didactic. Patients were informed that the overall aims of the intervention were to help: (1) to understand the nature and purpose of medication; (2) to find better ways of taking medication; and (3) to cope with any side-effects that were experienced. In the first part of session 1, detailed information about neuroleptic medication was offered and a standard United Kingdom Psychiatric Pharmacy Group leaflet on neu-roleptics was used, studied and discussed with the therapist. The leaflet covers what neuroleptics are for (the names: anti-psychotic and tranquilliser are also highlighted), who is prescribed them and problems and contra-indications (for example, kidney problems, other medications, pregnancy), as well as the non-addictive nature of neuroleptics and their interaction with alcohol. The patient is asked about current side-effects. The therapist stresses that doctors try to choose medications with few side-effects but that this can be difficult. Patients were informed of the difference between the approved and chemical names of their medication, using an analogy with baked beans, which are marketed with many different brand names. The effects of decreasing and increasing doses without doctors' advice were also discussed. It was stressed that people respond differently to neuroleptic medication, both in terms of benefits and side-effects. The intervention includes providing information about medication, its indications and potential side-effects, destigmatizing mental illness and medication-taking and behavioural strategies to help patients remember when to take their drugs. The philosophy behind this approach is similar to that of some of the earlier educational interventions – the patient is given strong advice that they should take their medical treatment as prescribed.

Box 13.2   Alliance intervention

The intervention was delivered in 8–12 half-hour sessions by two psychology gradu-ates, initially in hospital and then in the patients' own homes. It used a motivational interviewing approach, and builds on previous research that has focused on clients' experiences of medication (Day and Bentall 1998; Rogers et al. 1998).

A framework within which patients can choose the account of their difficulties which they find personally most helpful, while at the same time accepting that others (for example, mental health professionals) hold different and equally valid accounts. The main focus of sessions was on establishing rapport, and introducing the idea that there are many different ways of construing psychiatric disorders. The first session allows the patients to formulate their own model of mental health problems drawing on different accounts discovered or encountered. Patients are asked to recall any explanations of symptoms which had been entertained or recalled when hearing them discussed by someone else. Questions about medication were answered and a brief history of medication-taking elicited. Later sessions focused on the importance of communicating with professionals and informing them of both positive and negative effects of medication. The aim of these sessions was to empower the patients to act as rational consumers, asserting their rights to adequate treatment and becoming monitors of their own symptoms. It includes self-monitoring of symptoms and side-effects experienced by individuals, exploring ideas and beliefs about mental health problems and medication, and learning how to negotiate with mental health professionals by means of role play. The philosophy behind this approach is that the patient should be regarded as a rational participant, and encouraged to evaluate the value of medication for him- or herself. It is assumed that this will usually result in 'appropriate adherence' (i.e. enhanced adherence) if, and only if, the medication is experienced as having positive effects, overall, for the patient.

It can be seen from the boxes that the philosophy and delivery style of the two interventions differed and the trial was used to assess which was the most persuasive (if either) in bringing about a change in attitudes to adherence to medication. The *compliance* intervention (Box 13.1) was more didactic, formulaic and prescriptive than the *alliance* intervention (Box 13.2) which provided a framework within which patients could choose a preferred account of their difficulties, while at the same time accepting that others (for example, mental health professionals) might hold a different account of reality.

It can be seen from Table 13.1 that two qualitative studies were undertaken around different elements of the design and execution of the trial. The first qualitative study included interviews with 34 patients who were taking neuroleptic drugs under ordinary circumstances and were unconnected with the trial. The second qualitative study (which included a sub-sample of 16 participants followed up longitudinally), was directly linked to the trial. It involved interviews at two points: with recruits when they had agreed to participate in the trial and later on when they left the trial (one year after having received one of the two interventions).

Meaning and management of neuroleptic medication study

In this first qualitative study (Rogers et al., 1998) our research team wanted to gain an understanding of the ordinary situations of patients taking medication on an everyday basis. We wanted to use data from elicited accounts to describe the context within which the interventions forming part of the trial would be introduced. We also wanted to use the meaning, experience and existing practices of people taking neuroleptic drugs to help develop one of the interventions – a person centred intervention (the alliance intervention). As discussed above, change is commonly measured in trials against 'treatment as usual', which refers to normal services currently being provided to an individual (in this case medication prescribed in psychiatric services) and the existing activities of social actors in context are usually ignored. This study of the experience of suffering from and responding to a long standing mental health problem (undertaken prior to the trial with people who were not involved in the trial) generated rich descriptions of the strategies that lay people had already adopted in managing medication and that arose out of daily living and social context. Thus we considered that this was likely to provide a priori insights into how patterns of social interaction, and the demands of everyday life, influenced people's choices and actions.

We used a set of topics to explore patients' reasons for taking neuroleptics and the ways in which they self-regulated their medication on a daily basis. The data suggested that the main utility of taking neuroleptic medication was not only to control specific symptoms but, in a more generalized way, to gain a semblance of personal control in managing everyday life. This came at the cost of side-effects which at times equalized or outweighed the positive gains of neuroleptic medication. Everyday medication practices were influenced by social expectations of the need to control the behaviour of people with mental health problems living in the community and the fear of coercion and potential sanctions from mental health professionals. Thus medication-taking was linked to a wider context of the meaning and symbolic significance that schizophrenia holds in contemporary society, which in turn has consequences for patients in their everyday lives. Self-regulatory action and the notion of choosing when and how to take medication tended to be less evident than one would expect in medication-taking for other conditions. The difference lay in the presumed threat of external social control posed as a result of being a person diagnosed with a label of schizophrenia. There was nonetheless a number of ways in which people varied their medication-taking from the way in which it was prescribed. For example, through a process of trial and error, some people adjusted the medication depending on the perceived effect it had on their mood and actions.

The findings from this first qualitative study were used to inform the design of the trial to test two alternative interventions. From the data it was possible to identify how the routine everyday practices of patients were important in the self-regulation of medication. We explored the interaction between lay perspectives and situational constraints and used this to devise a patient centred training package (intervention). This included examples of the reality of patients' constructs, such as stressing patient control, the variations in how people took medication over the course of the week (for example, some individuals in the study reported delaying taking medication if a leisure activity such as going to the pub was involved) and the social context of medication-taking (Box 13.2). The intention was to devise an intervention for use in the trial which mirrored, or at least was sensitive to, the way in which people actually experienced the taking of neuroleptic medication and which might, therefore, be more likely to bring about change.

Pre- and post-trial qualitative study

The aim of the second qualitative study was different to the first in so far as we set out to explore the influences that might not be captured using the quantitative measures in the trial alone (Rogers et al., 2003). In this study, a purposive sample was drawn from the two active arms of the trial (alliance and compliance) according to positive or negative ratings on the key outcome measure – an attitudinal scale.[3] Qualitative interviews were conducted at the point of 'exiting' the trial, usually immediately after the final assessment (see Box 13.3)

We explored how the intervention worked by studying the meaning and processes behind the outcome measures for both the compliance and alliance interventions at the individual level. We wanted to make a contextualized link, using patient narratives, with the more de-contextualized outcomes of the quantitative measures based on standard scales.

Box 13.3 Post-trial interviews

Patients were interviewed in their own home and a semi-structured interview schedule was used to guide interviews with the patients. Topics guiding the interview centered on experiences relating to the intervention and also to mental health problems over the last year. Respondents were also asked about changes in attitudes to medication, medication practice, interaction with professionals, key events and aspirations in their lives over the last year and the impact these may have had on their mental health problem. Aspects of grounded theorizing and constant comparison were used as a means of identifying and developing themes iteratively from ongoing data collection and analysis and the thematic analysis. The themes from the two groups were summarised and compared to ascertain similarities and differences and focused on how the activities and delivery of the educational compliance and therapeutic alliance 'therapy' were understood and experienced.

Disrupting presumptions about change: patients' recall of the trial interventions

In the set of interviews carried out at the end of the trial, we asked people who had been subjected to the compliance and alliance interventions to recall the information and training they had received as a result of being assigned to one of these two groups. Participants' recollections of the trial were both general and positive (for example, 'I think it's a good thing') *but* there was a lack of recall about the details of the intervention to which they had been assigned. This may have been because of the length of time (one year) between the intervention and final assessment, which seemed to impact on the recall of fine detail such as the ward environment and circumstances within which the intervention was delivered and experienced by patients. Patient accounts referred to their state of mind and circumstances following admission to acute psychiatric hospital wards – drowsiness, confusion and disruption associated with entering the hospital environment meant that recall may have been curtailed. However, a global response was usually followed by a more detailed account in which judgements were based on comparisons with past experiences of routine management and prior contact with mental health services. Respondents alluded to being provided with more information and personal attention than they had experienced previously.

The interviews also successfully tapped into the salience of specific situations within which the interventions were administered. Most of the respondents we spoke to had come to expect little engagement or challenge from routine contact with mental health staff about the provision of information. Additionally, they valued *any* form of communication with someone interested in eliciting subjective viewpoints about medication management. Exceptionally, descriptions about the interventions coalesced with the designated principles of the interventions. However, generally, patient accounts of their experience challenged the assumption that there was a clear demarcation between the delivery of the intervention (the training element) and the follow-up assessments undertaken subsequently. The fact that the interventions were not based on drugs or other technologies, but were predicated on 'talk' might have made patients less able to discriminate between the 'talk' of the training sessions and the 'talk' entailed in filling in face to face assessment questionnaires.

Measuring outcomes and perceptions of change

The trial was designed to discriminate clearly between the two interventions. However, it was clear that, for some, the more didactic compliance condition implicitly triggered a response which was expected and associated with the therapeutic alliance intervention. The latter was designed to motivate individuals to think more expansively and act with greater autonomy and assertiveness. This was evident in a number of the responses given by people who had been in the compliance training group. The language people used to describe medication change implied the personal ownership of medication-taking (for example, referring to 'my' medication). The interviews produced evidence of the efforts to self-regulate the taking of medication through a process, over several months, of unilateral and strategic reduction of medication. These self-possessed attitudes to medication-taking were indirectly linked to opportunities that patients had for exercising control over other key aspects of their lives, such as domestic and working conditions. Moreover, this type of narrative was markedly absent from the qualitative accounts of medication and lifestyle management of those *not* having received either of the two interventions where external rationales for medication-taking were prioritized. Thus, narrative analysis pointed to a range of fine grained processes that would otherwise not have been revealed had the trial been used on its own. It also suggested the 'mechanisms' via which positive and negative results occurred (Rogers et al., 1998). Initial analysis of the main quantitative trial showed little in the way of statistically significant differences between the outcomes for the two groups of patients receiving either the alliance or compliance intervention but there was evidence of a difference in outcomes between these and the control group. Therapeutic alliance scores also predicted attitudes towards drugs and hospital admissions at follow-up. Data from the trial also showed that the quality of relationships with clinicians during acute admission appeared to be an important determinant of patients' attitudes toward treatment and adherence to medication (Day et al., 2005).

Discussion

So in summary what did the two qualitative studies reveal about change? Together they helped reveal aspects of the experience of taking neuroleptic medication that could feed into designing an intervention that reflected context and people's everyday experiences, feelings and thoughts about medication *and* illuminated aspects of process and outcome of the trial which would otherwise have remained latent. The findings of the qualitative components linked with, and extended to, an understanding of the positive outcomes of efforts to improve attitudes to medication by illuminating how aspects of personal control and management can change as a result of participation in a trial. Following receipt of the interventions, patients talked in a way which suggested a change in their sense of agency and self-confidence in making choices about their medication-taking, and a willingness to formulate and express critical and more informed opinions to mental health professionals. The qualitative results also showed that the understanding of the process and purpose of the trial differed for the participants taking part, and differed from the professional researchers' starting assumptions. The design of the two interventions incorporated different philosophies and, as researchers, we expected to establish which intervention would be shown to be 'best'. However, patients did not readily discriminate between the content, form and function of the different interventions. Instead, they indicated a continuum of experience. For patients, the reported benefits of participating in the trial were the common experience of increased levels of communication and opportunity for self-expression.

Involvement and learning from this research extends to the wider policy environment in health and illness, where patient initiated care is being actively promoted through complex interventions such as this. Within health services research there is an increasing focus placed on patient response and involvement in complex interventions and thus an important aspect of this is an understanding of the conditions necessary to accommodate and embed complex interventions into the routine elements of the health and illness 'work' undertaken by patients. While self-care interventions and patient initiated care are increasingly promoted as effective strategies for improving quality of life and health outcomes for individuals with long-term health conditions, evaluations tend to centre on presumptions of staged models of change and psychological behavioural outcomes (for example, self-efficacy), or attitudes to successful management derived from 'positive' psychology. They do not necessarily consider prior management strategies, relationships and context. Using the example above I have tried to show how responses to formal self-management can be extended to incorporate other aspects of people's lives. These also illuminate some of the ways in which policy initiatives are mediated and translated from a macro to a micro level.

Notes

For further details of the research design and results please refer to the following articles Day et al. (2005) and Rogers et al. (1998, 2003).

1. Unlike simple interventions, for example which test one generation of a drug against another.
2. The DAI is predictive of compliance and has been found to correlate with other measures of neuroleptic adherence (Day et al., 2005).
3. Patient attitudes to drugs were measured prior to the intervention, immediately after completing the intervention and approximately 1 year after completion of the intervention

References

Applebaum, P.S., Roth, L.H., Lidz, C.W., Benson P. and Winslade, W. (1987) 'False hopes and best data: consent to research and the therapeutic misconception', Hastings Center Report.

Bury, M. (1982) 'Chronic illness as biographical disruption', *Sociology of Health & Illness*, 4 (2): 167–82.

Bury, M. (1991) 'The sociology of chronic illness: a review of research and prospects', *Sociology of Health & Illness*, 13 (4): 451–68.

Corbin. J.M. and Strauss, A. (1991) 'A nursing model for chronic illness based upon the trajectory framework', *Scholarly Inquiry for Nursing Practice*, 5 (3): 155–74.

Day, J.C., Bentall, R.P., Roberts, C., et al. (2005) 'Attitudes toward antipsychotic medication – the impact of clinical variables and relationships with health professionals', *Archives of General Psychiatry*, 62 (7): 717–24.

Donovan, J., Mills, N., Smith, M., Brindle, L., Jacoby, A., Peters, T., et al. (2002) 'Improving design and conduct of randomised trials by embedding them in qualitative research: ProtecT (prostate testing for cancer and treatment) study', *BMJ*, 7367 (325): 766–70.

Gerhardt, U. (1989) *Ideas About Illness: An Intellectual and Political History of Medical Sociology.* New York: New York University Press.

Medical Research Council (2000) *A Framework for Development and Evaluation of Complex Interventions to Improve Health.* London: Medical Research Council.

Paterson, C., Baarts, C., Laila, L. and Verhoef, M. (2009) 'Evaluating complex health interventions: a critical analysis of the "outcomes" concept', *BMC Complementary and Alternative Medicine* 2009, 9: 18.

Pawson, R. and Tilley, N. (1997) *Realistic Evaluation.* London: Sage.

Robinson, D. (1971) *The Process of Becoming Ill.* London: Routledge and Kegan Paul.

Rogers, A., Day, J.C., Williams, B., et al. (1998) 'The meaning and management of neuroleptic medication: a study of patients with a diagnosis of schizophrenia', *Social Science & Medicine*, 47 (9), 1313–23.

Rogers, A., Day, J., Randall, F., et al. (2003) 'Patients' understanding and participation in a trial designed to improve the management of anti-psychotic medication – a qualitative study', *Social Psychiatry and Psychiatric Epidemiology*, 38 (12): 720–7.

Rogers, A., Lee, V. and Kennedy, A. (2007) 'Continuity and change? Exploring reactions to a guided self-management intervention in a randomized controlled trial for IBS with reference to prior experience of managing a long term condition', *Trials*, 8 (6). Available at: http://www.trialsjournal.com/content/8/1/6

Wright, E., Gronfein, W. and Owens, T. (2000) 'Deinstitutionalization, social rejection, and the self esteem of former mental patients', *Journal of Health and Social Behaviour*, 41 (March): 68–90.

FOURTEEN

Exploring the Narrative Potential of Cohort Data and Event History Analysis

Jane Elliott

Introduction

Narratives and numbers are usually thought of as belonging to two quite separate cultures. While researchers are often interested in narratives or numbers there are relatively few who are comfortable with analysing both. However, the aim of this chapter is to suggest that some research designs that collect quantitative data, and some forms of quantitative analysis, do have an implicit narrative structure. Indeed, by paying greater attention to the narratives embedded within longitudinal data researchers can overcome some of the criticisms typically made of quantitative analysis, namely that it runs the risk of focusing on the relationships between variables at the expense of understanding the social and historical context within which the data has been collected (Blumer, 1956).

Given that the argument that structured surveys collecting quantitative data can yield analyses that have narrative features is a somewhat unusual one, it is important to offer a definition of narrative before proceeding any further. The simplest is perhaps that a narrative is a story with a beginning, a middle and an end, and in this chapter the focus will be on temporality as a key feature of narrative form. In an influential paper, Labov and Waletzky state that narrative provides a 'method of recapitulating past experiences by matching a verbal sequence of clauses to the sequence of events that actually occurred' (1967: 12). As will be discussed in more detail below, if this placing of events in a sequence is understood as a defining feature of narrative then there are clear parallels with research designs that collect information on the timing of salient events in individuals' lives.

The first section of this chapter will focus on the narrative properties and narrative potential of longitudinal cohort studies, which collect detailed information from a large, representative sample of individuals through their lives. The second section focuses more specifically on a group of statistical techniques known as event history analysis, which is particularly appropriate for the analysis of life history data of the kind collected in the British cohort studies, as well as in other large-scale longitudinal studies such as the British Household Panel Survey and the Panel Study of Income Dynamics in the USA. This section of the chapter discusses two examples of research that have used data from the British Birth Cohort Studies both to understand factors that affect the timing and sequence of events in the lives of groups of cohort members and to understand social change by making comparisons between cohorts. The final part of the chapter will discuss some of the limitations of the types of narrative that can be produced using event history analysis and will briefly describe a qualitative interview study that is currently being carried out with a sub-sample of members of the 1958 cohort study and which will provide further resources for analysis using more narrative and case-based approaches.

Many of the themes discussed in this chapter resonate with the approaches to research discussed by Nazroo (Chapter 15, in this volume). In particular the research examples provided here underline the need to theorize and study period influences in order to understand changes between age cohorts.

Cohort studies: a narrative research design?

Britain is unique in the world in having three national birth cohort studies that have followed individuals, born in a specific week of the year, through childhood and adolescence and into adult life. Further details of these specific studies are provided in Box 14.1. The focus here, however, is on the extent to which these types of studies can be understood to have a narrative research design. A key feature of longitudinal cohort studies is that by maintaining contact with a large sample of individuals and re-surveying them at regular intervals it is possible to build up a rich and detailed record about the life of each member of the study, a type of quantitative life story. For example, the collection of datasets which currently constitute the 1958 cohort study include over 15,000 variables (or pieces of information) about each cohort member. In addition, the fact that these studies are designed as multipurpose resources for use by a wide range of researchers with different disciplinary backgrounds means that the data collected provide an insight into many different aspects of each cohort member's life including employment, housing, relationships, fertility, social participation, and physical and mental health.

Box 14.1   British Birth Cohort Studies

The 1946 National Survey of Health and Development was initially set up to understand more about the use made of obstetric, medical and midwifery services and
their role in preventing premature and infant death in the years before the establishment of the National Health Service in 1948. The initial survey covered over 16,500
births and was promoted by the Royal College of Obstetricians and the Population
Investigation Committee, and funded by the Nuffield Foundation. A follow-up survey
was designed to examine the health and development of a representative sample
(5362) of this population, which has now been studied 22 times, most recently at
age 60 years. Since the early 1960s the study has been funded by the Medical
Research Council, and the focus has been on collecting information about individuals'
health and well being.

Twelve years after the inception of the 1946 cohort study, a second study was
launched to examine the social and obstetric factors associated with stillbirth
and death in early infancy. Information was gathered about almost 17,500
babies. Initially the 1958 British Birth Cohort Study was not planned as a longitudinal study, but subsequently the National Children's Bureau was commis-
sioned by the Central Advisory Council for Education (The Plowden Committee)
to retrace the cohort at age 7 and monitor their educational, physical and social
development. Further surveys took place when the children were aged 11 and
16. The cohort was followed up in young adult life at age 23, in 1981, and
cohort members have been re-contacted on four subsequent occasions, at ages
33, 42, and 46 years, with the most recent survey at age 50 in 2008/9. In
contrast to the MRC 1946 National Survey of Health and Development, the
1958 cohort has developed into a multipurpose study and the information collected on individuals' lives has been analysed by researchers from across a
number of different disciplines including epidemiology, economics, demography,
education, sociology and psychology.

A further 12 years after the 1958 cohort study, the 1970 British Birth Cohort Study
(BCS70) began as the British Births Survey, when data was collected about the births
and social circumstances of over 17,000 babies born in England, Scotland, Wales
and Northern Ireland. Data was collected using a questionnaire completed by the
midwife who had been present at the birth and, information was extracted from
clinical records. The study aimed to examine the social and biological characteristics
of the mother in relation to neonatal morbidity, and to compare the results with those
of the 1958 National Child Development Study. The cohort was surveyed during
childhood at ages 5, 10 and 16 years. Initially it was not clear that funding was
available to follow the cohort into adult life, but contact was maintained and a
postal survey of over 9000 cohort members took place when the cohort was aged
26 in 1996. Both the 1958 and the 1970 cohort studies are now managed by the
Centre for Longitudinal Studies at the Institute of Education, London. This has made
it possible to ensure that comparable data is collected from both cohorts, and further
surveys of the 1970 cohort have now been carried out at ages 30, 34 and 38
years.

The Millennium Cohort Study (MCS) represents the fourth British Birth Cohort Study and has already collected detailed information about children and their parents at ages 9 months, 3, 5 and 7 years, with the next data collection planned at age 11.

It is beyond the scope of this chapter to provide a summary of the wide body of research based on information collected in these studies. However, there are a number of brief descriptive accounts of the history of the 1946, 1958 and 1970 cohort studies included in existing publications which present some of the main results of the studies (Elliott and Shepherd, 2006; Ferri et al., 2003; Power and Elliott, 2006; Wadsworth, 1991).

The majority of information collected in all of the British cohort studies is quantitative, and the researchers who use these resources adopt almost exclusively a quantitative analytic approach, for example, estimating multivariate and longitudinal models in order to understand more about the ways that different variables are associated with each other. However, as is discussed below, the detailed and longitudinal nature of the studies, and the fact that cohort members are explicitly located in a specific historical context, means that the studies have a number of narrative properties.

First, the collection of detailed life history data in each of the surveys of adult cohort members could be understood as similar to asking each respondent to provide a standardized narrative about their life. Adapting Labov and Waletzky's definition, researchers aim to match a sequence of variables to the sequence of events that actually occurred in individuals' lives. This also means that it is possible to conduct event history analysis that focuses on the timing and sequencing of events within individuals' lives, as will be discussed in more detail below. Second, longitudinal research based on data from a group of individuals all born at the same time has considerable potential for allowing researchers to frame the results of their analyses within a specific historical and cultural context (Elliott, 2005, 2008). Third, when cross-cohort comparisons are made, there is potential for examining how changes in society might shape the way that individuals experience particular events or difficulties in their lives. For example, it is plausible that the negative impact of parental divorce on children may have been reduced as its incidence increased during the 1960s and 1970s. Research by Margaret Ely et al. (1999), which examined the association between having divorced parents and educational outcomes for the three cohorts of British children born in 1946, 1958 and 1970, was able directly to test this *reduced effect hypothesis* and found little evidence that the impact of divorce has diminished for more recent cohorts of children. Furthermore, by comparing the results of event history analysis carried out on different cohorts of individuals it is possible to construct a narrative of social change. The next section describes the type of life history data that is collected in the cohort studies and provides a brief introduction to event history analysis.

Event history data and event history analysis

A quantitative life history or 'event history' is a systematic record of *when* particular events have occurred for an individual. In this context an event corresponds to any qualitative change occurring at a specific point in time. The birth of a child, the date of starting a job and the date of getting married could all therefore be described as events within an individual's biography. Elder defines a life history as 'a lifetime chronology of events and activities that typically and variably combine data records on education, work life, family, and residence' (1992: 1122). The cohort studies, described above, have focused on five key domains: employment, relationships, fertility, housing and qualifications. Information has been collected on the month and year in which key events or transitions have occurred for individuals. In theory, almost any event could be recorded in an event history. However, because event history data are mostly collected retrospectively, there is a tendency to focus on culturally significant events whose dates are likely to be remembered easily by respondents. In many cases therefore an event marks a change in status – from unemployment to employment, from living alone to cohabiting or from being single to being married, for example. In addition, in order to allow for quantitative analysis, the collection of the event history data must be standardized. In other words the choices of events to be recorded are made by the team of researchers conducting the study, and they have to be the same for all respondents.

The retrospective and chronological properties of event history data suggest the possibilities of analyses with a narrative structure. Indeed Labov and Waletzky's definition of narrative, quoted at the beginning of the chapter, with its emphasis on a 'sequence of events', may be almost directly applied to the event history data collected within the cohort studies. By collecting this type of data, social scientists are in some senses requesting that individuals provide a formalized or standardized narrative about various aspects of their lives. However, what is clearly missing from these formalized narrative records is the perspective of the individual respondent on the events that are recorded. An event history can record the date at which someone changes job or moves house but cannot reveal what the experience of that job change or house move *means* for the individual concerned (Elliott, 2005). This point will be returned to below.

Event history modelling

In many respects event history models resemble more widely understood regression models, such as ordinary least squares regression and logistic regression (where the dependent variable is dichotomous). The emphasis is on determining the relative importance of a number of independent variables or 'covariates' for 'predicting' the outcome of a dependent variable. However, event history modelling differs from standard multiple regression in that the dependent variable is not a measurement of an individual attribute (such as income or qualifications), rather it is derived from the occurrence or non-occurrence of an event and the timing of that event. For example, if age at first co-resident partnership is the dependent variable of interest, the model is able to take account of whether the individual has ever entered a co-resident partnership and also the age at which this first occurred. Other examples of data amenable to event history modelling include the duration from redundancy to becoming re-employed, the duration from release from prison to re-arrest, the duration until the birth of a first child and the duration from cohabitation to marriage. Figure 14.1 provides an illustration of the form of these types of data. Standard regression techniques are not appropriate in the case of event history data, which focus on the timing of events. There are two reasons for this. First is the problem of what duration value to assign to individuals or cases that have not experienced the event of interest by the time the data is collected – these are termed 'censored cases'. In Figure 14.1 cases 4 and 6 are examples of censored cases. A second problem, once a sample is observed longitudinally, is the potential for the values of some of the independent covariates to change. The issue then arises as to how to incorporate these 'time-varying' covariates into the analysis.

These two problems have led to the development of modelling techniques specifically intended for the analysis of event history data. In essence, these techniques allow us to evaluate the relative importance of a number of different variables, or covariates, for predicting the chance, or 'hazard,' of an event occurring. The hazard is a key concept in event history analysis, and is sometimes also referred to as the 'hazard rate' or 'hazard function'. It can be interpreted as the probability that an event will occur at a particular point in time, given that the individual is at risk at that time. The group of individuals who are at risk of the event occurring is therefore usually referred to as the 'risk set'.

Although event history data clearly has narrative properties, in that it records information about a whole sequence of events for each individual in the sample, it could be argued that event history analysis, with its focus on predicting a single transition, is less narrative in character than sequence analysis? (Abbott, 1992). However, if the covariates within the model include information about circumstances and events that occurred earlier in each individual's life then the event history model can be seen to move closer to a narrative structure with the dependent variable or transition providing the resolution of the narrative.

Approaches to event history modelling

One of the most common approaches within the social sciences is to use Cox's (1972) proportional hazard models or 'Cox Regression'. This provides

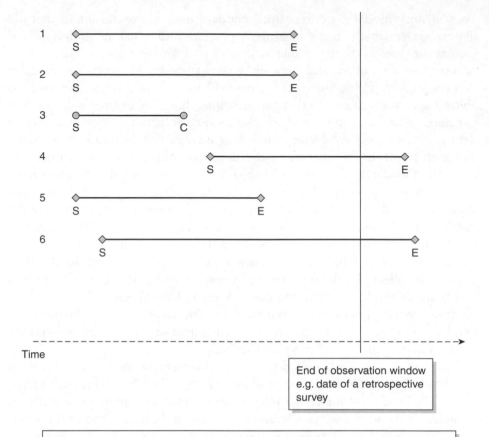

Figure 14.1   Diagrammatic representation of event history data

a method for modelling time-to-event data and allows the inclusion of predictor variables (covariates). For example, a model could be estimated for duration of marriage based on religiosity, age at marriage and level of education. Cox Regression will handle the censored cases correctly, and will provide estimated coefficients for each of the covariates, allowing an assessment of the *relative importance of multiple covariates and of any interactions between them*. Cox regression is known as a continuous time approach because it is assumed that the time that an event occurs is measured accurately.

Although the Cox model is one of the most popular and widely applied approaches it has two main disadvantages. First, it is relatively inflexible in terms of modelling duration dependence, that is, for specifying exactly how the hazard may change over time; and, second, it makes it difficult to incorporate time-varying covariates. For this reason, many researchers with an explicit interest in how the probability of an event occurring changes over time prefer to use a 'discrete time' approach. This requires that the data have a specific format. A separate unit of analysis is created for each discrete time interval. Each record therefore corresponds to a person-month or person-year (depending on the accuracy with which events have been recorded). Once the data has been reconfigured in this way, the unit of analysis is transferred from being the individual case to being a person-year (or person-month), and logistic regression models can be estimated for the dichotomous dependent variable (whether the event occurred or not) using maximum likelihood methods (Allison, 1984). This approach facilitates inclusion of explanatory variables that vary over time because each year or month that an individual is at risk is treated as a separate observation. It is also easy to include more than one measure of duration. Discrete time methods are therefore thought to offer a preferable approach when the researcher wants to include several time-varying covariates. A good example is provided by Heaton and Call's (1995) research on the timing of divorce. This analytic approach is also frequently used by those looking at recidivism and wanting to understand the timing and correlates of repeat offending (Baumer, 1997; Benda, 2003; Gainey et al., 2000).

A major limitation with the simple approach to the analysis of discretized longitudinal data described above, is it does not take account of the fact that the unit of analysis is the person-year and therefore the individual cases are not fully independent (as they should be for a logistic regression), but are clustered at the level of the person. For example, in an analysis modelling duration of marriage, an individual who had been married for 10 years would contribute 10 observations or person-years to the dataset. In analytic terms, because these observations are treated as independent the narrative properties of the data are lost. In a well-crafted story we expect one event to lead to the next in the sequence, but when data is discretized and analysed using logistic regression it is as if the chain of events is broken into separate pieces. Another way to understand this problem is to consider that there may be additional variables that have a strong association with the dependent variable but which are not included in the model. The existence of such 'unobserved heterogeneity' will mean that models are misspecified and in particular spurious duration effects may be detected. The use of more sophisticated models including fixed or random effects models can overcome these problems and allow the researcher to produce more robust estimates of duration dependence. The use of these models therefore enables the separate pieces of the chain to be linked and re-introduces a narrative character to the analysis. It is beyond the scope of this chapter to discuss these models, but for a more detailed introductory treatment, see Elliott (2002), Davies (1994) and Box-Steffensmeier and Jones (2004).

Analysis as narrative

The individual event histories that are provided in longitudinal studies, such as the British Birth Cohort Studies, have something of a narrative character because they consist of a sequence of events. However, it could also be argued that, at the level of the individual case, these very structured records are more similar to chronicles than narratives because they merely record that events took place rather than attaching any meaning to those events or suggesting how different events may be interrelated (Elliott, 2005; White, 1987). Once a researcher uses these data to estimate a model, however, the model itself could be said to take on some of the characteristics of a narrative. For example, the estimation of a model allows the researcher to ascertain what the most important factors in determining the outcome are. In the same way that a successful narrative or story involves the selection of relevant events or episodes, by estimating an event history model a researcher is able to evaluate the relative importance of a number of different variables or covariates, and these are then selected for inclusion in the model. In the next section two examples of research using event history data from the British Birth Cohort Studies are discussed in order to exemplify the types of research narratives that can be constructed using this type of data.

An excellent example of the way in which event history data collected in cohort studies can be used to provide the foundation for a narrative about social change is provided in a paper by Joshi and Hinde (1993). This focuses on women's employment behaviour and specifically on the time that women spend out of the labour market following the birth of a child. Cox proportional hazard models are used by the authors to model the duration between the birth of a child and a mother returning to work. In other words the dependent variable is the time between a birth and the next entry to paid work. Joshi and Hinde use data from the 1946 birth cohort study, known as the National Survey of Health and Development, which provides information on mothers' employment before and after bearing a child in 1946 and on a second generation of mothers – the cohort members themselves, who mainly had their children during the 1970s. Their aim is to look for changes in the patterns and determinants of mothers' employment over the 30 years since the Second World War. Joshi and Hinde report aggregate changes in women's employment patterns following the birth of a child and find that the break in employment after childbearing had at least halved between the years around 1950 and those around 1970. In addition Joshi and Hinde examine the factors that are most strongly associated with a return to employment and once again uncover profound differences between the two generations of women. Whereas for the generation giving birth in 1946, husbands' occupation and region were strongly associated with employment behaviour, for the generation born in 1946 their own education and the age at which they had their first child became much more important predictors of the speed of returning to work. As Joshi and Hinde state, 'Whereas just after the war, where a woman lived and what her husband did were among the most important determinants of her employment behaviour, by the 1970s they were not. Multivariate analysis of individual data from two cohorts confirms a picture of class and regional class convergence in women's employment behaviour' (1993: 218). Joshi and Hinde's paper therefore documents a dramatic change in individual women's life stories in a single generation, from including a long spell out of the labour market caring for children to much more continuous attachment to the labour market with only a relatively short break for childbearing.

A more recent example of the way that retrospective event history data can be used to construct narratives at both the individual and societal level is provided in a paper by Steele et al. (2007), which focuses on women's partnership formation and fertility. Steele et al. use data from both the 1970 and 1958 cohort studies and focus specifically on women who had formed at least one non-marital, co-residential (that is, cohabiting) union, by their 30th birthday. This paper is similar to the paper by Joshi and Hinde in that it uses the event history data to model the trajectories of women at an individual level but it also makes comparisons between the two cohorts. In this case a kind of meta-narrative or 'secondary narrative' is constructed about social change with respect to marital and cohabiting behaviour. For example, Steele et al. find that by age 30 the majority of women in both cohorts (approximately 56 per cent) had had just one co-residential partnership (either marital or cohabiting). However, focusing on the differences between marriage and cohabitation the authors find that whereas for the 1958 cohort only 39 per cent of women in the cohort had cohabited by age 30, this figure had risen to 73 per cent for women in the 1970 cohort. In other words more women in the 1958 cohort made the transition directly into marriage, whereas for the 1970 cohort there was sharp decline in direct marriage so that many women cohabited first, and indeed may never marry. Steele et al. also report that the duration of cohabiting unions changed so that the median was 25 months for the 1958 cohort, but 34 months for the 1970 cohort. They suggest that this is largely due to the lower rate of marriage for the more recent cohort.

Steele et al. find, therefore, that for women born in 1958 a typical trajectory was to move directly into marriage, while those who cohabited tended to live in these *de facto* unions for a relatively short time before moving into marriage. Furthermore women born in 1958 who became pregnant while cohabiting had a relatively high probability of marrying before the baby was born. In contrast, many more of the women in the 1970 cohort chose to cohabit rather than to marry, and while some cohabited first and then legalized their union it was not unusual for women to continue cohabiting over relatively long durations. Steele et al. also report that for the 1970 cohort of women, a conception during cohabitation was less likely to be immediately followed by marriage. Thus, in comparison with the 1958 cohort, for the 1970 cohort there were many more births to cohabiting, rather than married, mothers. The detailed event history data collected in the 1958 and 1970 cohort studies therefore made it possible for Steele et al. to analyse data at an individual level and to provide a detailed description of typical relationship and fertility trajectories for women. Furthermore, by making comparisons between the cohorts they are able to describe social change and to document the fact that for many couples cohabitation seems to replace marriage rather than simply being a precursor to marriage.

Individual cases in longitudinal research

A number of authors have argued that a major shortcoming of quantitative approaches to research is that they do not pay enough attention to individual cases (Abbott, 1992; Bertaux, 1981; Farran, 1990; Pugh, 1990). At the simplest level, quantitative analysis can be understood to obscure the individual because it aims to provide a summary description of the characteristics of a group or aggregation of people rather than focusing on the unique qualities of each case in the sample. For researchers trained in more qualitative approaches to research, reports on quantitative or statistical analyses can appear to neglect the vibrant and unique individuals who have provided the information on which analyses are based. This can also present a problem for those reading research reports based on statistical aggregations. Lay audiences and those wanting to use research to inform policy can find descriptive and multivariate statistical analyses rather dry and impenetrable. For this reason, some sociologists have experimented with providing case studies of individuals to illustrate or augment the results of their research. Bynner et al. (1997) provide descriptions of trajectories followed by a number of 'typical' individuals from the 1958 and 1970 British cohort studies with basic skills difficulties to complement their statistical descriptions of the longitudinal data. For example they provide the following 'thumbnail' sketch of 'Daryl':

> Daryl has very low literacy and numeracy skills. He left full-time education at 16 with 7 exam passes. He has spent over 20 years in full-time employment. He has never been promoted or been on a training course. He works more than 40 hours every week. From 1985 he has been employed as a Dyers Operative and earns £170 per week. Daryl has never married and still lives with his parents in Yorkshire. He reports to be very satisfied with his life. (Bynner et al., 1997: Appendix 4)

In addition to using case studies to illustrate the results of more conventional quantitative analysis, some authors have argued for constructing case studies, based on longitudinal quantitative data, as a *precursor* to quantitative analysis. For example, Singer et al. (1998) use data from the Wisconsin Longitudinal Study of individuals graduating from high schools in 1957, in their research on the varying pathways leading to four different mental health outcomes for middle-aged women. Specifically they aim to understand the processes that lead to women being resilient, healthy, vulnerable or depressed in mid-life. The Wisconsin Longitudinal study consists of three waves of data collection so that data is available on the same group of respondents for 1957, 1975 and 1992. The most innovative aspect of the approach, proposed by Singer et al., is that the analysis begins by using three waves of survey data to piece together individual life stories. Thus conventional quantitative data, coded in terms of responses on a wide variety of variables, is used to construct a narrative biographical story for a small sub-sample of individuals. As Singer et al. explain, they aim to do something with survey data that is rarely attempted, that is, to 'generate all of the information that exists about a single respondent and weave it together as a narrative account. We assert that the crafting of whole life stories is fundamental to comprehending the processes we seek to understand' (Singer et al., 1998: 19).

The detailed information collected on cohort members through their lives, coupled with the potential for understanding analysis of individual trajectories within specific historical and social contexts, goes some way to allowing researchers to construct narrative biographies or case histories of individuals within these studies. However, cohort members have, to date, been given limited, if any, opportunity to tell their own life stories. The types of narratives deriving from event history analysis or from constructing individual case histories described above are very different from the narratives told by the Fortune family (see Thomson, Chapter 4, this volume). The narratives that can be constructed from existing quantitative data are therefore likely to reflect the interests of the researchers who have contributed to the content and design of the studies, rather than the perspectives of the people whose lives have been charted in detail over the past five decades.

It should be made clear that, by using quantitative data in this way, it is the researcher who remains the narrator of each biography. The individuals whose lives are being presented do not have a voice. The meanings that they might attach to specific experiences or circumstances during their lives are obscured from view. It is the researcher who selects what appears to be most interesting or significant from the wealth of material that is available and who crafts the life stories which can never fully represent the reflexive individuals, who have their own stories to tell.

In the future there will be new opportunities for linking qualitative narrative material with quantitative longitudinal data from the cohort studies.

A qualitative sub-study of 180 cohort members is being carried out as part of the data collection from members of the 1958 cohort at age 50 in 2008/9. Following the structured quantitative interview, which represents the main data collection instrument for the age 50 sweep of the study, a sub-sample of cohort members are being invited to take part in an in-depth biographical interview. This qualitative interview is semi-structured and uses a topic guide rather than a standardized set of questions. The biographical interview covers six main areas: neighbourhood and belonging; social participation and leisure activities; social networks; the cohort member's own life story; identity; and, finally, the experience of being part of a longitudinal cohort study. Each interview is being digitally recorded and transcribed and will be archived so that transcripts are available for secondary analysis, either as qualitative data or in tandem with the rich quantitative data that already exists about members of the cohort. By eliciting the cohort member's own life story as part of the interview it is possible to examine the extent to which the event history information collected in the structured interviews mirrors the salient events recounted by individuals as they provide a narrative about their life.

In summary, the detailed longitudinal quantitative data available from the cohort studies already allows for approaches to analysis, such as event history modelling, that have a narrative dimension. In addition information can be extracted in order to construct narrative case studies or biographies, either as illustrative material in research reports or in order to generate hypotheses that can be tested using quantitative analyses. However, all of these 'narrative' approaches lack the perspective of the cohort members themselves. The collection of qualitative life histories from a sub-sample of the 1958 cohort will therefore provide a rather different kind of narrative resource that can be analysed alongside and in tandem with the existing quantitative data.

Further information about the British Birth Cohort Studies

The 1958, 1970 and Millennium Cohort studies, which are introduced in this chapter, are all managed by the Centre for Longitudinal Studies at the Institute of Education. Further details of the studies, including information about the content of the surveys, information about workshops and seminars, and an extensive bibliography of publications based on the studies, can be found on the CLS website at: www.cls.ioe.ac.uk

The data from these three cohort studies is available free of charge for analysis by bona fide researchers. Data is distributed by the Economic and Social Data Service (longitudinal) at the UK Data Archive. Further details are provided on the website (http://www.esds.ac.uk/longitudinal/)

The 1946 British Birth Cohort Study, known as the MRC National Survey of Health and Development (NSHD) is managed by the MRC Unit for

Lifelong Health and Ageing (LHA). Further details of the study including publications, key findings and collaborations, can be found on the LHA website (http://www.nshd.mrc.ac.uk/)

References

Abbott, A. (1992) 'What do cases do?', in C. Ragin and H.S. Becker (eds), *What Is a Case?* Cambridge: Cambridge University Press. pp. 53–82.

Allison, P.D. (1984) *Event History Analysis: Regression for Longitudinal Event Data.* Beverly Hills, CA: Sage.

Baumer, E. (1997) 'Levels and predictors of recidivism: the Malta experience', *Criminology*, 35: 601–28.

Benda, B.B. (2003) 'Survival analysis of criminal recidivism of boot camp graduates using elements from general and developmental explanatory models', *International Journal of Offender Therapy and Comparative Criminology*, 47 (1): 89–110.

Bertaux, D. (1981) 'From the life-history approach to the transformation of sociological practice', in D. Bertaux (ed.), *Biography and Society*. Beverly Hills, CA: Sage. pp. 29–46.

Blumer, H. (1956) 'Sociological analysis and the variable', *American Sociological Review*, 21: 683–90.

Box-Steffensmeier, J. and Jones, B. (2004) *Event History Modeling*. Cambridge: Cambridge University Press.

Bynner, J., Ferri, E. and Shepherd, P. (1997) *Twenty-something in the 1990s: Getting on, Getting by, Getting nowhere*. Aldershot: Ashgate.

Cox, D.R. (1972) 'Regression models and life tables', *Journal of the Royal Statistical Society*, B (34): 187–202.

Davies, R.B. (1994) 'From cross-sectional to longitudinal analysis', in A. Dale and R.B. Davies (eds), *Analysing Social and Political Change: A Casebook of Methods*. London: Sage Publications. pp. 20–40.

Elder, G.H. (1992) 'Life course', in B.E.F. and M.L. Borgatta (eds), *Encyclopedia of Sociology*, Vol. 3. New York: Macmillan. pp. 1120–30.

Elliott, B.J. (2002) 'The value of event history techniques for understanding social processes: modeling women's employment behaviour after motherhood', *International Journal of Social Research Methodology*, 5 (2): 107–32.

Elliott, J. (2005) *Using Narrative in Social Research: Qualitative and Quantitative Approaches*. London: Sage.

Elliott, J. (2008) 'The narrative potential of the British Birth Cohort Studies', *Qualitative Research*, 8 (3): 411–21.

Elliott, J. and Shepherd, P. (2006) 'Cohort Profile: 1970 British Birth Cohort (BCS70)', *International Journal of Epidemiology*, 35 (4): 836–43.

Ely, M., Richards, M.P.M., Wadsworth, M.E.J. and Elliott, B.J. (1999) 'Secular changes in the association of parental divorce and children's educational attainment – evidence from three British Birth Cohorts', *Journal of Social Policy*, 28 (3): 437–55.

Farran, D. (1990) 'Seeking Susan: producing statistical information on young people's leisure', in L. Stanley (ed.), *Feminist Praxis*. London: Routledge. pp. 91–102.

Ferri, E., Bynner, J. and Wadsworth, M.E.J. (2003) *Changing Britain, Changing Lives: Three Generations at the Turn of the Century*. London: Institute of Education.

Gainey, R.R., Payne, B.K. and O'Toole, M. (2000) 'The relationship between time in jail, time on electronic monitoring, and recidivism: an event history analysis of a jail-based program', *Justice Quarterly*, 17 (4): 733–52.

Heaton, T.B. and Call, V.R.A. (1995) 'Modeling family dynamics with event history techniques', *Journal of Marriage and the Family,* 57: 1078–90.

Joshi, H. and Hinde, P.R.A. (1993) 'Employment after childbearing in post-war Britain: cohort study evidence on contrasts within and across generations', *European Sociological Review*, 9 (3): 203–27.

Labov, W. and Waletzky, J. (1967) 'Narrative analysis: oral versions of personal experience', in J. Helm (ed.), *Essays on the Verbal and Visual Arts*. Seattle, WA: University of Washington Press. pp. 12–44.

Power, C. and Elliott, J. (2006) 'Cohort profile: 1958 British Birth Cohort (National Child Development Study)', *International Journal of Epidemiology*, 35 (1): 34–41.

Pugh, A. (1990) 'My statistics and feminism – a true story', in L. Stanley (ed.), *Feminist Praxis*. London: Routledge. pp. 91–102.

Singer, B., Ryff, C.D., Carr, D. and Magee, W.J. (1998) 'Linking life histories and mental health: a person-centred strategy', *Sociological Methodology*, 28: 1–51.

Steele, F., Kallis, C., Joshi, H. and Goldstein, H. (2007) *Changes in the Relationship between the Outcomes of Cohabiting Partnerships and Fertility Among Young British Women: Evidence from the 1958 and 1970 Birth Cohort Studies*. London: Centre for Longitudinal Studies.

Wadsworth, M.E.J. (1991) *The Imprint of Time: Childhood, History and Adult Life*. Oxford: Oxford University Press.

White, H. (1987) *The Content of the Form*. Baltimore, MD: Johns Hopkins.

FIFTEEN

Using Longitudinal Survey Data

Researching Changing Health in Later Life

James Nazroo

Introduction

In this chapter I set out to illustrate the value of longitudinal quantitative survey data, most particularly in terms of understanding causal relationships and where such data help resolve issues of time-order. However, I am also concerned to provide necessary cautions when using or interpreting such data. The chapter is not a statistical treatise, it does not contain an account of statistical theory, or methods for handling longitudinal data (such as multi-level modelling, or structural equation modelling); rather the focus is on a discussion of the broad principles guiding the use of such data, together with the strengths and limitations of particular approaches. To illustrate the methodological points being made, examples will be drawn from recent research examining ageing processes and the patterning of health in later life using data from the English Longitudinal Study of Ageing (Banks et al., 2006, 2008; Marmot et al., 2003). The next section provides a brief account of why this subject is both important and one that can be usefully studied with longitudinal survey data. But first a brief discussion of cause.

Questions of causality lie behind much of what we do in social science research. There are many ways of both conceptualizing and addressing issues of cause – this chapter focuses on those approaches that make use of quantitative individual-level data collected over time – but, regardless, we seek answers in relation to cause in order to inform approaches to solving problems. How problems are defined is, of course, another matter, but if our understanding of underlying causal processes is mistaken, the solutions we develop for the problems we have identified will fail to have the desired outcome. For example, if we consider the poorer behavioural outcomes of children in single-parent families to be a consequence of the trauma of separation and the absence of a father-figure, our approach to solving the problem will be very different than if we consider the crucial cause to be the socio-economic inequality faced by single-parent families (McMunn et al., 2001). Given the personal and political investment in many of the issues social scientists study, investigating causal processes is perhaps the most important thing we do. This is not to say that statistical models using quantitative data can pin down the answer to causal questions, but that with appropriate design they can be used to shed important light on theorized relationships. And it is here that longitudinal studies have strong advantages, which are discussed below.

Ageing societies

The challenges posed by the ageing of populations across the world as a consequence of increasing life expectancy are a dominant feature of policy discussion and academic research. Concern focuses on the need to minimize the implications of potentially growing numbers of dependent and frail people post-working life, and to maximize the social and economic contributions provided by healthy and active older citizens (European Union, 2002). While such discussions are generally premised on an inevitable and unchanging relationship between age and ill health, they also acknowledge the possibility that the ageing of our populations is transforming our societies and individual experiences of growing older. But these changes are happening in neither a predictable nor uniform way. If we are to develop policies that allow us to maximize the opportunities of ageing societies, then we need to understand the causal processes that lead to negative and positive outcomes at older ages. However, framing causal questions in the face of such significant and complex changes, let alone marshalling the data to address them, is not straightforward.

An obvious example is the concern that ill health among older people will create an unsustainable demand on society as the numbers of older people increase. If the main driver of the increase in numbers of older people is improvements in health leading to greater life-expectancy, and if there is marked heterogeneity (or inequality) across individuals in the relationship between age and health, then the relationship is not deterministic. Instead, the association is more complex and if we can determine those factors that lead to better, or worse, health in later life we can influence, and improve, outcomes. So, one important concern is with understanding, at an individual level, the factors that might be leading to changes in health at older age; that is, providing answers to questions concerned with causation. Which factors lead to good health at older ages, and which explain socio-economic inequalities in health at older ages, are important causal questions. The answers to them have the potential to influence social, health and economic policy in positive ways. To answer such questions the use of longitudinal, or panel, survey data comes into its own, because it enables the identification of time order – whether the proposed cause was present before the proposed effect. The remainder of this chapter will be concerned with exploring the strengths and limitations of approaches to understanding cause using panel survey data, taking the example of health in later life to illustrate the points being made.

Causal reasoning and longitudinal data in quantitative research

If X is the cause of Y, we have in mind that change in X produces a change in Y, and not merely that a change in X is followed by or associated with a change in Y. (Blalock, 1961: 9)

This quote encapsulates the principles underlying quantitative approaches to identifying and understanding causal relationships. Key elements of the quote are the need to identify change, the temporal order of change, and that change in the outcome is more than simply associated with change in the proposed cause. This line of reasoning clearly has its roots in the approaches of experimental natural sciences, where changes in the outcome can be assessed following the experimental manipulation of one element of the environment (the hypothesized cause). In the social world such experimental manipulation of hypothesized causes is, of course, only occasionally possible and, although many argue that such experimental manipulation is a 'gold standard' in attempts to understand causal processes in the social sciences (Oakley, 2004, 2005), it is neither possible, nor likely to be informative, to have such manipulation done in a way that is unconnected to other elements of the environment – social systems are 'open' and interactive (Lawson, 1997) even when we can conduct randomized trials of interventions. So, while experiments might help us understand causal processes within a specific 'closed' context, generalizing beyond that context will be far from straightforward. Understanding contextual specificities and influences is an important part of dealing with causal questions in the social sciences, meaning that we often rely on non-experimental observational data to draw causal conclusions (Cook and Campbell, 1979).

For example, among older people a simple examination shows a strong correlation between marital status and risk of future mortality. Those who are widowed have markedly lower survival rates than those who are currently married (Nazroo et al., 2008a). The causal processes that this association represents are undoubtedly worth examining, but marital status is not something that can be manipulated to examine the effects of a change in marital status and whether and why a change might relate to future mortality risk. It is also not something that is randomly distributed in the older population. Indeed, the non-random distribution of marital status and of changes in marital status indicate how the causal relationships we are likely to be interested in are complex, unfold over time, may be poorly represented by measurement at discrete time points, and involve the interaction of interconnected dimensions of social lives and relationships.

One solution is to ignore, or bypass, some of this complexity and to examine the impact of different marital circumstances (X in the notation used by Blalock in the quote above) on mortality (Y) among people who are similar on other relevant characteristics. To do this one would typically conduct a multivariate analysis that takes into account the other characteristics that are correlated with marital status and mortality (age, gender, smoking, socio-economic position and so on), thereby accounting for differences in the characteristics of people with different marital statuses and allowing for a direct comparison between different categories of marital status. This is an attempt to generate the equivalent of a controlled experiment; by adjusting for all relevant factors we simulate a random allocation into categories of the causal factor of interest (marital status). The difficulties such an approach generates are apparent, key factors may be missed out of, or poorly measured in, the model, and assumptions of causal direction (from X to Y rather than Y to X) may be mistaken, all resulting in other important causal processes unaccounted for (known as the problem of endogeneity). Nevertheless, this is a common and useful way of tackling the possibility that characteristics that lead to location in relation to the causal factor of interest (being married, for example) might be driving the association between causal factor – marital status – and outcome – mortality risk. In the case of marital status and mortality risk, such an analysis reveals that once some key factors are taken into account (age, gender, socio-economic position, health behaviours) those who are married have the lowest risk of mortality, while those who are separated or divorced, or who have never been married, have the highest risk, with those who are widowed somewhere between, rather than having the highest risk (Nazroo et al., 2008a).

Although this type of approach helps us get closer to an accurate estimation of the correlation between cause and effect (X and Y in Blalock's notation), it provides only a very preliminary examination of causal process, because it is restricted to examining the relationship between initial conditions (marital status) and future event (mortality). Ideally we would like to examine this further in two ways. First, by seeing whether a change in initial conditions (marital status) leads to a change in the risk of the future event to take us a bit further in specifying the causal process. Second, by examining why a characteristic such as marital status might increase risk of an outcome such as mortality. For example, one might hypothesize that becoming a widow increases risk of future mortality because of a consequent increase in loneliness, isolation and lack of social support. Figure 15.1 shows how such a causal model might be empirically elaborated in relation to another health

a. Simple correlation

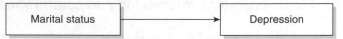

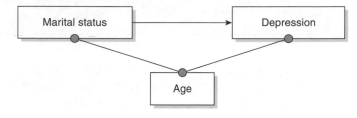

b. Controls for other correlated and causally prior variables (e.g. age)

c. An elaborated change model

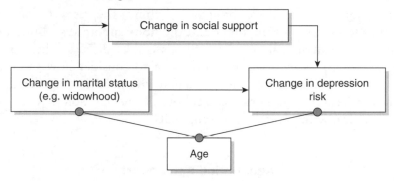

Figure 15.1   Elaboration of a variable based causal model: marital status and depression (arrows indicate the causal paths of interest)

outcome, depression (depression has been substituted for mortality so that issues of time order can be discussed – depression might proceed change in marital status, mortality clearly cannot).

Using the approach implied by Figure 15.1, we can examine how far a change in marital status leads to a change in risk of depression, after controlling for correlating factors not involved in the hypothesized causal connection and examine how far the relationship operates through a third, intervening, factor (social support in this example). The significance of time order, and the consequent need to use longitudinal methods, is immediately apparent. The change in marital status must precede these changes in depression, the change in social support must follow the change in marital status but precede the change in depression, and age should, conceptually at least, precede both marital status and depression. In more abstract terms, this is often described in terms of independent (marital status), intervening (social support), dependent (depression) and control (age) variables (see Box 15.1)

Box 15.1 Independent, intervening and control variables

Building on the earlier standardised notation: changes in X (independent variable, or causal factor) precede changes in Y (dependent variable, or outcome), while control variables precede both X and Y, and changes in intervening variables follow changes in X, but precede changes in Y.

Collecting data on the unit of investigation repeatedly over time – as longitudinal studies are designed to do – provides the resource to examine such interrelated changes and to begin to identify causal relationships. Hence the emphasis on the need for longitudinal survey data (Berthoud and Burton, 2008).

Having outlined the basic principles behind the use of longitudinal approaches to deal with time order and the non-random distribution of relevant factors in causal analyses, the methods will be discussed in more detail shortly. But first it is worth a short diversion to consider how the focus on change and time in studies of ageing leads to the need to consider the close relationships between age, period and cohort, a consideration that emphasizes the need to deal with context and complexity.

Age, period and cohort

If we observe that those aged in their 80s have poorer health than those aged in their 70s at a given point in time (so a cross-sectional observation), the temptation is to understand this as an age effect. However, there are alternative explanations that need to be considered. An obvious problem is that such an observation covers survivors from particular cohorts, so the differences observed may well be moderated by a survival effect (that those with the poorest health died before they reached their 80s) and in fact reflect larger differences in health between the cohorts (for an illustration of this see McMunn et al., 2009). This also points to the need to consider age groups in terms of cohorts. It may well be that differences in health between those in their 80s and those in their 70s are a consequences of the different histories they have lived through – so called cohort effects. So, improvements in childhood nutrition and public health might well lead to better health among cohorts who are born more recently (leading to both increased longevity and reductions in illness and disability), or the exposure of a particular cohort to a particular hazard, perhaps at a particularly vulnerable age, might lead to poorer health than other cohorts. And cross-cutting these age and cohort explanations are period effects where, for example, a particular policy might impact differentially on the health of different age groups.

Within cross-sectional data, then, age and cohort effects cannot be separated (different cohorts are different ages), and period effects cannot be directly tested. And, although, longitudinal data allow us to examine all three of age, period and cohort, the interdependence of these three dimensions makes it impossible empirically to separate out all three of their effects, even with repeated observations over time (Sacker and Wiggins, 2002). So:

- Observed changes over time for a specific age cohort, such as rising disability rates, could be a consequence of both period and age effects, which change together (they are co-linear), and may be cohort specific.
- When changes over time are observed for more than one age cohort:

  o Age and cohort effects can be separated, for example the disability rates of different cohorts at the same age, but this will be at different points in time so there will remain the possibility of a period effect;
  o Period and cohort effects can be separated, for example disability rates of different cohorts at the same point in time, but there will remain the possibility of an age effect; and
  o Age and period effects can be separated, for example the disability rates of different age groups at a particular point in time, compared with their disability rates at the same age but at different points in time, but, as described above, observed differences may be cohort effects.

As Menard (1991: 7) pointed out, age, cohort and period are each a linear function of the other. Cohort (year of birth) = period (year of observation) – age (years since birth), so they cannot be separated empirically in a straightforward manner.

Nevertheless, in many cases it is worth considering how such a separation might be achieved. The question of the relationship between age and disability and how this relates to cohort, or period, influences is undoubtedly worth pursuing, but is a question that can only be pursued if analyses are theoretically informed. For example, a period effect can be more convincingly tested if there is a clear hypothesis regarding what it is about the period that may be important (for example, a flu epidemic), and even better if the hypothesis can be directly tested in the analysis and contrasted with other hypothesized explanations. But none of this can be done without access to longitudinal data covering the different cohorts, periods and ages of interest, hence the importance of such data.

Tackling endogeneity: value and limits of panel data

As described above, in the social sciences causal relationships are typically examined with quantitative observational (rather than experimental) data using multivariate models, such as linear regression. In such models, the relationship between the outcome (dependent variable) and cause (independent variable) is modelled in a way that allows us to assess the size of the effect of the independent variable on the dependent variable, the causal effect that is of paramount interest, and to estimate the degree of error in the model. However, if our measurement of the independent variable is correlated with the error in the model our estimate of the size of its effect will be wrong. This can occur for a number of reasons: key factors correlated with the independent and dependent variables have not been included in the model (for example, control variables such as age), the independent variable itself has been poorly measured, and the causal relationship between the 'dependent' and 'independent' variables runs in both directions. For a slightly more detailed, but still easy to follow description, read Box 15.2.

Box 15.2   Tackling endogeneity

Using the earlier standardised notion, where Y represents the dependent variable and X the independent variable, regression models typically take the form:

$Y = \beta_0 + \beta_1 X + \varepsilon_1$

Here:

- β_0 is described as the intercept, the value of Y when X is zero;
- ε_1 is the error in the model; and
- β_1 is the size of the effect of X on Y for each unit change in X.

So, in a causal model β_1 is the parameter we are trying to estimate. However, the error term, ε_1, is also important, because in observational studies endogenous effects will arise if X is correlated with the error term. This can occur for three principle reasons:

- if the error term contains omitted variables that are correlated with X and Y;
- if X contains significant measurement error, so its true value is not observed accurately enough; and
- if causality runs in both directions, from Y to X as well as X to Y – so-called reverse causation.

In such circumstances X can be described as endogenous, and β_1 as not identified (that is, it cannot be estimated with accuracy).

This brief description of the nature of endogeneity shows that the key value of panel data for causal analysis is the increased ability it gives us to deal with reverse causation. If we observe a relationship between a change in the hypothesized independent variable (say marital status) and a later change in the dependent variable (say depression), we can be confident that any causal relationship we may be observing flows in the hypothesized direction. This does

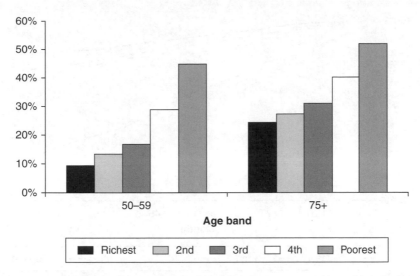

Figure 15.2   Observed cross-sectional relationship between wealth and health for men: percent with fair or poor health by wealth quintile
Source: English Longitudinal Study of Ageing, Wave 1, 2002–3.

not deal with the other potential sources of endogeneity (omitted variables and measurement error), but does solve a common and very important problem.

For example, take the relationship between socio-economic position and health. This has been repeatedly documented and the direction of causation (does poor health lead to lower socio-economic position or vice versa) has been debated. Although the weight of evidence strongly suggests socio-economic position leads to better health rather than vice versa, the debate is less well clarified in the case of older populations, where it has been documented that poor health is a driver of retirement, part-time working and personal expenditure on health and social care (Smith, 2004). All of this is *prima facia* evidence that poor health may lead to deteriorating economic position.

Figure 15.2 shows the consistency of the relationship between health and wealth that is observed in cross-section for two older age groups of men. For both groups the richest fifth of the population have a considerably lower risk of fair or poor health than the poorest fifth, and the relationship is graded across wealth categories. Given comments above, an obvious way to examine causal direction is to observe changes in wealth and health over time. Figure 15.3 does this by examining survival rates for women over a 70-month period by wealth quintile at the start of the follow-up period (so subsequent changes in wealth are ignored). It shows a clear and graded relationship between wealth and survival rates, with those who were in the richest fifth at the start of the period having the highest survival rates and those in the poorest fifth having the lowest survival rates. Effectively this is a model of change in the dependent variable (Y = mortality) by the value of the independent variable

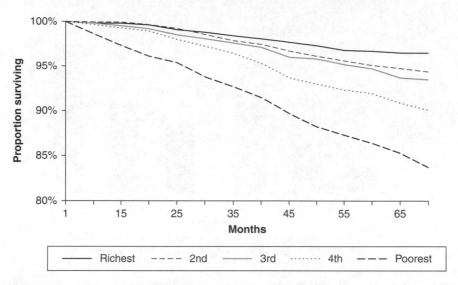

Figure 15.3   Survival rates by wealth quintile, women aged 50 or older
Source: English Longitudinal Study of Ageing, Waves 1 to 3, 2002–7.

(X = wealth) at time 1. And the model can be made more effective by including control variables that reflect items which may contaminate the wealth–health relationship, thereby reducing the omitted variables problem. A model including gender, marital status, level of physical activity, smoking behaviour, alcohol consumption, level of education and occupational class, retains a strong relationship between wealth at time 1 and mortality over the following 70 months, with the poorest fifth of the population having a more than 50 per cent greater risk of dying compared with the richest fifth (Nazroo et al., 2008a).

Such an analysis does not, however, deal with the possible influence of health on wealth prior to time 1, and how this might lead to an observed correlation between wealth and mortality. So, as Figure 15.4 shows, a form of reverse causation may remain in the model – earlier poor health may lead to both a deterioration in wealth position and an increased risk of mortality.

One solution to this is to control for health at time 1 in the model (so to remove the association shown in Figure 15.2). This will produce a parsimonious estimate of the effect of wealth on health, because it removes any prior effect of wealth on health, as well as any prior effect of health on wealth. An alternative is to stratify the analysis by level of health at time 1, or only analyse those who are, as far as can be estimated, healthy at time 1. This latter strategy is shown in Figure 15.5 for those aged 75 or older. Although mortality risks are much lower for the healthy than they are on average, the relative size of the difference in risk between the rich and the poor remains.

Even better than accounting for health at time 1, however, would be to observe changes in wealth that are unrelated to health (so called exogenous changes) and

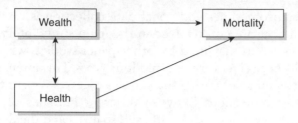

Figure 15.4   Simple wealth, health and mortality model

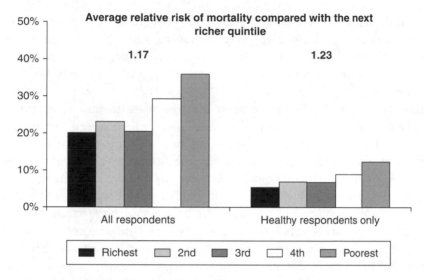

Figure 15.5   Mortality rates by wealth quintile, healthy respondents compared with all respondents, those aged 75 or older
Source: English Longitudinal Study of Ageing, Waves 1 to 3, 2002–7.

subsequent change in health, or change in mortality risk. However, when exploring changes in values of both independent and dependent variables establishing the relative time order of changes becomes, once again, problematic.

Time order, periodicity of data collections and anticipated events

Panel surveys are labour intensive, expensive and time consuming for participants. For example, the English Longitudinal Study of Ageing collects data from around 11,000 respondents every two years. The core of the data collection involves a face to face interview, lasting on average 70 minutes, followed by a short self-completion questionnaire. And in approximately two-thirds of cases two people within the household are interviewed. In addition, every second interview is followed (so every four years) by a lengthy assessment with a nurse, and sometimes additional data collection is carried out in the year the respondents are not involved in the main study interview. This type of rhythm is similar to that used by other panel studies, with frequency of contact typically between every one and four years. This intensity reflects the desire to collect a range of data – the causal processes we are typically interested in involve connections between different domains of peoples' lives (economic, social, psychological, health, and so on) – and the desire to observe changes as closely as possible to when they occur, so that time order can be established. However, even with a yearly contact clearly identifying the timing of change, and the time order of related changes, is problematic. And establishing accurate timing is particularly difficult when we are concerned with less discrete and more subjective changes, such as a change in health, mood or attitude, rather than a house move, marriage, or job change. This then means we are less confident that accurate timing has allowed reverse causation to be ruled out.

Take, for example, the relationship between health and retirement – if they are found to be associated, does poor health lead to retirement or vice versa? In theory, longitudinal data collection that charts both change in health and change in economic activity can identify when changes occur, and whether a change in health precedes or follows the change in economic activity. In practice, however, it is quite possible that both a change in health and a change in economic activity will have occurred in the period between interviews – the life events literature suggests that changes in health occur within a matter of weeks following an event (Brown and Harris, 1989). And it is equally possible that in many cases a change in employment status will follow reasonably soon after a health event. Of course, we can collect additional data to help establish time order (when did the job change and the heart attack occur), but in some cases it is harder to be precise with timing (for example, a change in level of depression), although careful data collection can help (for example, collecting information on reason for job change). Perhaps more importantly, a careful test of a theoretically grounded hypothesis can be convincing even if time order cannot be empirically established.

One such example is the relationship between retirement and depression. Without spelling out the background literature in detail (see, for example, Gall et al., 1997), it seems reasonable to assume that those who are, or become, depressed are more likely to retire from work. It also seems possible that those who retire might become depressed, perhaps because of the difficulty of accommodating to role changes. Connecting these observations with discussions of socio-economic inequality and agency, perhaps those who choose to retire in positive economic circumstances will have a reduction in their level of depression, while those who retire in negative economic circumstances will have an increase in their level of depression. Assuming that both retirement and the change in mood occur between waves of data collection, we cannot confidently determine which event occurs first, but a carefully designed analysis might help us draw conclusions on causality. An analysis of change in mood (mood at time 2 controlled for mood at time 1) predicted by change in employment and controlled for factors such as age, gender and physical health, shows that those who retire are no more likely to have a change in mood than those who remain working. However, if retirement is differentiated between those who do and do not retire wealthy, the model suggests that those who retire wealthy have an improvement in mood compared with those who remain working, while those who retire not wealthy have a decline in mood (see Nazroo et al. [2008b] for full details of this analysis). Such evidence is more strongly suggestive of a retirement effect on mood than a mood effect on retirement. While the former relationship might well be differentiated by wealth, we have no reason to hypothesize that the impact of depression on retirement would be differentiated by wealth (would a decline in mood be more likely to lead to retirement for the not-wealthy than the wealthy?).

The difficulty of capturing the relative timing of events, because of the periodicity of waves of data collection, is only part of the problem. Those we study both react to and anticipate events. To extend the example in relation to job change and depression, those working in a sector of the economy hit during an economic recession may, prior to the event of unemployment, experience a decline in employment conditions and/or anticipate being made redundant. In such cases, mood change might occur before unemployment, even though the (unmeasured) changes leading up to unemployment might be conceptualized as part of the unemployment event, so the broader 'unemployment event' may have led to the mood change. One partial solution to this problem is to make use of innovative questions on 'expectations' that have been included in some panel studies. Such questions ask respondents to anticipate the likelihood of future events (for example, whether they will still be working in ten years time), and changes in such expectations might usefully be included in causal analysis. The work by Dwyer (2002) and Dwyer and Mitchell (1999) on the relationship between retirement and health is an interesting example of this.

The promise of instrumental variables

Returning to earlier discussions of the difficulty of determining causation in non-experimental research and of endogeneity, we can see that even high quality panel studies remain troubled with problems of measurement error, omitted variables and establishing causal direction. Careful design of data collection – ensuring as far as possible that relevant variables are collected, concepts are well measured and the timing of events is accurately identified – together with theoretically informed analytical models, helps to minimize these problems, often to a convincing level. But where uncertainties remain, the classic, but difficult to implement, strategy of using instrumental variables might help. The technique is fundamental to econometrics and has been well described elsewhere (Bascle, 2008; McFadden, 1999). In brief, when attempting to model a causal relationship this technique involves substituting the independent variable with an estimate of its value, separately modelled using instrumental variables that are theorized to have no causal relationship with the dependent variable. Effectively this produces a modelled value of the independent variable that is uncontaminated by reverse causation, measurement error, or other factors that correlate with the independent and dependent variable, thereby dealing with issues of endogeniety. Read through Box 15.3 for a more detailed, but still straightforward, explanation of this.

Box 15.3   Instrumental variables

When attempting to identify the size of the causal effect of X on Y the instrumental variable approach involves identifying one or more additional variables, represented by Z, which are correlated with X, but only with Y through the effect of X on Y. We can then use Z to estimate X and use this estimated variable to determine the impact of X on Y with endogenous effects (resulting from reverse causation, omitted variables and measurement error) removed. Effectively we determine three models (although the notation in model 2 is different from that in 1 and 3, the principle is the same):

1. $Y = \beta_0 + \beta_1 X + \varepsilon_1$
2. $\hat{X} = \alpha_0 + \alpha_1 Z + \xi_1$
3. $Y = \beta_0 + \beta_1 \hat{X} + \varepsilon_1$

Findings from model 3, compared with model 1, indicate the degree to which the estimates in model 1 are contaminated by endogenous effects

---

It is immediately apparent that the success of this approach depends on two issues. The first is that the instrumental variables (Z) are correlated with the independent variable (Y) only through their relationship with the independent variable (X). Such an assertion is clearly theory dependent, making the identification of potential instrumental variables (those that are correlated with the cause, but not with the outcome) difficult and often controversial. Second, the identification of an instrumental variable is made all the more difficult when we consider that it needs to be a powerful predictor of the independent variable, so that the estimated value of the independent variable is accurate. If this is not the case the modelling will be imprecise and underestimate the impact of the independent variable on the dependent variable.

A brief example will help to illustrate the method.[1] As described earlier, a central issue when examining the relationship between ageing and health is whether retirement negatively affects health, or whether any observed relationship is in fact a consequence of those who are ill being more likely to retire. A straightforward model using panel data suggests that retirement leads to a greater risk of chest pain (indicative of ischaemic heart disease), after taking into account a range of other relevant factors, including prior health (Nazroo et al., 2008b). Given difficulties in determining the relative timing of retirement and the first experience of chest pain, for the reasons described in the previous section, this model was developed further using the instrumental variable approach. For this it was hypothesized that a measure of pension accrual – the level at which pension wealth increases during employment – would be an adequate instrumental variable. Theoretically, it is proposed that the timing of retirement (the independent variable) will, in large part, be driven by the level of reward from continuing to work. In this case it is proposed that the incentive to retire (for older people) increases as the accumulation of pension entitlements decreases, for example, when contributions to a pension reach their allowed maximum and continuing to work no longer increases pension wealth. So the first condition of an instrumental variable is met, it is correlated with the hypothesized causal variable (retirement). And, it is proposed that the accrual of pension wealth is not causally related to the person's health, instead being driven by her/his employment and investment opportunities and choices, so the second condition, that it is not causally linked to the hypothesized dependent variable (health), would also be met. Using pension accrual as an instrumental variable when modelling the impact of retirement on the development of chest pain results in the negative effect of retirement on health – health becoming worse after retirement – being reduced to a very small and not statistically significant size (Nazroo et al., 2008b). This leads to the conclusion that the identified relationship between retirement and chest pain was endogenous, so retirement does not lead to an increased risk of chest pain. Of course it could be argued that the instrumental variable was inadequate, again highlighting the importance of theoretically robust approaches to modelling survey data.

Conclusion

This chapter has been concerned with illustrating the value, and limitations, of longitudinal survey data. The emphasis has been on the issue of causality, and how longitudinal data increase our ability to identify time order and likely direction of causality in circumstances where we might plausibly argue that causal relationships could flow in either direction (for example, in the retirement and health relationship). While longitudinal data can often resolve time order issues, it was shown that this is not always the case – sometime changes of interest in both dependent and independent variables happen between waves of data collection leaving timing uncertain, and often changes in one dimension might be a consequence of actors anticipating events in another dimension (for example, an anticipated redundancy leading to depression before unemployment occurs). And time order is only one dimension of the broader endogeneity problem, where measurement error and omitting important factors may be just as significant. In all cases the value of longitudinal data is enhanced by the use of carefully theorized and well specified empirical models, even when techniques designed to deal with endogenity, such as instrumental variables, are incorporated into the analysis. It is also enhanced by the use of a range of approaches to causal modelling, and the marshalling of alternative forms of data, such as biographical narratives.

Although the emphasis has been on issues related to establishing time order and related causal questions, longitudinal data are also an important resource when tackling questions around age, cohort and period. In cross-sectional data it is impossible to do more than identify relevant issues. The example of differences in health across age groups illustrates this well; such differences could simply be a consequence of ageing, but they could also be a consequence of differences in cohort specific exposures (for example, differences in the quality of childhood nutrition for the compared cohorts), or of particular period effects, which cannot be examined in cross-sectional data. Longitudinal data do not solve this problem, just as they cannot always resolve time order issues, because the collinearities between age, period and cohort means we cannot separate all three dimensions even over time. However, comparing changes in the experiences of cohorts over time greatly enhances our ability to do this.

Finally it is worth reflecting on the ambition behind using panel data to examine causal effects. At its most crude level the analyses we conduct involve correlating the changes in answers to one question with changes in the answers to another. Behind this is a causal model that can be complex and sophisticated given the depth and quality of data in many longitudinal data sources. Regardless of the quality of the approach to analysis allowed by longitudinal data, the key concern of how adequately variables capture underlying concepts and meanings remains. Marsh's (1982, particularly chapter 5) account of these issues and approaches to dealing with them remains pertinent. And as the description of cohort and period effects implies, the complex and open nature of social systems means that the application of learning from a study needs careful consideration of wider social, economic, political and cultural contexts.

Note

1. I am very grateful to Marcos Vera Hernandez, Alissa Goodman, Alistair Muriel and Gemma Tetlow for allowing me to draw this example from their work, which is reported in Nazroo et al. (2008b).

References

Banks, J., Breeze, E., Lessof, C. and Nazroo, J. (2006) *Retirement, Health and Relationships of the Older Population in England: The 2004 English Longitudinal Study of Ageing.* London: The Institute for Fiscal Studies.

Banks, J., Breeze, E., Lessof, C. and Nazroo, J. (2008) *Living in the 21st Century: Older People in England. The 2006 English Longitudinal Study of Ageing.* London: The Institute for Fiscal Studies.

Bascle, G. (2008) 'Controlling for endogeneity with instrumental variables in strategic management research', *Strategic Organization*, 6 (3): 285–327.

Berthoud, R. and Burton, J. (eds) (2008) *In Praise of Panel Surveys.* Essex: Institute for Social and Economic Research.

Blalock, H.M. (1961) *Causal Inferences in Nonexperimental Research.* Chapel Hill, NC: University of North Carolina Press.

Brown, G.W. and Harris, T.O. (1989) *Life Events and Illness.* New York: Guildford Press

Cook, T.D. and Campbell, D.T. (1979) *Quasi-Experimentation: Design and Analysis for Field Settings.* Chicago, IL: Rand McNally.

Dwyer, D. (2002) *Planning For Retirement: The Accuracy of Expected Retirement Dates and the Role of Health Shocks,* Working Paper 2001–08, Center for Retirement Research at Boston College.

Dwyer, D.S. and Mitchell O.S. (1999) 'Health shocks as determinants of retirement: are self-rated measures endogenous?', *Journal of Health Economics*, 18: 173–93.

European Union, Communication from the Commission to the Council and the European Parliament Europe's response to World Ageing (2002) *Promoting Economic and Social Progress in an Ageing World: A contribution of the European Commission to the 2nd World Assembly on Ageing,* Brussels, 18.3.2002, COM(2002) 143 final. Available at: http://europa.eu/eur-lex/en/com/cnc/2002/com2002_0143en01.pdf

Gall, T.L., Ebvans, D.R. and Howard, J. (1997) 'The retirement adjustment process: changes in the well-being of male retirees across time', *Journal of Gerontology: Psychological Sciences*, 52B (3): 110–17.

Lawson, T. (1997) *Economics and Reality.* London: Routledge.

Marmot, M., Banks, J., Blundell, R., Lessof, C. and Nazroo, J. (2003) *Health, Wealth and Lifestyles of the Older Population in England: The 2002 English Longitudinal Study of Ageing.* London: The Institute for Fiscal Studies.

Marsh, C. (1982) *The Survey Method: The Contribution of Surveys to Sociological Explanation.* London: George, Allen and Unwin.

McFadden, D. (1999) http://elsa.berkeley.edu/~mcfadden/e240b_f01/ch4.pdf

McMunn, A., Nazroo, J.Y., Marmot, M.G., Boreham, R. and Goodman, R. (2001) 'Children's emotional and behavioural well-being and the family environment: findings from the Health Survey for England', *Social Science and Medicine*, 53 (4), 423–40.

McMumm, A., Nazroo, J. and Breeze, E. (2009) 'Inequalities an health at older ages: a longitudinal investigation of onset of illness and survival effects in England', *Age and Ageing*, 38: 181-7.

Menard, S. (1991) *Longitudinal Research*. Newbury Park, CA: Sage.

Nazroo, J., Zaninotto, P. and Gjoncça, E. (2008a) 'Mortality and healthy life expectancy', in J. Banks, E. Breeze, C. Lessof and J. Nazroo (eds.), *Living in the 21st century: older people in England. The 2006 English Longitudinal Study of Ageing.* London: The Institute for Fiscal Studies. pp. 253–80.

Nazroo, J., Goodman, A., Marmot, M. and Blundell, R. (2008b) *Inequalities in Health in an Aging Population: Patterns, Causes and Consequences: Full Research Report and Appendix*, ESRC End of Award Report, RES-000–23–0590. Swindon: ESRC.

Oakley, A. (2004) 'Who's afraid of the randomized controlled trial? Some dilemmas of the scientific method and 'good' research practice', in C. Seale (ed.), *Social Research Methods: A Reader*. London: Routledge. pp. 510–18.

Oakley, A. (2005) 'Design and analysis of social intervention studies in health research', in A. Bowling and S. Ebrahim (eds), *Handbook of Health Research Methods*. Maidenhead: Open University Press. pp. 246–65.

Sacker, A. and Wiggins, R.D. (2002) 'Age-period-cohort effects on inequalities in psychological distress, 1981–2000', *Psychological Medicine*, 32 (6): 977–90.

Smith, J. (2004) 'Unravelling the SES-Health Connection', Institute for Fiscal Studies Working Paper W04/02, London: Institute for Fiscal Studies, doi: 10.1920/wp.ifs.2004.0402

Index

abortion, 192
Abrams, M., 172
abstraction of data from its context, 172
action research, 130
'adequate description' concept, 25, 107, 117–18
adjacency matrices, 81–2
age effects, 230–1
ageing populations, 226
aggregate constraint (of a vertex in SNA), 85–6
anthropological research, 78, 107, 109, 112
Applebaum, P.S., 196
Arber, S., 170
architectural research, 128–30; *see also* socio-architectural view of the world; Japanese architecture and design
arcs in social network analysis, 83
Atelier Bow-Wow, 129–30
Athens, 126–7, 130

Ballas, Dimitris, vii, 6, 8, 11, 22–4, 103–6, 168; *co-author of Chapter 10*
Bertaux, Daniel, 63, 176
Bertaux-Wiame, Isabelle, 63, 176
biographically-based research, 71
Bjerrum Nielsen, Harriet, 63
Blalock, H.M., 227–8
blockmodelling, 79–80, 87
Bott, Elizabeth, 174, 176
Brand, Ralf, 128, 130
British cohort studies, 91–2, 98, 101, 211–14, 218–22; narrative aspects of, 213, 218, 222
British Household Panel Survey (BHPS), 91, 98, 101, 157, 170, 211
'brothering', 8, 54–9
Brown, Richard, 177
Butler, Judith, 182
Byng-Hall, John, 63
Bynner, J., 220

Call, V.R.A., 217
Cameron, Lynne, 38, 40
Carr, E.H., 170

cartograms, 6, 8, 11, 23–4, 104, 151–62; creation of, 161–2
case histories and case study methodology, 66–71, 124–5, 176, 220–2
causal relationships, analysis of, 168, 225–33, 238–40
'censored cases', 167, 215–16
Census data, 169–70
centrality of vertices in social network analysis, 85–6
Centre for Longitudinal Studies, 222
change over time, 165–6; evidence for identification of, 166–8; historians' and social scientists' perspectives on, 169–73, 177–8
choropleth maps, 153, 159
Chowbey, Punita, vii, 6–7, 11, 15, 18, 20, 32, 104–6; *co-author of Chapter 9*
chronic illness, 134–5, 139, 142–7, 196–200; sociology of, 199–200
cities as locations for research, 103, 120–1, 125–6, 131
civil partnerships, 191
Clifford, J., 109
cliques within networks, 87
co-construction of technology, 122, 126, 128, 131
cohabitation, 219–20
cohesion in networks, 84–7
cohort effects, 230–1, 240
cohort studies, 210–11; *see also* British cohort studies
Commerzbank Tower, Frankfurt, 127–8, 130
community, concept of, 136
community researchers (CRs), 137–47
complete network data, 79
complex interventions (CIs) in health care, 198–9, 208
configurations as units of analysis, 64
context of research, 31–2; *see also* family context
coping processes, 200
Cowan, Ruth Schwartz, 126
Cox, D.R. (and Cox regression), 215–18

creative interview encounters, 36–40, 43–6
Crossley, Nick, vii, 6, 12–13, 17, 22–4, 27–8, 32; *author of Chapter 5*
cultural analysis, 67

Dale, Angela, vii, 6–7, 13, 16–19, 28, 32, 167, 170; *author of Chapter 6, co-author of Chapter 1 and co-editor*
data: collection and analysis of, 18–21, 80–1; generation of, 139–42, 146; nature of, 15–18; reading of, 21–2, 67–71
Davies, Katherine, viii, 9, 11–13, 15, 18, 24, 27–31; *co-author of Chapter 2*
density of networks, 84–5
depression, 228–9, 236–7
depth interviewing, 90, 95, 106, 134, 147
descriptive accounts, 107, 110
diameters of networks, 84
'digital divide', 124
'directed' relationships, 82–3
discourse analysis, 40
'discrete time' approach to event history modelling, 217
divorce: impact of, 213; timing of, 217
Donovan, Catherine, 183
Donovan, J., 196
Dorling, Danny, viii, 6, 8, 11, 22–4, 103–6, 168; *co-author of Chapter 10*
Douglas, Jack, 36
Drug Attitude Inventory (DAI), 201–2
Duberman, M.B., 181
Dwyer, D.S., 237

Economic and Social Data Service (ESDS), 91, 101, 222; Qualidata Archive, 173, 175
edges in social network analysis, 83
educational attainment, determinants of, 98–9
ego-net data, 28–31, 79, 81
Elias, Norbert, 64
Elliott, Jane, viii, 9–10, 14, 16, 18–19, 23–4, 32, 165–7; *author of Chapter 14*
Ely, Margaret, 213
endogeneity, 228, 232–3, 238–40
English Longitudinal Study of Ageing (ELSA), 7, 235–6
epistemology, 107, 184–5
ethnic identities, 144–5
ethnic minorities, 135–6
ethnographic interviews, 140
ethnographic research, 19–20, 25, 34, 36, 66, 78, 103–13, 116–18, 125, 129
event history analysis, 30, 32, 167–8, 211–15, 221
event history modelling, 9–10, 14, 214–19, 222
expectations, use of questions on, 237

experimental methods of research, 40–4, 227–8
expert knowledge, 22–3, 108

facial recognition, 43
family context, 100
family dynamics, 63–4
Family Expenditure Survey, 170
family relationships: examples of, 93–5; survey data on, 90–101
family resemblance, 33–47
Family Resources Survey, 100
family size related to educational attainment, 98–9
'fateful moment' concept, 188–9
Felman, Shoshana, 51
feminism, 186, 190
fieldwork and field notes, 19–20, 24, 66, 109, 112, 129, 139, 146–7, 173
Fink, B., 52
focus groups, 34, 46
Foucault, Michel, 182, 185
Frankfurt, 127–8, 130
Freud, Sigmund, 50
Frosh, Stephen, viii, 8, 14, 16–17, 21–2, 25–6, 28, 30, 32, 52, 58–9; *co-author of Chapter 3*

Gastner, M.T., 152–4, 157–8, 161
Geertz, C., 25
General Household Survey, 7, 93–4, 100, 170
generalization of research findings, 23–5
Georgaca, E., 52, 60
Ghanaian communities, 136, 142–6
Giddens, Anthony, 188
Goffman, E., 44
Goldthorpe, John, 171–2
Google Earth, 162
'Grant', 28, 32, 54–9
graph theory, 78, 83
Guy, Simon, viii, 10, 16–18, 20–1, 103, 105–6, 122, 128–30; *co-author of Chapter 8*

Halsey, A.H., 169
happiness, subjective measures of, 157–8
Hardisty, Frank, 161
Hardy, Thomas, 33, 35
Harrison, Tom, 172
Harriss, Kaveri, viii, 6–7, 11, 15, 18, 20, 32, 104–6; *co-author of Chapter 9*
Harvey, Penny ix, 4, 10–12, 14–15, 18–20, 22, 24–5, 32, 103, 105, 111–12, 168; *co-author of Chapter 7*
Hasselt, Belgium, 128, 130
hazard functions in event history analysis, 215
health of older people, 226–7, 236–40
Heaphy, Brian, 183

Heaton, T.B., 217
Hinde, P.R.A., 218–19
Hirschfeld, Magnus, 185
historians' perspective on change, 169–73, 177–8, 185
History Workshop movement, 181
HIV/AIDS, 183, 190–1
Hockey, J., 34
homosexuality, 184–6, 189–92
homunculus portrayal of the body, 153
horizontal reading of data, 67–8, 71
household types, 94–5
human cartography, 151–3, 162

Iacovou, M., 99
ideographic understanding of social change, 23
incidence matrices in social network analysis, 82
individualistic bias in sociological methods, 75
infrastructure developments, 124, 128, 130
Inglehart, Ronald, 171–2
instrumental variables, use of, 19, 237–40
interpretations, psychological, 51
intersubjectivity, 52–3
interview data, 125; combined with survey data, 95–8; *see also* creative interview encounters; ethnographic interviews; narrative interviews; post-trial interviews; qualitative interviews
intra-family relationships, 100
'invisible resources', 143–4

Jackson, Brian, 177
Japanese architecture and design, 105, 128–30
Jenkins, J., 6, 100
Jennings, Humphrey, 172
Joshi, H., 218–19

Kaika, Maria, 126–7, 130
Karvonen, Andrew, ix, 10, 16–18, 20–1, 103, 105–6; *co-author of Chapter 8*
Kehily, M.J., 67–8, 70–1
knowledge practices, 108–9, 117
knowledge production, 18–21, 147
Knox, Hannah, ix, 4, 10–12, 14–15, 18–20, 22, 24–5, 32, 103, 105, 111–12, 168; *co-author of Chapter 7*
Konvitz, J.W., 121
Kuhn, Thomas, 121

labelling of perspectives on social science research, 3, 14
Labour Force Survey, 96–7, 100
Labov, W., 210, 213–14
Lacan, J., 52–3, 59–60
Lander, Karen, 41
language's role in research, 24–5

Law, J., 130–1
Lefebvre, Henri, 129
life-course transitions, 165
life histories and life narratives, 17, 213–14
'living apart together' (LAT) couples, 92
'locationless logics', 108
locations for research, choice of, 104–5
London parliamentary constituencies, 154–6
longitudinal studies, 14, 30–1, 71, 91, 98–101, 166, 170, 210–13, 217–22, 225–31, 236, 239–40

MacKenzie, D., 122
Madge, Charles, 172
Mannheim, Karl, 62–3, 67
mapping methods, 104–5, 150–63
Marcus, G., 109
marital status: and depression, 228–9; and mortality risk, 227–8
Marquand, D., 181
Marsh, C., 240
Mason, Jennifer, ix, 9, 11–13, 15, 18, 24, 27, 29, 31, 177; *co-author of Chapters 1 and 2 and co-editor*
Mass-Observation, 166–7, 172–6
Menard, S., 231
Mercator, Gerardus (and Mercator projection), 150
Millburn Report (2009), 98
Millennium Cohort Study, 213
Millennium Development Goals, 159–60
Mitchell, O.S., 237
Mitchell, T., 108
Moore, Niamh, 177
Moore, Steven, 127, 130
motherhood, 27–8, 31, 62–72; and age, 67–8; intergenerational narratives of, 68–72; *see also* single parents

narrative, 68, 113, 117, 185–8, 221–2; definitions of, 210, 214; quantitative analysis of, 210
narrative analysis, 207
narrative interpretive method, 65
narrative interviews, 17
National Child Development Study, 98–9, 170
National Survey of Health and Development, 212, 218, 222–3
Nazroo, James, ix, 7, 9–10, 14, 16, 18–19, 24, 30–1, 165–8, 211; *author of Chapter 15*
neo-liberalism, 187–8, 191
neuroleptic medication, 204–5
Newman, Mark, 152–4, 157–8, 161
nomethetic understanding of social change, 23

Ocongate, Peru, 111
Office for National Statistics, 97

Ogden, Thomas, 52
only children, 99
ontology of social research, 3–5, 8–18, 107
opinion polling, 170

Pakistani communities, 96–8, 136, 142, 144
panel surveys, 7, 14, 170, 226–7, 235–7, 240
participant observation, 34
Pawson, R., 196
pension entitlements, 239
period effects, 230–1, 240
photo elicitation, 31, 37–8
photo shoots, 44–6
place: concepts of, 103, 107; politics of, 117; significance of, 106, 135, 145; *see also* locations for research
place-making, 115
Plummer, K., 182, 185
post-materialist values, 172
post-trial interviews, 205
poverty: reduction of, 159; spatial distribution of, 155–6
Proctor, M., 170
professional families, 98
psychoanalysis, 21–2, 49–60; and language, 52; and literature, 51–2; distortion of, 51; Lacanian, 52–3, 59–60; misappropriation of, 50, 53; as a process of reading the social, 52
psychological testing, 43–6
punk scene in London and Manchester, 85

qualitative interviews, 166, 222
qualitative quasi-experiments, 41–3
qualitative research, 95–6, 124. 126. 168, 173–8, 220; combined with randomized controlled trials, 195–208
quota sampling, 65

racialized processes, 135
randomized controlled trials (RCTs), 9, 22, 166, 168; combined with qualitative research, 195–208
'rapid appraisal', 135–6, 139–42
reciprocated relationships, 82–3
reflexivity, 20–1, 32,, 183, 193; *concentric*, 53–4
relational data, handling of, 78
relationship: analysis of, 30; different conceptualizations of, 27–9
relationship matrices, 93–4
representativeness of samples, 176–7
retirement: and depression, 236–7; and health, 236, 239
reverse causation, 232–8
risk sets in event history analysis, 215

road-building, 107–11, 115–17, 168
Robb, Jim, 174
Rogers, Anne, ix, 9, 16, 18, 25–6, 166, 168; *author of Chapter 13*
Rosenthal, Gabriele, 69
Rowbotham, S., 181
Rudberg, Monica, 63

Salway, Sarah, x, 6–7, 11, 15, 18, 20, 32, 104–6; *co-author of Chapter 9*
sampling, 23–4, 65, 176–7
Savage, Mike, x, 16, 23, 25–6, 165–7; *author of Chapter 11*
Saville Young, Lisa, x, 8, 14, 16–17, 21–2, 25–6. 28, 30, 32; *co-author of Chapter 3*
Scapetoad software, 161
science and technology studies (STS), 121–2
secondary analysis of survey data, 170, 173–8, 222
Section 28 of the Local Government Act, 190–1
self-management of long-term medication, 196–9, 204–8
sewer systems, 123
Sexual Offences Act (1967), 190–1
'sexual revolution' (1960s), 188
sexuality, history of, 181–93
Singer, B., 221
single parents, 95–6
skyscrapers, 123
sociability (in health clubs), 76
Social Action for Health, 136
social class, changes in experience of, 166
social constructionism, 122, 182, 196
social mobility, analysis of, 172
social network analysis (SNA), 6, 12–13, 17, 23, 27–32, 75–88; data analysed in, 79–80; data gathering for, 80–1; definition of, 77; history of, 78
social psychology, 32
Social Science Research Council Data Archive, 170
social structures, 75
social trends, analysis of, 169
sociality, 58–9
socio-architectural view of the world, 5–7
socio-economic status related to health, 233
sociograms, 83
The Sociological Society, 173
sociotechnical study of cities, 120–31; examples of, 126–30
standardized and non-standardized data, 166–75
statistical analysis, 167; *see also* sampling
Steele, F., 219–20
stories as part of the social world, 4–5

structural adjustment policies, 187
student networks, 77, 79
subjectivity, 58–9, 63; *see also* intersubjectivity
suffragette movement, 76–80
sustainable development, 128
Swinden, Ed, 45
Szegö, Janos, 151

Tarr, J.A., 121
technological development, 121–30; contextual nature of, 123; as a *contingent* process, 123
Thatcher, Margaret, 190
theorizing process, 19–22
'thick description', 25
Thompson, E.P., 181
Thompson, Paul, 63, 69
Thomson, Rachel, x, 4, 15, 20, 27, 30–1, 67–8, 70–1, 168; *author of Chapter 4*
Tilley, N., 196
time, sense of, 106
Tokyo, 105, 128–30
Tsukamoto, Yoshiharu, 129–30
two-mode analysis, 80

UK Household Longitudinal Survey, 101
underweight children, 159–60

United Nations: Children's Fund (UNICEF), 160; Millennium Development Goals, 159–60
United States, survey data on, 101, 211, 221
urban history, 121–2

vertical reading of data, 68–71
vertices in social network analysis, 81–6
visualization as part of research, 24, 37
vox pop encounters, 44–6

Wacjman, J., 122
Waletzky, J., 210, 213–14
water supply networks, 126–7
Watts, Helen, 77–80
wealth: spatial distribution of, 155–7; and survival rates, 233–5
Webb, J., 169
Weeks, Jeffrey, x, 5, 16, 22, 25–6, 165–7; *author of Chapter 12*
Wickham, Lee, 41
Wolfenden Report (1957), 189–92
women's employment patterns, 96–8, 218–19
World Bank, 187
world views, 13
Worldmapper project, 158–62

zeitgeist concept, 4–5, 27, 62–3, 71